MOVING TOWARD MATURITY SERIES

LEADER'S GUIDE

VICTOR BOOKS®

A DIVISION OF SCRIPTURE PRESS PUBLICATIONS INC.
USA CANADA ENGLAND

MOVING TOWARD MATURITY LEADER'S GUIDE

Other resources by Barry St. Clair that will help you in your personal growth and ministry:

The Youth Ministry Puzzle Video
This video package takes a serious look at the essential ingredients for a youth ministry strategy in the local church. Youth workers and leaders can view and discuss together this presentation of effective youth ministry strategy taught by Barry St. Clair.

Building Leaders for Strategic Youth Ministry
Training leaders is the key to an excellent ministry. Adult lay leaders can experience personal spiritual growth, order their priorities, and learn the skills necessary to work effectively with students. When lay leaders complete Building Leaders they are equipped to minister to students.

The Facts of Life
Talking to friends about Jesus Christ is one of the greatest challenges Christians face at school. This booklet, written specifically to reach young people, is a dynamic tool for outreach.

Getting Started
An excellent booklet to give to a new Christian. Its hard-hitting approach will help a new believer know what steps to take to follow Christ. And it provides positive answers to how to communicate their new found faith to their parents and friends.

Time Alone with God Notebook
This notebook is for use in your personal quiet time. Each notebook has a 10-week supply of application-oriented material.

ISBN: 0-89693-298-2

2   3   4   5   6   7   8   9   10   Printing/Year   95   94   93   92

CONTENTS

FOLLOWING JESUS

Leader's Guide
prepared by
Juanita Wright Potter

Introduction

Moving Toward Maturity is a five-part discipleship training series for young people. It is designed to help them become so independently dependent on Jesus Christ that they can teach others to do the same. This series has three main purposes:

1. To train young people in the "how to's" of Christian living.
2. To help young people develop strong, Christlike characters.
3. To move young people from the point of getting to know Jesus Christ to the point of sharing Him with others.

Following Jesus, the first book in the series, introduces students to the basics of discipleship: becoming God's child; developing a relationship with Jesus Christ, discovering God's purposes, love, and will; learning to study the Bible and pray, putting God first. It contains 10 Bible studies, 10 memory verse cards, and a "Bible Response Sheet" for use in a daily study of 1 John (see session 7).

The other four study books in the series, and related materials, are described on the outside back cover of this Leader's Guide.

Discipleship Family

Commitment is the key to a successful group study of *Following Jesus*. So limit the study group to those young people who will commit themselves to study the book and Bible on their own and will faithfully take part in every group meeting. This group of committed young people and their leader are called a Discipleship Family. (Turn to page 11 in *Following Jesus* and read the commitments required of each person.)

By making and keeping these commitments, each Discipleship Family member will:

1. Learn to depend on Jesus Christ.
2. Develop personal discipline in Bible study, prayer, witnessing, establishing and following priorities, and seeking and obeying God's will.
3. Experience the rich fellowship and love of a committed, caring Christian community.

The young people and leaders who commit themselves to this discipleship training will move toward Christ's goal for the church: "His gifts were made that Christians might be properly equipped for their service, that the whole body might be built up until the time comes when, in the unity of common faith and common knowledge of the Son of God, we arrive at real maturity—that measure of development which is meant by 'the fullness of Christ' " (Eph. 4:12-13).*

*Quoted from *The New Testament in Modern English*, © by J. B. Phillips, published by The MacMillan Company. Used by permission.

You, the Leader

Being a leader of a Discipleship Family will require more time and personal involvement than most Bible studies or Sunday School classes you may have taught in the past. As a member of the group (not just its leader) you should take part in all the commitments, activities, and assignments of the Discipleship Family. To get started, here are some things you will need to do.

1. Get familiar with the Moving Toward Maturity series (see back cover) **and your role as a Discipleship Family leader.** Besides the introduction of this Leader's Guide, two other resources by Barry St. Clair can clarify your role: the book *Building Leaders for Strategic Youth Ministry* and the six-part video "The Youth Ministry Puzzle." Both are available in Christian bookstores or from Victor Books or Reach Out Ministries.

2. Read through *Following Jesus* **and this Leader's Guide.** As you read, ask God to reveal to you those young people who should be a part of this study group. Ask Him to direct your steps as you organize and lead your Discipleship Family.

3. Organize your Discipleship Family. Announce plans for the formation of your Discipleship Family to all the young people in your church. Explain what will be involved in meetings, assignments, etc. Read the commitment sheet (page 11, *Following Jesus*) that all group members will be expected to sign. Invite everyone who is interested, to meet you at a specific time and place for an in-depth introduction (see session 1, page 12). Before that meeting, speak privately with young people you feel should be part of the group and encourage them to join. Your group will be most effective with 4 to 8 members, and should not exceed 12. If more people are interested, a second group should be formed.

4. Purchase all of the materials you will need well in advance of the first meeting. Each Discipleship Family member (including yourself) should have his own copy of *Following Jesus*. Everyone who is leading a Discipleship Family group should have his own copy of the Leader's Guide. Make sure every group member has his own Bible.

5. Decide the best time and place to meet. Have everyone bring their school and work schedules to the first meeting so they can decide as a group when and where to meet for the next 10 sessions. If possible, plan to hold the meetings in your home or the home of one of the group members. Meeting in the informal atmosphere of a living room or around a dining room table will help people open up and join in discussions.

6. Allow up to two hours for each meeting. Suggested time allotments for each part of the meeting are given in this Leader's Guide. A total of 60 minutes is suggested for the introductory meeting (session 1); 75 minutes are suggested for sessions 2-11. Since these are not instructional classes, but meetings designed to build relationships and share insights, they should be open-ended. If you finish a session in 75 minutes, fine. But you should have the freedom to meet for two hours (never longer) if necessary.

7. Get the group together for a fun activity. Before or after session 1, plan a fun get-acquainted activity (softball game, bike hike, retreat, pizza party, picnic) for the young people who are interested in joining a Discipleship Family. This will help them relax and feel more at ease with one another.

Building relationships

Your role in the Discipleship Family is that of leader, not teacher. By explaining that you and all members of the group are in the process of becoming more mature disciples of Christ, you will begin to establish yourself as one of the group rather than as the "instructor." But because you are more mature in years and in experience than the young people in your Discipleship Family, they will look to you for organization, guidance, and example. If they can see that you genuinely love God and that you care about them as individuals, they will more likely form solid, loving relationships with God, with you, and with one another.

1. Meet with each group member. Schedule an appointment with each member of your Discipleship Family during the first week or two. Get to know his needs, interests, concerns, and goals. Share those things about yourself as well. This will help you see one another as unique, important individuals with feelings and ideas. It will also result in more meaningful discussions during your group meetings.

2. Keep a notebook during this 10-week study. In it, write your observations about members of your Discipleship Family. Regularly pray for each one by name. Keep track of individual needs and achievements. If someone misses a session, contact him personally. Help him when he has trouble understanding something from Scripture. Talk with him if he seems to be breaking his commitments. Call on him for his opinions during meetings. Build him up so he will be valued and appreciated by the group.

You can also use this notebook for writing your evaluation of each session, what you plan to do to improve as a leader, and your own responses to the studies in 1 John that begin with Bible study 6.

3. Keep your pastor and church informed. While you're building relationships in your Discipleship Family, build relationships within the church as well. Keep your pastor informed as to what is happening in your group. Encourage group members to be involved in the church and to strengthen their relationships with other believers—particularly other young people who are not a part of a Discipleship Family. Group members need to form strong relationships with one another, but they should avoid becoming a "clique."

4. Limit group membership. Because your Discipleship Family will be building trust based on shared experiences, don't take in any new members once the group has been established. (If several new people are interested in joining, start a now Discipleship Family for them at a later date.) After completing the study of *Following Jesus*, challenge each person to renew his commitment and to continue with the group in the study of *Spending Time Alone with God*.

Effective meetings

The Discipleship Family's meetings are based on biblical principles of discipleship. Each session has at least one *Group Life* and one *Individual Growth* goal. It's important that you work toward accomplishing both.

1. Be prepared. Begin your preparation for each session at least five days in advance. Do the Bible study in *Following Jesus*, answering the questions for yourself, not as you think the students might answer. Then skim through the Leader's Guide suggestions to see if there is anything you need to do right away. Later in the week (one or two days before the meeting) finalize your preparation: Review the *Following Jesus* material, and study the Leader's Guide suggestions, adapting activities according to the particular needs of your group.

2. Start on time. Since Discipleship Family meetings can last up to two hours, ask everyone to come on time, or even a few minutes early. (Those who arrive early can use the time to get to know each other better or review Bible memory verses.)

3. Help students keep their commitments. Students are to complete their assignments in *Following Jesus* **before** each session so the meeting can be devoted to building on what the students are learning on their own. For that reason, the "Exploring God's Word" section of each session does not contain a verbatim review of the Bible study material in *Following Jesus*. Instead students are given an opportunity to quickly look over the Bible study content and their written responses. Then the discussion that follows builds on and reinforces what students have learned during the week prior to the meeting.

Be sensitive to group members who may lack self-discipline and need extra encouragement and motivation to keep their commitments. Be positive. Recall how Christ loved, encouraged, and disciplined the early disciples; then follow His example in helping His new disciples along.

4. Develop skill in leading discussions. Initially you will probably have to guide discussions by asking a question, getting a response, then asking another question. But if you keep your group small, this question/answer time will develop into group conversations as members get to know one another better. The sharing of insights from individual Bible study will give Scripture a greater impact in each person's life. As group members become more comfortable in speaking with one another about their lives in Christ, they will also be more at ease in speaking to others outside the group.

Here's how to keep your Discipleship Family discussions on track so each member can contribute and learn during each session:

►*State questions clearly and concisely.* You're more likely to get specific answers if you ask specific questions.

After you ask a question, allow time for the group to think. Don't be afraid of short periods of silence. And don't jump in with your own answers or opinions. Don't make a contribution to the discussion that someone else in the group can make.

►*Respect each person's comments.* Encourage each one to say what he thinks, not just what he thinks he should say. Ask additional questions to help him amplify his thoughts and move from ideas to applications.

►*Stay close to Scripture.* The Bible is the authority for this study and for your group discussions. Encourage group members to base their ideas on biblical principles.

►*Challenge trite or superficial answers.* Don't let group members get away with simply rattling off a cliché or a Bible verse. Ask them to explain what they mean or give an illustration.

►*Ask review questions when appropriate to help the group think through things they've studied up to that point.* Use this time for members to raise previously-discussed issues with which they're still having problems.

►*If some group members are hesitant to take part in the discussions, ask them direct questions relating to their personal opinions or experiences.* Let them know that you care about them and what they think.

►*If some members answer all the questions, begin addressing your questions to others by name so everyone may be heard.* If a member continues to monopolize the discussions, you may want to talk with him privately after the meeting. Let him know you appreciate him and his contributions, but ask him to give others more opportunity to take part.

5. Evaluate each session. Within 24 hours of each meeting, evaluate how the session went and note the emerging needs of group members. The "After the Meeting" section of each session in this Leader's Guide can help you do this.

As you prepare to lead each meeting, pray that God will help you model the life of a true disciple. Be enthusiastic about growing spiritually, helping others grow, and sharing your faith with non-Christians. Your spirit can be contagious.

If group meetings are enjoyable and helpful to a Discipleship Family member, he will not only grow in his relationships with Christ and the rest of the group, but will probably be eager to commit himself to the Discipleship Family until all five books in the Moving Toward Maturity series have been completed.☐

Becoming a Discipleship Family

OVERVIEW

Key Concept   To benefit most from a group study of *Following Jesus*, we must commit ourselves to the disciplines of a Discipleship Family.

Goals   *Individual Growth:* To accept the responsibilities and commitments of the Discipleship Family.
Group Life: To establish a foundation for developing strong fellowship ties within the group.

BEFORE THE MEETING

1. Study pages 6-10 of this Leader's Guide for important background information.
2. In *Following Jesus,* study pages 5-11, and put together the memory verse packet located in the back of the book.
3. Call each person who said he'd come to the first meeting. Remind him to bring his school and work schedules. Express your personal interest in his becoming a part of the Discipleship Family.
4. Based on your knowledge of the young people who are coming to this first meeting, make a note of each one's needs. Ask God to help you present the challenge of discipleship in such a way that each person will want to study *Following Jesus* as a part of the Discipleship Family.
5. Gather materials for the meeting:
   Bible
   Following Jesus (one for each person)
   Package of construction paper of various colors
   Pencils
   3" x 5" cards
   Memory verse packet

BUILDING THE GROUP *(20 minutes)*

As each person arrives, ask him to write his name, address, and phone number on a 3" x 5" card. Then have him choose a sheet of construction paper and tear or fold it into a shape that symbolizes what he hopes God will do in his life as a result of being a part of this Discipleship Family. (Take part in this activity.)

Have everyone respond to each of the following questions before moving to the next question. (You go first.)

1. What is your full name? **3. What are your favorite activities?**
2. Where do you live? **4. Describe your symbol.**

FOCUSING ON LIFE *(5 minutes)*

Ask: **What can make belonging to a family a good experience?** (love, encouragement, sharing, etc.) Record responses.

EXPLORING THE CHALLENGE *(20 minutes)*

Read Ephesians 4:11-16, emphasizing how we as Christians can help each other grow and become mature in Christ.

Describe the Moving Toward Maturity series and the purpose of the Discipleship Family (page 6 of this Leader's Guide). Share your own enthusiasm about what this study experience can do for all of you. Stress how disciplined commitment to God and to other group members is the key to success.

Give everyone a copy of *Following Jesus.* Review the contents and read the group disciplines (page 11). Discuss any questions students have about the commitments they are expected to make.

Briefly discuss the time (one-and-a-quarter to two hours per week with the group plus individual study time) and the number of weeks (10 more). Decide on a specific time and place to meet.

CONSIDERING THE CHOICE *(15 minutes)*

Review the positive characteristics of being a part of a family listed earlier. Ask the group to silently consider how those characteristics can apply to a Discipleship Family. Ask each person to write on his paper symbol the one group discipline in which he feels he will need the most encouragement and group support. Ask each one to share what he wrote. (If you share first, other group members will find it easier to share.)

Challenge the group to think and pray about making the commitment to a Discipleship Family. Encourage them to talk it over with their parents. Anyone who decides not to become a part of this particular 10-week Discipleship Family should let you know before the next meeting and return his unmarked copy of Following Jesus. Those who choose to join should come to the next meeting with all assignments in Bible study 1 completed. Encourage everyone to set aside a specific time each week to do the Bible study assignments for the next week (preferably at least five days in advance). This will give them several days to work on the memory verse and carry out any extra assignments that may be given in the Bible study.

Pray for each person by name and for his decision about joining this Discipleship Family. Thank God for what He is going to do in all of your lives as you commit yourselves to Him and to each other.

Assignments for Next Week   Be enthusiastic as you give the following assignments in your own words:

1. In Following Jesus, **read pages 5-10, study and sign the "Personal Commitment" (page 11), complete Bible study 1, and put together the memory verse packet in the back of the book.** Show the group your made-up packet.

2. Memorize 1 John 5:11, as indicated at the end of Bible study 1.

3. Bring a Bible, a pen or pencil, and Following Jesus **to every meeting.**

Before students leave this first meeting, try to talk with them individually. See if they have any questions or problems. Encourage them to join the group, and let them know you care about each of them and their concerns.   •

AFTER THE MEETING

1. Evaluate the meeting: Did each person become involved in sharing his ideas and feelings? How can you more effectively involve each person in next week's discussions? Review "Effective Meetings," page 9 of this Leader's Guide.

2. This week, and every week, begin preparing for the next session at least five days in advance. Complete the Bible study in Following Jesus, and read through the Leader's Guide suggestions.

Are You Sure?

Bible Study 1

OVERVIEW

Key Concept
Spiritual growth can begin when we are confident that God has received us as His children.

Memory Verse
1 John 5:11

Goals
Individual Growth: To claim and thank God for the assurance of salvation made possible through Jesus Christ.
Group Life: To accept and affirm one another as important members of the group.

BEFORE THE MEETING

1. Pray for each group member by name and ask God to give you wisdom in guiding each one into a life of committed discipleship.
2. In *Following Jesus,* do Bible study 1, writing your personal answers to each question. In the margins jot down other observations you may want to share or discuss with the group.
3. Memorize 1 John 5:11.
4. Contact each person who attended last week's session. Answer his questions and remind him of the meeting time and place. If for some reason he has decided not to join this Discipleship Family, assure him of your continued love for him and the hope that he will be able to join a future group.
5. Make a list of the names, addresses, and phone numbers of all of the group members (from the 3" x 5" cards filled out last week). Make a copy of the list for each person.
6. Gather materials for the meeting:
   Bible
   Following Jesus
   List of group members' names and addresses
   Memory verse packet

BUILDING THE GROUP *(20 minutes)*

Greet each person. Make him feel at home. Welcome him as an important part of this Discipleship Family. Have everyone turn to the "Personal Commitment" sheet (page 11, *Following Jesus*). Read it together. Ask anyone who hasn't already done so to sign his sheet. (Be sure to sign yours too!) Then, as a symbol of mutual commitment and support, have everyone sign everyone else's commitment sheet.

Ask each person to say one word that describes how he feels about committing himself to the Discipleship Family for 10 weeks (fear, excitement, uncertainty, etc.). Briefly discuss how any negative emotions can be overcome. Ask volunteers to offer short prayers about the emotions expressed and ask God to give you all a vision for what He wants to do in your lives during the next nine weeks.

Enthusiastically assure the young people of your availability and desire to help each one successfully complete this discipleship study.

FOCUSING ON LIFE *(10 minutes)*

Discuss: **Have you ever belonged to a group (band, baseball team, school club, etc.) and doubted your acceptance by others in the group? Is so, how did you feel? How was your contribution to the group affected? How did your doubts cause you to react to others in the group?**

Explain that we can have these same feelings and reactions toward God and other Christians if we have doubts about our salvation. Share an example of this from your own experience or ask several volunteers to give examples.

EXPLORING GOD'S WORD *(35 minutes)*

[NOTE: Each week this section is based on the work students have done in Following Jesus. The discussion questions are usually not identical to those in the study book, but they draw from the same

Scriptures and assignments. This technique helps students think through what they've studied rather than just parroting written answers.]

Allow time for everyone to review his written responses to Bible study 1 in *Following Jesus.* Then discuss:

1. What would you tell a person who says, "I feel fine just the way I am. Why should I become a Christian?" *Responses can be based on students' answers under "What is a Christian?"*

2. In what ways did you find it hard to take any one of the five steps to salvation listed on page 17? (For example, someone might say that he was too proud to admit his need of Christ till he realized that by admitting his need he could actually *become* what he could otherwise only *pretend* to be.)

3. How can you know if you're truly a Christian? *Refer to the "Knowing You're God's" section, page 23.* In summary, answers should include:

1 John 2:3-6	True belief leads to obedience.
3:14	Love for others develops.
3:24; 4:13	Christ's Spirit lets you know that He is with you.
4:15	Christians tell others about Christ.
5:1	God promised that by believing in Christ we can be His children.

4. Of the five assurances given in 1 John, which one is most meaningful to you? Why? *Give everyone an opportunity to answer.*

As a group, quote today's memory verse (1 John 5:11). Then offer sentence prayers of thanksgiving for the salvation God has given through His Son, Jesus Christ.

APPLYING GOD'S WORD *(10 minutes)*

Ask each person to write in response to Bible study 1: (1) One thing he will do this week to affirm his salvation. (Examples: Thank God every day that He remains true to His promises; tell someone else about what it means to him to be a Christian.) (2) One thing he will do this week to demonstrate his commitment to another member of the Discipleship Family. (Examples: Offer a ride to someone who may have a hard time finding a way to the next meeting; call someone during the week just to encourage him as a fellow member of the group.)

Assignments for Next Week As you give the following assignments, be positive. Let the young people know that you have faith in their desire and ability to be accountable.

1. Complete Bible study 2 in *Following Jesus.* Don't forget to memorize the Scripture verse.

2. Be prepared to share the results of what you do this week to affirm your salvation and to demonstrate your commitment to someone else in your Discipleship Family.

AFTER THE MEETING

1. Evaluate the meeting: Was the atmosphere relaxed? Did everyone feel free to take part? If not, jot down some possible causes and things you can do to improve the situation next week.

2. If anyone seemed uncertain about his salvation, be sure to get together with him or call him sometime this week.

The Great Discovery
Bible Study 2

OVERVIEW

Key Concept — Spiritual growth is based on knowing what God wants us to do and to become.

Memory Verse — Philippians 1:6

Goals — *Individual Growth:* To discover God's purposes for His children and to begin taking the steps necessary to fulfill those purposes.
Group Life: To encourage one another in pursuing the goals of developing a close relationship with God; a mature, Christlike character; and a life that represents Christ to the world.

BEFORE THE MEETING

1. Pray for all group members by name, asking God to assure each one of His presence and His love.
2. Complete Bible study 2 in *Following Jesus.* Remember, as a member (not just the leader) of this Discipleship Family, take part in all group activities and discussions, but be careful not to dominate.
3. Memorize Philippians 1:6; review 1 John 5:11.
4. Gather materials for the meeting:
   Bible
   Following Jesus
   Bible memory packet.

BUILDING THE GROUP *(20 minutes)*

Ask volunteers to share what they did this past week to (1) affirm their salvation and (2) demonstrate their love for someone in your Discipleship Family. Briefly discuss the results of what they did: How did they feel? How did others respond?

Ask the group to think about the behavior of people in general. Discuss:

1. What are some of the life purposes many people seem to have? (Having a good time, making lots of money, getting by, etc.)

2. What evidences indicate that many people have no purpose for their lives? (Boredom, unfinished projects, constantly changing plans, fear of the future, etc.)

3. How would having a significant purpose for living change the way they act?

FOCUSING ON LIFE *(10 minutes)*

Discuss:

1. Have you ever asked yourself, "Why am I here? Why was I born?"

2. What answers did you give before you were a Christian?

3. Have your answers changed at all since you studied this week's assignment? *Refer group members to their responses on pages 28, 30, and 31 in* Following Jesus.

4. Why do you think having a purpose in life is important?

EXPLORING GOD'S WORD *(30 minutes)*

Have students silently review their work on Bible study 2 in *Following Jesus*. Then discuss:

1. What are three purposes God has for our lives? (To establish a love relationship with God, to mature in Christ, and to witness for Christ.)

2. How would you describe a Christian's love relationship with God? (It begins with spiritual birth; it involves continual communication with God; etc.)

3. **What control do we have over our relationships with God?** *Refer to the sections on restoring and maintaining fellowship under "God's Purpose #1," pages 28-29, for answers.* (We can break our fellowship with God by sinning; we can restore it by confessing our sins; we can maintain it by communicating with Him; etc.)

4. **What are some characteristics of a "grown-up" or mature Christian?** *Have students check Galatians 5:22-23 and Romans 12:2.* (He is loving, joyful, peaceful, patient, kind, etc.; he looks at things from God's point of view, not from the world's.)

5. **Name at least three things you think God uses to help us become more like Christ.** (His Spirit, His Word, and the events and people around us.)

6. **In 2 Corinthians 5:20 Paul describes Christians as "Christ's ambassadors." In other words, we are like diplomats sent from one country to another—we are sent from the kingdom of God to represent Him on earth. What are two ways we can fulfill our mission as ambassadors?** *Refer students to the two main points under "God's Purpose #3."* (By our attitudes and actions toward others; by talking with others about Christ and God's kingdom.)

APPLYING GOD'S WORD *(15 minutes)*

Ask each group member to think about his life before he became a Christian and compare it with his life since he received Christ. Have each person (including yourself) share one example of how his life has changed and how that change could be a witness to others about Christ.

Have each one review silently what he wrote on page 33 to describe his purpose in life. Ask him to think of specific ways he can begin to act on his statement of purpose this coming week and to write them down in the book. If necessary, suggest some possibilities: how he spends his free time in the evenings or on weekends; how he responds to his parents when asked to do something; what he talks about when he is with friends; or the attitude he has toward homework. Share your own purpose in life and how you plan to act on it this week. Then ask volunteers to do the same.

Ask two people to pray, asking that each group member will be able to move toward the goal of God's purpose for his life in the coming week.

Quote this week's memory verse (Philippians 1:6), then ask students to quote it with you. Review 1 John 5:11. Encourage group members to work in pairs between meetings to help each other with the memory program.

Assignments for Next Week Give the following assignments:
  1. In *Following Jesus*, complete Bible study 3, "Lots of Love."
  2. Find one or two other people in the group with whom you can work on memorizing Scripture.

AFTER THE MEETING

1. Evaluate the meeting: Did discussions stay away from cliches and abstractions, focusing on specific, practical, life-related ideas? If not, ask God to help you know when to probe deeper in next week's discussions.

2. If some group members are having difficulty keeping up with the assignments, call them during the week. Encourage them to stay with the group. Answer any questions they may have. Offer to help them work out a schedule.

Lots of Love
Bible Study 3

OVERVIEW

Key Concept

Spiritual growth is rooted in an active love relationship with God.

Memory Verse

John 3:16

Goals

Individual Growth: To become aware of the character and quality of God's love and to consider ways to express love to God.
Group Life: To explore ways to express love to God and God's love to one another as a body of believers.

BEFORE THE MEETING

1. Pray for each member of the group and for the development of group unity.
2. In *Following Jesus*, complete Bible study 3, studying all Scripture passages mentioned.
3. Note breakdowns of human attempts at love which you may hear or read about during the week. Be ready to use one as an example to get discussion started during the second activity of the meeting.
4. Gather materials for the meeting:
   Bible
   Following Jesus
   Bible memory packet.

THE MEETING

BUILDING THE GROUP *(20 minutes)*

Ask the group to name and jot down the five characteristics of God's love outlined in Bible study 3 (unconditional, sacrificial, serving, forgiving, creative).

Ask them to think of specific instances either out of their own or someone else's experience where human love has broken down (broken friendships, quarrels with parents, divorce, runaways, etc.). As each member gives an example, have the group decide which of the five characteristics of God's love was the primary missing element in that particular instance.

Discuss how God's love differs from what usually passes for love in daily life. (Enliven the discussion by suggesting that they think of how advertisers use the promise of love as an end result of using their products.)

FOCUSING ON LIFE *(10 minutes)*

Discuss: **Have there been times when you have doubted God's love for you? Why? How can we get rid of such doubts?** (Focus on what God says.) Then say, **God does love us, but He wants us to love Him too. How can we express our love to God? Let's check it out.**

EXPLORING GOD'S WORD *(30 minutes)*

Give everyone a few minutes to review the contents and their written responses to Bible study 3 in *Following Jesus.*

Discuss the following issues, encouraging each person to contribute his thoughts and to jot down the ideas of other group members.

1. If someone told you, "The way to love God is to go to church, read the Bible, and pray," what would you say? (That's only the beginning—a small part of what it means to love God.)

2. From what you know of Jesus' life on earth, what are some specific ways He expressed His love for God to God? to others? (He took time to pray, rejected Satan's tempting offers, obeyed His Father even to death; fed the hungry, healed the sick, loved those whom others found unlovable.)

3. How do Jesus' expressions of love to God and to others relate to the five characteristics of God's love outlined in today's Bible study? (They demonstrate God's kind of love.)

4. What can you do to express your love for God with your heart? your soul? your mind? your body? *Answers may be based on students' written responses to "Making It Personal."*

5. How can your love for God be expressed by the way you treat your family? your friends? the guy who keeps annoying you in study hall? the teacher who is a little too hard on you?

APPLYING GOD'S WORD (15 minutes)

Discuss:

1. How can we as a group express our love to God? *Suggest planning a special time of worship—praying and singing or reading hymns—as a good beginning point and as a way to ask God for His answer to this question.*

2. How might our relationships with one another express God's love? *Suggest that during the week they list ways they can make their relationships with each person in the group more serving, more forgiving, more creative, more sacrificial, and more unconditional.*

Encourage each member to meet with at least one other member of the group for a time of sharing and praying before the next meeting. If he needs to mend or restore a strained or broken relationship with anyone in the group, he should meet with that person first. Strengthened relationships between individuals will help the whole Discipleship Family.

Quote today's memory verse (John 3:16) together. In response to God's sacrificial love for them, have several group members pray, thanking God for His love and asking for His guidance as they seek to express their love for Him this coming week.

Assignments for Next Week   Motivate students to do next week's assignments by saying **Do you ever have trouble loving yourself or others? Your Bible study this next week will help you learn to accept yourself and others by exercising God's kind of love.**

1. Complete Bible study 4. Write down any comments, questions, or pertinent thoughts.

2. Get together with one person from the group during the week for prayer.

AFTER THE MEETING

1. Evaluate: Are two or three people dominating the discussions at each group meeting? If so, talk with them privately. Let them know you appreciate their contributions; but ask them to work with you in helping everyone take part.

2. If there is a person in the group with whom you need to mend or strengthen your relationship, set a time and place to meet with him.

Love to Spare

Bible Study 4

OVERVIEW

Key Concept Spiritual growth involves learning to love ourselves and others with God's kind of love.

Memory Verse 1 John 3:23

Goals *Individual Growth:* To gain a new sense of self-worth and begin expressing love to those who seem especially unlovable.
Group Life: To become a source of acceptance, appreciation, and love for one another.

BEFORE THE MEETING

1. Pray that the relationships between individuals in your Discipleship Family will be stengthened during the coming weeks.
2. Complete Bible study 4 in *Following Jesus.*
3. Write one thing you like about each person in your Discipleship Family.
4. Gather materials for the meeting:
   Bible
   Following Jesus
   Bible Memory Packet.

THE MEETING

BUILDING THE GROUP *(20 minutes)*

Ask volunteers to share their experiences of this past week as they talked and prayed with other group members. What did they learn about the other person? about themselves? Suggest that they all try to meet with each person at least once during the next six weeks.

Say: **Under "Loving Yourself" in Bible study 4, you were to make two lists: (1) things you don't like about yourself; (2) things you do like about yourself. How many of you had difficulty thinking of** things to put on that first list? How many of you found it harder to come up with things to put on that second list? Since most of us find it much easier to think of things we do like about ourselves, let's help each other add to our lists of likable things. Ask each person in the group to name one thing he likes about each of the other group members—you begin. Let this be a fun, relaxed time.

FOCUSING ON LIFE *(10 minutes)*

Discuss:

1. **What relationship is there between how you feel about yourself and how you feel about other people?** *Have students make a list of things they don't like about other people and compare it with the list of things they don't like about themselves.*

2. **How does this comparison relate to what Jesus said in Mark 12:31?** (He did not simply command us to love our neighbors. He knew that was impossible if we don't love and value ourselves.)

EXPLORING GOD'S WORD *(30 minutes)*

Have each person review "Loving Others," Bible study 4. Then discuss:

1. **Why is it important for Christians to love other people?** *Refer to insights from 1 John 4:7-19 for the answers.* (God is love; He loved us first and His love is made complete by our love for others; God lives in us; we can have confidence on the day of judgment; love drives out fear; we can't love God and not love others; God has commanded it.)

2. **How can we begin to love other people when we don't feel like loving them?** *Refer again to 1 John 4:7-19.* (By knowing and relying on God's love because love comes from God; God gives us His Spirit who lives in us and fills us with God's love.)

3. **What did Jesus say was the best way for the world to know that we are His disciples?** *Refer to John 13:34-35.* (By our visible expressions of love for each other.)

4. **How can we stop simply talking about loving others and begin to truly love right now?** *Refer to the"Loving Others" section, page 49.* (Ask God for His Love; believe that He has given it; do a good and loving deed for someone you find hard to love.)

APPLYING GOD'S WORD *(15 minutes)*

As a group, quote today's memory verse (1 John 3:23). Then ask each person to share his experience this past week in showing God's love to a person he has found hard to love. (Refer to their responses under "Making It Personal.") Ask if they realize that while they are trying to express love to others, that doesn't necessarily mean that others will love them in return.

Ask: **How can we help each other when we get frustrated, angry, or discouraged by the actions of others?** (Call one another when we are having a hard time following through with God's love.)

Close the meeting in prayer, asking God to help each of you realize that you have love to spare because God's love has the power to transform not only your lives but the life of each person you deal with each day.

Assignments for Next Week Give the following assignments in your own words and with enthusiasm:

1. Complete Bible study 5.
2. Review all memory verses and be prepared to recite them.
3. Read "The Guest Who Took Over" in the back of *Following Jesus,* as required in Bible study 5.

Mention that beginning with Bible study 6, each person will need a notebook for writing responses to daily Bible reading assignments in 1 John. Group members may already have extra notebooks at home they can use. If not, offer to buy inexpensive notebooks for everyone who needs them. Students can reimburse you for the cost when you hand them out at next week's meeting.

AFTER THE MEETING ———————————————————————

1. Evaluate: Was the atmosphere of the meeting relaxed and comfortable? If not, why? The room itself could be the problem if it is too hot or cold, lacks a homey warmth, has poor lighting or uncomfortable chairs, or isn't protected from outside interruptions. Find ways to improve the room, or look for a better meeting place. If the problem lies in poor group dynamics, review the suggestions for effective meetings on page 9 of this Leader's Guide.

2. If any group members seem to be on the fringe, either not being accepted fully by the others or just not taking part in the discussions and activities, pray specifically for them this week. If possible get together with them before the next meeting to express your love for them and to encourage them to share their thoughts and ideas.

Alive in You
Bible Study 5

OVERVIEW

Key Concept   Spiritual growth is made possible by the transforming power of Jesus Christ living in us.

Memory Verse   John 15:5

Goals   *Individual Growth:* To discover what it means to "remain in Christ" and to identify and develop the characteristics of a life in Christ. *Group Life:* To encourage development of the Spirit's fruit in group members' relationships with one another and with their families, classmates, and other Christians.

BEFORE THE MEETING

1. Pray for each member of your Discipleship Family by name. Ask that they will all develop an understanding that being Christ's disciples does not depend on their efforts, but on Christ who lives in them and will work through them.
2. In *Following Jesus*, complete Bible study 5; read "The Guest Who Took Over."
3. Review all Bible memory verses.
4. Consider specific ways you can express love, joy, peace, patience, kindness, goodness, gentleness, and self-control to each group member when you talk or meet with him this week.
5. Gather materials for the meeting:
   Bible
   Following Jesus
   Bible memory packet
   A houseplant
   Notebooks (one for each group member who needs one—see last week's assignment section, page 27, in this Leader's Guide)

BUILDING THE GROUP *(15 minutes)*

Divide the group into pairs and have partners take turns reviewing Bible verses memorized so far. Encourage those who know their verses well to help those who don't by meeting with them during the week for practice. Ask volunteers to share any benefits they have received so far from hiding God's Word in their hearts.

Since you're halfway through this discipleship study, take a few minutes to review the main points of the first four Bible studies. Ask:

1. How can we know we are truly Christians?
2. What are three purposes God has for our lives?
3. What are five characteristics of God's love?
4. Why is it important for Christians to love other people?

Ask each person to share at least one thing he has learned that has been especially important in his life. Ask for any questions, comments, problems, or suggestions about the Discipleship Family, things you have studied, or the group meetings.

During a time of prayer, reaffirm the commitment of the group to Christ and one another, asking for guidance and wisdom in dealing with any problems mentioned in the preceding discussion, and thanking God for the truths that have been learned so far.

FOCUSING ON LIFE *(15 minutes)*

Discuss "The Guest Who Took Over," page 120 in *Following Jesus:*

1. What do the different rooms described in the article represent in your life? *Refer members to their responses on page 55.*

2. What difference does it make to know that Christ is with you, not just when you are in church or when you pray or read the Bible, but all of the time? *Encourage group members to share how this knowledge makes them feel and the difference it makes or could make in their attitudes and actions.*

EXPLORING GOD'S WORD *(30 minutes)*

Allow a few minutes for each person to review the rest of his responses to the assignments in Bible study 5, *Following Jesus.* Then discuss:

1. What are some things you can do to allow Christ to have consistent control of your life? (Confess sins; accept His control.)

2. How does this compare with how we learned to restore and maintain our fellowship with God? *Refer to Bible study 2, page 28.*

3. What image did Jesus use to describe our relationship with Him? *Refer to John 15:5.* (Vine and branches.) To make this image more tangible, hold up a houseplant and remind the group of the interrelatedness of each part of a plant. Point out that there is no great effort expended by each branch to produce the leaves, flowers, or fruit that characterize the plant—they are simply the natural result of being a part of the plant. The fruit comes from the nature of the plant, not from the hard work of each branch.

4. How are our lives in Christ like branches on a plant? (The power and fruit of the Christian life come from the nature of God—if we stay with Him, we will grow and become like Him.)

5. How are our lives different from a plant's branches? (We have the freedom to abide in Him or to go our own way.)

Refer to "Exploring the Results" section in *Following Jesus*, page 58; ask the following questions:

1. What does it mean to "remain in"? *After each person has read his written definition, try to summarize all contributions into one statement.*

2. What are the results of remaining in Christ and Christ remaining in us? *Refer to John 15:5-11.* (We will bear much fruit; our prayers will be answered; God will receive glory; our discipleship will be proved; our obedience will result in experiencing His love for us and the joy that He gives.)

3. What does God do to produce more fruit in us? *Refer to John 15:2-3.* (He trims away the deadwood—sinful characteristics that keep us from bearing fruit; and He nurtures spiritual fruit.)

4. What basic tool does He use for trimming and nurturing? (His Word.)

Go over the list of deadwood characteristics that Paul gives in Galatians 5:19-21 (see "Making It Personal," page 60, *Following Jesus*). Make sure the meanings of the words are clear to everyone. For example, "debauchery" (NIV) or "lasciviousness" (KJV) more simply defined mean "lustfulness" or "immorality." Then discuss:

1. Why are these characteristics considered "deadwood" for a Christian? (Because God's goal for a Christian is to be like Christ, and those things are not part of His character.)

2. Which of these is most prominent among young people today?

3. How does "deadwood" express itself in each of our lives? *Have each person share one piece of deadwood he sees in his own life—you share first.*

4. How can we help each other trim the deadwood out of our lives? (Encourage one another; be accountable to one another.)

Say: When God trims us, He doesn't leave gaping holes in our lives so we have stubby, ugly lives. Instead He heals and nurtures us to produce beautiful fruit. Then discuss:

1. What words does Paul use to describe this "fruit-filled" life? *Refer to Galatians 5:22-23.* (Love, joy, peace, patience, kindness, goodness, faithfulness, gentleness, and self-control.)

2. How prominent are these characteristics among the people we know at school, work, church, and home?

3. What is likely to be the result of our developing these characteristics in our lives—being kind, gentle, patient, good, etc.—and expressing them in the world around us?

APPLYING GOD'S WORD *(15 minutes)*

Say: While it is true that allowing Christ to live out the fruit of the Spirit in us will make us different from most of the crowd and give us new challenges to face, having the fruit of the Spirit will also help us handle the normal frustrations we face in our daily lives.

Ask group members to look over the list of frustrations they wrote on page 53 in *Following Jesus,* and to think of specific ways that the fruit of the Spirit will help them handle those frustrations. Give them time to write down any new ideas they have. Then ask volunteers to share one or more of their ideas. (Examples: expressing thanks instead of complaints to parents; showing self-control and patience with little brothers or sisters; being faithful in responsibilities at school or work; being at peace about dating relationships; not constantly speculating or worrying; being faithful to friends through hard times; practicing self-control to overcome negative thoughts, actions, and habits.)

Go over the section "Giving Christ Control," page 56. Then quote the memory verse (John 15:5) together. Follow with a time of silent prayer during which each person asks God for guidance in the specific areas of life he is having trouble with right now. Close by leading a prayer of thanksgiving for God's consistent presence, control, and power in your lives.

Assignments for Next Week   Give the following assignments:

1. Complete Bible study 6.

2. Spend at least 10 minutes each day in Bible study as explained at the end of Bible study 6. *If you brought notebooks for students to use for this assignment, give them out now.* (See session 5, "Assignments for Next Week.")

3. Bring your notebooks to the rest of our meetings so you can share with the rest of us what God is teaching you in 1 John.

1. Evaluate: Do you find yourself giving more answers to the discussion questions than the students are? If so, perhaps you're not giving them enough time to collect their thoughts. If there is a silent moment after a question is asked, don't rush in with hints or answers. Give everyone a chance to think through what they want to say and let them say it. Remember, as a Discipleship Family leader, you guide group members toward discovering and sharing biblical insights for themselves. Though you should correct any wrong interpretations, you should not lecture.

2. Be alert for anyone who may need to talk with you alone. As Bible study assignments and specific life applications increase, some members may feel too pressured or have questions or problems they can't answer or solve by themselves.

God Says . . .
Bible Study 6

OVERVIEW

Key Concept   Spiritual growth is nourished by getting into God's Word on a regular basis.

Memory Verse   Psalm 119:9

Goals   *Individual Growth:* To begin studying the Bible every day and to apply what is studied to daily life.
Group Life: To encourage one another to study God's Word every day and to remind one another of what has been learned.

BEFORE THE MEETING

1. Pray that each person will make time to study the Bible each day this week and that God will speak to each in a special way.
2. In *Following Jesus*, complete Bible study 6, including the special Bible studies in 1 John.
3. Think of things you have learned and things people have told that have helped you develop the habit of studying the Bible. Be prepared to share these with the group at the meeting.
4. Talk with several group members during the week to encourage them in their study and to let them know you care about them.
5. Gather materials for the meeting:
   Bible
   Following Jesus
   Fiber-tipped pens in various colors
   Plain sheets of paper
   Notebook (containing your notes on 1 John)
   Bible memory packet

BUILDING THE GROUP *(15 minutes)*

Ask for reports on the 10 minutes of daily Bible study as assigned at the end of Bible study 6 in *Following Jesus*. Ask: **Were you able to set a specific time? Did you find a quiet place where you could be alone? Were you able to concentrate? Did you find the "Bible Response Sheet" easy to duplicate and use in your own notebook?** Let this be a time where group members share ways to overcome specific difficulties or problems in following through on the Bible study time. Give examples from your own experience.

Ask several people to share one important insight they have gained from their study of 1 John so far.

FOCUSING ON LIFE *(10 minutes)*

Referring to the beginning of Bible study 6, page 65, *Following Jesus*, ask:

1. **What can we learn about Jesus' study of God's Word from His encounter with Satan, recorded in Matthew 4:1-10?** (He knew Scripture and used it to resist temptation.)

2. **What would most people's response have been to the offer of bread after 40 days without eating anything?** (Thanks a lot! I'm starving!)

3. **What would have been their response to being offered all the land within sight from the top of a mountain?** (Wow!)

Say: **Because Jesus knew God and His Word so well, He knew what to say to Satan. He was able to recognize that Satan was tempting Him. Studying the Bible can make us more aware of what is going on around us and give us the insight and wisdom needed to deal with real life.**

EXPLORING GOD'S WORD *(40 minutes)*

Give everyone a few minutes to review his work on this week's Bible study. Then discuss:

1. **Why is the Bible such an important source of help for us as we seek Christ's control of our lives?** *Refer to "Counting on God's Word," page 66.* (It is inspired by God for teaching, correcting, training, and equipping; it is alive and can change attitudes, thoughts,

spirits, and souls; it is authoritative—tells us God's will; it is the truth—and truth gives us freedom to truly live life at its fullest.)

2. **What are some benefits we gain from studying and obeying God's Word?** *Refer to "Discovering the Benefits of God's Word," page 68.* (Maturity, prosperity, wisdom, understanding, light, guidance, a clean life, God's love and companionship [friendship], faith, ability to obey God.)

3. **If all we have talked about so far is true, and it is, then knowing God's Word should be one of our top priorities in life. But how do we go about knowing the Word?** *See "Experiencing the Benefits of God's Word," page 68.* (Hear, read, study, memorize, meditate.)

Talk about what "hearing" the Word means. Encourage group members to attend church services regularly, take notes on messages given by the pastor and other Bible teachers, and write specific things they can do to apply each message to their lives.

Discuss the difference between "reading" the Word and "studying" it. Though everyone in the Discipleship Family is studying a small portion of Scripture each day, encourage them to start reading whole chapters or books at one sitting to get an overview of God's Word.

Turn to the 1 John, Daily Bible Reading Assignments on page 127, *Following Jesus.* Select one of the first five passages listed and work through it together, answering: Who? What? When? Where? Why? What does it say? What does it mean? How does it apply to me? What am I going to do about it?

Ask if Bible study 6 has clarified the purpose of the Scripture memory they have been doing for the past five weeks. Have each person recite one of the verses, personalizing it by inserting his own name where there are pronouns or words like "the world" or "the man." (Example: "I am the Vine; Jane is the branch. If Jane remains in Me and I in her, Jane will bear much fruit; apart from Me Jane can do nothing," John 15:5).

Give each person a sheet of paper and a pen. Then ask everyone to draw a picture which illustrates Psalm 1:1-3. Allow about five minutes. Have them display their work and then discuss how this simple exercise helped them dig deeper into the verses and apply what was said to their lives.

APPLYING GOD'S WORD (10 minutes)

Encourage each person to continue in the 10-minute daily study of 1 John as outlined on page 72. If someone is having trouble scheduling his time, offer to help him work out a schedule after the meeting. Say: **Remember, the purpose of studying God's Word is not just so we can all answer the questions at our weekly meetings. His Word is to become a part of everything we are. We are to use it, speak it,** rely on it, share it, and let it affect every area of our lives. For this to happen, we must develop the habit of thinking about God's Word in every situation. For example: When we're discouraged by grades or work, angry at someone, or nervous about telling someone about God, we should ask ourselves, "What would Jesus say or do in this situation? What specific Scripture passage gives a principle that applies to this situation?" By consciously reminding ourselves of Scripture, our minds will turn there first when we need guidance or encouragement. And God will bring to mind actual Scripture passages to guide us in many daily situations. To reinforce this, quote today's memory verse (Psalm 119:9) together.

Ask several volunteers to close in prayer; have them pray for perseverence in their study of God's Word.

Assignments for Next Week   Motivate group members to:
   1. Complete Bible study 7.
   2. Continue daily study of 1 John and begin a daily prayertime as explained at the end of Bible study 7.

Be available as students leave to help anyone who needs suggestions for scheduling a regular time for Bible study (get up a little earlier, cut out some TV watching, etc.).

AFTER THE MEETING ——————————————————————

1. Evaluate: Did everyone participate freely in all of the meeting activities? If some group members still seem to be on the edge of the group life, ask one or two of the more mature members to give them special support and companionship during the next weeks. Also, think of ways you can make them feel more a part of the group meetings (ask them to read Scripture; call on them by name occasionally, etc.).

2. Are some of your group members finding daily Bible study and prayer to be more of a chore than a joy? Commitment, determination, and self-discipline are needed for developing a relationship with God. But Bible study and prayer should be experiences that are enjoyed—not rituals that are endured. Try to talk with each person during the next couple of weeks to help him through any problems he may be having in this area.

Talking with God
Bible Study 7

OVERVIEW

Key Concept Spiritual growth is stimulated by communicating with God through daily prayer.

Memory Verse John 16:24

Goals *Individual Growth:* To explore the importance of prayer as a part of a disciple's life and to begin praying daily.
Group Life: To understand why prayer is an important part of loving and encouraging others and to begin praying for one another on a regular basis.

BEFORE THE MEETING

1. Pray for each Discipleship Family member by name, asking that each will want and develop a closer relationship with God.
2. In *Following Jesus*, complete Bible study 7, including the daily Bible study in 1 John and the prayertime.
3. Write specific prayer requests to share.
4. Gather materials for the meeting:
   Bible
   Following Jesus
   Notebook (your notes on 1 John)
   Bible memory packet

THE MEETING

BUILDING THE GROUP *(15 minutes)*

Use the first five minutes to discuss any questions, problems, or observations the group members would like to share about their experiences with the daily time of Bible study and prayer.

Ask each person to name one characteristic of a close friendship. Suggest they write down each characteristic as it's mentioned. After everyone has contributed, discuss: **Which characteristics can immediately be identified as true of your relationship with God? Which cannot? Why? How does your relationship with your closest friend and your relationship with God differ?**

FOCUSING ON LIFE *(10 minutes)*

Discuss: **Do you think that prayer really changes things? Why? Name one experience you have had in your prayer life that resulted in change. How did that make you feel? Name one experience you have had when you felt that your prayer was not heard. How did you feel? Do you think God always answers your prayers? Someone once said, "Prayer doesn't change things; prayer changes people." Do you agree or disagree? Why?**

EXPLORING GOD'S WORD *(20 minutes)*

Allow several minutes for group members to review Bible study 7 and their written responses. Then discuss:

 1. **When is the best time to pray?** (Anytime, all the time.)
 2. **What kind of mood do you need to be in to pray effectively?** (It doesn't matter; moods do not affect the effectiveness of prayer *[have students give examples from David's life]*; God wants to hear from us when we're feeling good and when we're feeling discouraged or need help.)
 3. **What are some things we can pray for?** *Refer to Matthew 6:9-14.* (Daily needs, forgiveness, guidance, deliverance and protection, God's will to be done, God to be given glory.)
 4. **According to John 14:13; 15:7; and 16:24, what does God promise to do in response to our prayers?** (Give us whatever we ask.)
 5. **What are the conditions attached to these promises?** (We must ask in His name and according to His will; we must obey His Word and pray with God's interests and kingdom in mind.)
 6. **Why is prayer important for us as Christ's disciples?** (It's one of the only two ways we get to know and communicate with the Master Teacher—God. Bible study is the other way.)

Discuss and say today's memory verse (John 16:24) together.

APPLYING GOD'S WORD *(30 minutes)*

It's important to learn about prayer, but it's more important to pray. Use the remaining time of this meeting for group prayer. Divide the prayertime into three parts:

1. Prayers of thanksgiving. Have each person share something with the group for which he is thankful today. Then ask everyone who will, to pray, thanking God for the things mentioned and anything else that comes to mind.

2. Prayers for personal needs. Ask that each person share personal prayer requests with the group (you begin) and again have a time of prayer when everyone who wants to can pray for the requests. Suggest that everyone write the requests in the space on page 83, in *Following Jesus*, so they can pray for one another during the coming week.

3. Prayers for others. Ask each person to suggest a prayer request for other people—your local church, local government, national issues, or world issues like hunger, peace, and justice. If they are familiar with any specific missionaries and mission work, include those too. Close the meeting by asking everyone to pray for one or more of the requests mentioned.

Assignments for Next Week Be enthusiastic as you remind students to:
1. **Complete Bible study 8.**
2. **Continue the daily Bible study and prayertime.**
3. **Review all Bible memory verses.**

If any group members expressed significant problems when sharing prayer requests, try to talk with them before they leave the meeting or call them tomorrow. Assure them of your prayers and your availability to help them if you can.

AFTER THE MEETING ————————————————————

1. Evaluate: Were group members open and relaxed with one another during the prayertime? Was there evidence of their love and concern for one another as they discussed prayer requests and the things they were thankful for? If you're meeting for prayer before or after the last three meetings, plan ways to vary the prayer time. For example: (a) Have brief sentence prayers with each person adding to what the last person said. (b) Have everyone hold hands. Each person takes his turn and squeezes the next person's hand when he's finished. If the next person doesn't want to pray aloud, he squeezes the hand of the next person.
2. During the week, note specific answers to prayers offered today. Share them during the group's next prayertime.

In His Image
Bible Study 8

OVERVIEW ————————————————————

Key Concept   Spiritual growth is ongoing when we are committed to following Jesus regardless of the cost.

Memory Verse   Matthew 4:19

Goals   *Individual Growth:* To discover what it means to be a disciple and to decide to follow Christ daily as His obedient disciple.
Group Life: To learn the cost of following Christ as disciples and to begin to realize the benefits of having a group of loving, caring, and forgiving friends who are on the same road.

BEFORE THE MEETING ————————————————

1. Pray that each group member will have a strong and continual desire to follow Christ, whatever the cost.
2. In *Following Jesus*, complete Bible study 8, and continue daily Bible study and prayertime.
3. If you get a phone call from anyone in the group this week when they reach page 90 in *Following Jesus,* make it a priority to meet with him the same day.
4. Gather materials for the meeting:
   Bible
   Following Jesus
   Notebook (your notes on 1 John)
   Bible memory packet

BUILDING THE GROUP *(20 minutes)*

Ask group members to share what they experienced as they continued their daily Bible study and prayertimes. (For example: special insights from 1 John, answers to prayer, new appreciation for daily Bible study and prayer, triumphs or defeats in battling the daily time schedule, etc.) Discuss their reactions to the group prayertime last week. Would they like to have a similar time of prayer before or after each weekly meeting? If so, make plans to begin next week.

Give the group a few minutes to think about the different people who have influenced their Christian lives. These may be family members, personal friends or acquaintances, authors of books, radio or TV personalities, etc. Ask each one to share the name of one person and how or why that person has influenced him in his Christian walk. (Be prepared to share your own example first.)

FOCUSING ON LIFE *(10 minutes)*

Say: **Almost everyone looks to someone or to some group for acceptance or direction. For example, think about some groups at your school. How can you tell which group a person belongs to?** (Who he's with, how he acts, how he dresses, where he goes, etc.) **Think about society as a whole. Where do most people get their ideas about what to do, what to wear, what to think, what to say? Who do people follow around and eagerly listen to?** (TV and film stars, sports figures, politicians, musicians, disc jockeys, etc.) **It's hard to find anyone who isn't patterning his life after someone or something. (Even people who claim to be "doing their own thing" are following a philosophy that's endorsed by many well-known people.) So the issue isn't so much whether we will follow anyone at all, but of whom will we choose to follow. Who is worthy to be followed?**

EXPLORING GOD'S WORD *(30 minutes)*

Allow a few minutes for group members to review Bible study 8 and their responses to it. Then discuss:

Following Jesus / 41

1. According to your research this week, what is a disciple? *Ask them to read their definitions.* Then summarize: **A disciple is one who learns, follows, and passes on what he has learned to others.**

2. What are the sure signs of being a disciple of Christ? *Refer to the list of characteristics from the Gospel of John, page 87.* (Faith, knowledge of God's Word, obedience, love, unity with other disciples, fruit of the Spirit, caring for other people, etc.)

3. How do we become Christ's disciples? *Refer to Colossians 2:6; Hebrews 11:6.* (By faith, believing in Him.)

4. We all took that step when we became Christians. But, how do we continue on the road of discipleship without getting detoured? *See Colossians 2:7.* (We must be rooted in Christ, built up in Christ, strengthened in the faith, and overflowing with thanksgiving.)

5. Sounds good, doesn't it? But what do those words mean to us in real life? How do we become "rooted in Christ?" (Through personal Bible study and prayer, meditation, etc.—the underground "root system" of a strong Christian faith.) **What can we do to be "built up in Christ"?** (Building up means to grow. We grow by applying God's Word to our lives, and by allowing Him to make us more like Christ.) **According to Colossians 3:12-16, what are some of these Christlike qualities?** (Compassion, kindness, humility, gentleness, patience, forgiveness, peaceableness, thankfulness, wisdom.) **How are we strengthened in the faith?** (By meeting with other believers, hearing God's Word preached and discussed, reading books about Christian life and thought, etc.) **What will happen when we are "overflowing with thankfulness"?** (We will be telling other people about Christ and our lives in Him; we will be a source of encouragement and strength for other disciples; we will glorify God.)

6. What are some possible hindrances that could make it hard for you to stay on the road of discipleship? *Have the group refer to their responses on page 89.* **How can they be overcome?** (By Christ's power.)

7. Christ has certainly promised that the life of discipleship will be worthwhile and full of benefits, but He never said it would be easy. According to Luke 9:23-26, what did He say is the cost of discipleship? *Refer to page 90.*

8. Think about the examples we gave earlier of Christians who have encouraged us to keep on following Christ. In what ways do their lives show that they have paid the costs of obedient discipleship? What can we learn from their examples of following Christ no matter what the costs?

APPLYING GOD'S WORD *(15 minutes)*

Quote today's memory verse (Matthew 4:19) together. Then say: **Christ calls us all to follow Him as committed disciples. How will we**

respond? Don't ask for verbal answers. Instead, allow a few minutes of silence so each group member can think through the implications of this study and pray about his commitment to be a 100-percent-sold-out disciple of Christ.

Refer to the "Making It Personal" section, page 94. Have each person review his response to the third assignment and write specific ways he will begin practicing the qualities he thinks God wants to build into his life. Next, have several people share their responses to the fourth assignment—ways God can use them as disciples to share his life with others. Then as a group, discuss specific ways you can put these into practice this week.

Assignments for Next Week   Be enthusiastic as you give the following assignment.
1. Complete Bible study 9.
2. Continue daily Bible study and prayertime.
3. Review all Bible memory verses.
4. Talk with a non-Christian about your life in Christ.

AFTER THE MEETING ─────────────────────────────

Evaluate: How did the group respond to this study? Is there a feeling of excitement? Are there any signs of fear? uncertainly? boredom? What are your feelings? How do you think your feelings affect the responses of the group members? Pray that God will give you a contagious enthusiasm for growing as a disciple and sharing your faith with others.

Blueprint for a Disciple
Bible Study 9

OVERVIEW

Key Concept   Spiritual growth is adventurous when we learn to make decisions based on God's will.

Memory Verse   Proverbs 3:5-6

Goals   *Individual Growth:* To learn the principles that help us know God's will and to use them as we make decisions.
Group Life: To understand how important the counsel of other Christians becomes when we make decisions; to begin to ask for their prayers and counsel when we face hard decisions.

BEFORE THE MEETING

1. Pray for each member of the group by name, asking God to guide him in any decisions he is facing this week.
2. In *Following Jesus,* complete Bible study 9 and continue daily Bible study and prayertime.
3. Review all Bible memory work.
4. Tell someone you know who is not a Christian about your life in Christ. Be ready to share your experience with the group.
5. If the Discipleship Family agreed to meet for prayer before this week's meeting, call everyone to remind them to come 15 minutes early.
6. Gather materials for the meeting:
   Bible
   Following Jesus
   Notebook (your notes on 1 John)
   Bible memory packet

THE MEETING ──────────────────────────

BUILDING THE GROUP *(15 minutes)*

Ask various group members to recite one of the Bible memory verses. Do this till everyone recites at least two verses.

Ask volunteers to share their experiences this past week in talking to other people about their lives in Christ (include yourself). Ask: **What did you say? What was the person's response? How did you feel before and after? What has this experience taught you about the importance of talking about Christ to others?** There may be some in the group who didn't do this assignment because they were afraid; others may have had an unpleasant experience. Be understanding. Encourage them by saying that as they grow in Christ, sharing Him with others will become more natural and easy. Mention the rest of the books in the Moving Toward Maturity series. Emphasize how each book will help them grow in their relationships with God and in their ability and confidence to share Christ with others (see the back cover of this Leader's Guide).

FOCUSING ON LIFE *(15 minutes)*

Have each person share an important decision he has made in the past, telling how he made it and what happened as a result. Ask: **Are you confident that your decision was based on God's will? Not so sure? Sure it wasn't? Why do you feel the way you do?**

Ask: **Do you think God really cares about all of the details and decisions of our lives? Let's look at Psalm 139; Proverbs 5:21; and Matthew 6:25-34 to see.** *Briefly summarize the contents of each passage.* **What if we make a wrong turn?**

EXPLORING GOD'S WORD *(25 minutes)*

Have everyone review Bible study 9. Then discuss:

1. According to this week's study, what things do you know are God's will for every Christian? (He should be *saved*—looking to and believing Christ; *sanctified*—living a holy and honorable life; *Spirit-filled*; *suffering* for doing good and enduring it well; *submitting to God*—obeying His written, known will.)

2. How can you find out what God wants you to do in a specific

situation? *Refer to Proverbs 3:5-8.* (Trust God; consider all alternatives and commit them to God; leave the matter in God's hands; spend time alone with God in prayer and Bible study specifically seeking His will on the matter; make the decision that gives you peace in God's presence.)

3. What do you usually think of when you talk to others about "God's will for my life"? (A life plan, career, etc.)

4. What do you think the Bible means when it speaks of "God's will" for your life? (A day-by-day decision to follow and obey God, not worrying about the future.)

Have everyone read over the seven practical pointers for knowing God's will on page 108, under "Some Things to Remember." Briefly discuss each one.

APPLYING GOD'S WORD *(20 minutes)*

Ask volunteers to share difficult decisions they are facing right now. As each person describes the decision he needs to make, let other group members suggest alternatives, mention Scriptures that apply, share their own experiences with similar decisions, and simply offer encouragement. After three or four people have received input on their particular decisions, ask each person to review what he wrote under the "Making It Personal" section, pages 105-109, regarding his own decision that needs to be made. Encourage each person to write down any new insights he has gained during this meeting that will help him in making that decision.

Recite today's memory verse (Proverbs 3:5-6) together. Then close the meeting in prayer, asking several group members to pray specifically for the decisions that have been discussed.

Assignments for Next Week Express your appreciation for the commitment of each person in the group, as you remind them of what they need to do before the next meeting:

1. Complete Bible study 10.

2. Continue daily Bible study and prayertime. If you have finished the 1 John study, you may want to begin studying the Gospel of John at your own rate.

3. Review all Bible memory verses.

AFTER THE MEETING

Evaluate: Did everyone get involved in today's discussions? Was there an atmosphere of warmth, caring, and true concern when group members shared decisions they were facing? Did you let group members counsel one another without stepping in too quickly with your own suggestions?

Good, Better, Best
Bible Study 10

OVERVIEW

Key Concept   Spiritual growth is increased when we set priorities based on God's purposes for our lives.

Memory Verse   Matthew 6:33

Goals   *Individual Growth:* To set specific goals for spiritual growth, plan the steps needed to meet those goals, and begin taking those steps.
Group Life: To set goals for the group and plan how to reach them as well as to encourage each other in individual goals.

BEFORE THE MEETING

1. Pray for each group member, asking that God will guide him in his study as he plans goals and sets priorities for his life. Pray that the group as a whole will continue as a growing, maturing body of believers.
2. In *Following Jesus,* complete Bible study 10 and continue the daily Bible study and prayertime.
3. Call each group member during the week and ask him to be thinking of goals he would like the group itself to set and move toward. Ask him to pray about renewing his commitment to continue in the Discipleship Family for the study of the next book.
4. List the goals you would like the group to reach in the coming weeks.
5. Gather materials for the meeting:
   Bible
   Following Jesus
   Notebook (your notes on 1 John)
   Bible memory packet
   Spending Time Alone with God

BUILDING THE GROUP *(20 minutes)*

Since this is the last meeting in this introductory discipleship study, ask all members of the group to share specific things they have appreciated about being part of a Discipleship Family. Then ask what they liked best and least about the book, *Following Jesus;* about the group meetings; about the assignments; etc. Jot down their ideas so you can include them in your own evaluation of this 10-week study and how it can be improved. (See the questionnaire on page 51 of this Leader's Guide.)

After everyone has shared their thoughts, have a brief time of prayer, thanking God for allowing each one the opportunity to be a part of this group and for teaching you all important truths.

Review the main points of the past nine Bible studies by asking:

1. How can we know we are truly Christians?
2. What are three purposes God has for our lives?
3. What are five characteristics of God's love?
4. Why is it important for Christians to love other people?
5. What are the results of Christ living in us and we in Him?
6. What five things can we do to get to know God's Word?
7. Why is prayer an important part of a Christian's life?
8. What are sure signs of being a disciple?
9. How can we find God's will in specific situations?

Recite the first nine memory verses together.

FOCUSING ON LIFE *(10 minutes)*

Say: **Are you ever overwhelmed with all the things you have to do each week? Do you ever wish you had 30-hour days or 8-day weeks? Everyone has the same number of hours each day, so the difference between a person who accomplishes a great deal in his life and one who barely manages to survive must be in the ways each chooses to spend his time. Let's see where our time is going, by checking out how we spent the 168 hours of last week.**

Have everyone write the number of hours they spent sleeping, in school, eating meals, studying, etc. Then have them total their hours. Most of them will still have 20 or so hours unaccounted for. Suggest that it is how they spend those unaccounted hours that will determine whether they reach the goals they set for themselves in this week's Bible study.

EXPLORING GOD'S WORD *(25 minutes)*

Give everyone a few minutes to review Bible study 10 and their written responses. Then discuss:

1. **What are some of the world's definitions of "success"?** (Attainment of wealth, fame, or power.)

2. **What is your definition of success?** *Refer them to their written responses on page 112.*

3. **How will we know when we become successful?** (By reaching set goals; following priorities.)

4. **As disciples, what should be our first concern when we begin to set goals for our lives?** (Finding out what God's goals are for us.)

5. **What are some of God's goals for us as His disciples?** (Seeking His kingdom, being conformed to His image, doing everything for His glory, knowing Christ, becoming like Christ.)

Ask two or three people to share the life goal each wrote for himself on page 114. (You go first.) Discuss: **What does this goal mean in day-to-day living? How will it affect the way you live? What habits will you have to change to make it happen?**

Discuss how the commitment and goals accomplished by the Discipleship Family during the past 10 weeks have changed their lives: **What are some things that happened as a result of spending a specific amount of time each day in Bible study and prayer? What encouraged you to finish the Bible study assignment before each meeting? How did you resolve the conflict when another activity was scheduled at the same time the Discipleship Family met?**

Impress on the group that this week's study is about *life* goals, *life* commitment, *life* changes—not short-term activities. Discuss how, as a result of keeping their commitments to the group and achieving the goals that were set, they now have a positive foundation on which to build life goals.

APPLYING GOD'S WORD *(20 minutes)*

Share your list of priorities from before and after you put Christ first in your life. Explain why you made the changes you did. Ask if anyone else would like to share his priority list, or if anyone has a question about how to set priorities. Say: **All parts of our lives—mental, spiritual, social, and physical—are important to Christ. Playing basketball, learning to play the piano, studying French, going to parties, taking walks, etc.—everything we do can be done for the glory of God. He made us the way we are so that we** can do all those things *and* have fellowship with Him. Quote today's memory verse (Matthew 6:33) together.

Since this is the last week in this particular study, ask group members to suggest future goals for the group itself. Do they want to continue as a "family"? Describe the next book in the Moving Toward Maturity series, *Spending Time Alone with God.* Suggest that studying it together would be a good way to build on the foundation established during the past few weeks of work and study. How can the group, as a part of the body of Christ, fulfill the goals that God has for it (seeking His kingdom, knowing Christ, and making Him known)?

Ask them if they want to renew their commitments to this Discipleship Family or to stop meeting. If they decide to continue, challenge each one to be faithful to God and to the group. Determine how soon, when, and where they'd like to begin the study of Book 2. (They may wish to wait a month or two, but in the meantime they could continue to meet for weekly prayer.) Make sure they have completed all assignments in *Following Jesus* before beginning the studies in *Spending Time Alone with God.*

Close the meeting with a time of prayer. Ask for specific requests any of them may have; then have several volunteers pray.

Try to talk with everyone individually before leaving the meeting place. Thank each for his faithfulness to the group and encourage each one to continue to be a part of whatever the Discipleship Family decides to do. Also encourage each to continue with a personal time of Bible study and prayer.

No Assignment

AFTER THE MEETING ————————————————————————

1. Evaluate: Carefully remove page 51 from this Leader's Guide, and use it to evaluate your 10-week experience with a Discipleship Family. Mail your comments to us right away. Your input is important to us.
2. If the group set a time to begin a study of *Spending Time Alone with God,* be sure to call everyone during the week to remind them of where and when to meet.

Dear Discipleship Family Leader,

After completing your group study of *Following Jesus,* please fill out and mail this evaluation sheet to the editor. Thanks for your input!

1. Did you and your young people enjoy this study? _____

Why? _____

_____

2. How many people were in your Discipleship Family group? _____

3. What benefits and problems did you experience as a Discipleship Family?

Benefits: _____

_____

Problems: _____

_____

4. Do you plan to continue the series as a Discipleship Family? _____

Why? _____

_____

5. What did group members like best and least about the student book?

Best: _____

_____

Least: _____

_____

6. What are the strengths and weaknesses of this Leader's Guide?

Strengths: _____

_____

Weaknesses: _____

_____

**SonPower Youth Sources Editor
1825 College Avenue
Wheaton, Illinois 60187**

SPENDING TIME ALONE WITH GOD

Leader's Guide
prepared by
Nancy Spitler

Introduction

Moving Toward Maturity is a five-part discipleship training series for young people. It is designed to help them become so independently dependent on Jesus Christ that they can teach others to do the same. This series has three main purposes:

1. To train students in the "how to's" of Christian living.
2. To help students develop strong, Christlike characters.
3. To move students from the point of getting to know Jesus Christ to the point of sharing Him with others.

Spending Time Alone with God, the second book in the series, will walk students through the process of developing their personal times with God. Your group members will discover the purpose and individual benefits of a daily time alone with God, the importance of Bible study and Scripture memory, and the elements of an effective prayer life (praise, thanksgiving, confession, petition, and intercession).

The other four study books in the series, and related materials, are described on the outside back cover of this Leader's Guide.

Discipleship Family

Commitment is the key to a successful group study of *Spending Time Alone with God.* So limit the study group to those young people who will commit themselves to study the book and Bible on their own and will faithfully take part in every group meeting. This group of committed young people and their leader are referred to as a *Discipleship Family.* (Turn to page 11 in *Spending Time Alone with God* and read the commitments required of each person.)

By making and keeping these commitments, each Discipleship Family member will:

1. Learn to depend on Jesus Christ.
2. Develop personal discipline in Bible study, prayer, and Scripture memory.
3. Experience the rich fellowship and love of a committed, caring Christian community.

The young people and leaders who commit themselves to this discipleship training will move toward Christ's goal for the church: "His gifts were made that Christians might be properly equipped for their service, that the whole body might be built up until the time comes when, in the unity of common faith and common knowledge of the Son of God, we arrive at real maturity—that measure of development which is meant by 'the fullness of Christ' " (Eph. 4:12-13).*

---

*Quoted from *The New Testament in Modern English,* © 1972 by J. B. Phillips, published by The MacMillan Company. Used by permission.

You, the Leader

Being a leader of a Discipleship Family will require more time and personal involvement than most Bible studies or Sunday School classes you may have taught in the past. As a member of the group (not just its leader) you should take part in all the commitments, activities, and assignments of the Discipleship Family. To get started, here are some things you will need to do.

1. **Get familiar with the Moving Toward Maturity series** (see back cover) **and your role as a Discipleship Family leader.** Besides the introduction of this Leader's Guide, two other resources by Barry St. Clair can clarify your role: the book *Building Leaders for Strategic Youth Ministry* and the six-part video "The Youth Ministry Puzzle." Both are available in Christian bookstores or from Victor Books or Reach Out Ministries.

2. **Read through** *Spending Time Alone with God* **and this Leader's Guide.** Call each person from your original *Following Jesus* group, describe to him the purpose of Book 2 and ask him if he is planning to continue with the Moving Toward Maturity series. Explain the need for him to renew his commitment for the next 10 weeks.

3. **Organize your Discipleship Family.** Pray that the Lord will cause those who need to continue the series to make that commitment. If some students have gone through *Following Jesus* on their own, or have been members of another Discipleship Family, allow them an opportunity to join your group if there is room. Your group will be most effective with 4 to 8 members, and should not exceed 12. If more people are interested, a second group should be formed.

4. **Purchase the materials you will need well in advance of the first meeting.** Everyone who is leading a Discipleship Family group should have his own copy of the Leader's Guide. Each Discipleship Family member (including yourself) should have his own copy of *Spending Time Alone with God, a Bible,* a 5¹/₂" x 8¹/₂" looseleaf notebook, a set of *Time Alone with God Notebook Inserts* (you can photocopy them from pages 249-264 of this Leader's Guide), and a supply of paper.

5. **Decide the best time and place to meet.** Have everyone bring their school and work schedules to the first meeting so they can decide as a group when and where to meet for the next 10 sessions. If possible, plan to hold the meetings in your home or the home of one of the group members. Meeting in the informal atmosphere of a living room or around a dining room table will help people open up and join in discussions.

6. **Allow up to two hours for each meeting.** Suggested time allotments for each part of the meeting are given in this Leader's Guide. A total of 60 minutes is suggested for the introductory meeting (session 1); 75 minutes are suggested for sessions 2-11. Since these are not instructional classes, but meetings designed to build relationships and share insights, they should be open-ended. If

you finish a session in 75 minutes, fine. But you should have the freedom to meet for two hours if necessary (never longer).

7. Get the group together for a fun activity. Before or after session 1, plan a fun get-acquainted activity (softball game, bike hike, retreat, pizza party, picnic) for the participants of the Discipleship Family. This will help them renew the relationships they have developed with one another.

8. Plan to have a half day of prayer to conclude your study of *Spending Time Alone with God.* Detailed suggestions for this activity are on page 95, but set a date early.

Building relationships

Your role in the Discipleship Family is that of leader, not teacher. By explaining that you and all members of the group are in the process of becoming more mature disciples of Christ, you will begin to establish yourself as one of the group rather than as the "instructor." But because you are more mature in years and in experience than the young people in your Discipleship Family, they will look to you for organization, guidance, and example.

1. Meet with each group member. Schedule an appointment with each member of your Discipleship Family during the first week or two. Strengthen your relationship with each person. Check on his needs, interests, concerns, and any goals he set as a result of studying *Following Jesus.* Share those things about yourself as well. This will help you see one another as unique, important individuals with feelings and ideas. It will also result in more meaningful discussions during your group meetings.

2. Keep your own Time Alone with God Notebook during this 10-week study. In addition to the student notebook assignments, also write your observations about members of your Discipleship Family. Regularly pray for each one by name. Keep track of individual needs and achievements. If someone misses a session, contact him personally. Help him when he has trouble understanding something from Scripture. Talk with him if he seems to be breaking his commitments. Call on him for his opinions during meetings. Build him up so he will be valued and appreciated by the group. You can also use your notebook for writing your evaluation of each session as well as what you plan to do to improve as a leader.

3. Keep your pastor and church informed. While you're building relationships in your Discipleship Family, continue to build relationships within the church as well. Keep your pastor informed as to what is happening in your group. Encourage group members to be involved in the church and to strengthen their relationships with other believers—particularly other young people who are not a part of a Discipleship Family. Group members should continue in the strong relationships they have built with one another, but they should avoid becoming a "clique."

4. Limit group membership. The people who are a part of this group should come from those who studied *Following Jesus* with you last quarter, and possibly others who have finished *Following Jesus* and want to join the group. Because your Discipleship Family will be building trust based on shared experiences, don't take in any new members once the group has been established. You should also make sure that everyone who plans to join this group has completed all previous group commitments. Anyone who has dropped out of a prior group should not move on until he finishes his work on that book. After completing the study of *Spending Time Alone with God*, challenge each person to renew his commitment and to continue with the group in the study of *Making Jesus Lord* (Book 3 in the Moving Toward Maturity series).

Effective meetings

The Discipleship Family's meetings are based on biblical principles of discipleship. Each session has at least one *Group Life* and one *Individual Growth* goal. It's important that you work toward accomplishing both.

1. Be prepared. Begin your preparation for each session at least five days in advance. Do the Bible study in *Spending Time Alone with God*, answering the questions for yourself, not as you think the students might answer. Then skim through the Leader's Guide suggestions to see if there is anything you need to do right away. Later in the week (one or two days before the meeting) finalize your preparation: Review the *Spending Time Alone with God* material, and study the Leader's Guide suggestions, adapting activities according to the particular needs of your group.

2. Start on time. Since Discipleship Family meetings can last up to two hours, ask everyone to come on time, or even a few minutes early. (Those who arrive early can use the time to share with other group members or review Bible memory verses.)

3. Help students keep their commitments. Students are to complete the appropriate Bible study in *Spending Time Alone with God* **before** each session so the meeting can be devoted to building on what the students are learning on their own. For that reason, the "Exploring God's Word" section of each session does not contain a verbatim review of the Bible study material in *Spending Time Alone with God*. Instead students are given an opportunity to quickly look over the Bible study content and their written responses. Then the discussion that follows builds on and reinforces what students have learned during the week prior to the meeting. Group members should also have a regular time each week to share results of their personal times with God.

Be sensitive to group members who may lack self-discipline and need extra encouragement and motivation to keep their commitments. Be positive. Recall how Christ loved, encouraged, and disciplined the early disciples; then follow His example in helping His new disciples along.

4. Continue to develop skill in leading discussions. Here are a few ways to keep your Discipleship Family discussions on track so each member can contribute and learn during each session:

►*State questions clearly and concisely.* You're more likely to get specific answers if you ask specific questions.

After you ask a question, allow time for the group to think. Don't be afraid of short periods of silence. And don't jump in with your own answers or opinions. Don't make a contribution to the discussion that someone else in the group can make.

►*Respect each person's comments.* Encourage each one to say what he thinks, not just what he thinks he should say. Ask additional questions to help him amplify his thoughts and move from ideas to applications.

►*Stay close to Scripture.* The Bible is the authority for this study and for your group discussions. Encourage group members to base their ideas on biblical principles.

►*Challenge trite or superficial answers.* Don't let group members get away with simply rattling off a cliché or a Bible verse. Ask them to explain what they mean or give an illustration.

►*Ask review questions when appropriate to help the group think through things they've studied up to that point.* Use this time for members to raise previously-discussed issues with which they're still having problems.

►*If some group members are hesitant to take part in the discussions, ask them direct questions relating to their personal opinions or experiences.* Let them know that you care about them and what they think.

►*If some members answer all the questions, begin addressing your questions to others by name so everyone may be heard.* If a member continues to monopolize the discussions, you may want to talk with him privately after the meeting. Let him know you appreciate him and his contributions, but ask him to give others more opportunity to take part.

5. Evaluate each session. Within 24 hours of each meeting, evaluate how the session went and note the emerging needs of group members. The "After the Meeting" section of each session in this Leader's Guide will help you do this.

As you prepare to lead each meeting, pray that God will help you model the life of a true disciple—especially when it comes to having your own time alone with God. Be enthusiastic about growing spiritually, helping others grow, and sharing your faith with non-Christians. Your spirit can be contagious.

If group meetings are enjoyable and helpful to a Discipleship Family member, he will not only grow in his relationships with Christ and the rest of the group, but will probably be eager to commit himself to the Discipleship Family until all five books in the Moving Toward Maturity series have been completed. □

Continuing Your Discipleship Family

OVERVIEW

Key Concept   To benefit most from a group study of *Spending Time Alone with God*, we must commit ourselves to the disciplines of a Discipleship Family.

Goals   *Individual Growth:* To accept the responsibilities and commitments of a Discipleship Family for another 10-week period.
Group Life: To continue the strong fellowship ties within the group established during the *Following Jesus* Discipleship Families.

BEFORE THE MEETING

1. Study pages 54-58 of this Leader's Guide for important background information.
2. In *Spending Time Alone with God*, study pages 5-11, and put together the memory verse packet located in the back of the book.
3. Call each person who said he'd come to the first meeting. Your group should consist of members who have been through *Following Jesus* Discipleship Families or who have completed *Following Jesus* on their own. Ask everyone to bring their school and work schedules.
4. Be prepared to present the purpose and format of the Moving Toward Maturity series to the group. Place special emphasis on the content of *Spending Time Alone with God*.
5. Gather materials for the meeting:
   Bible
   Spending Time Alone with God
   3" x 5" cards
   Pencils
   Memory verse packet
   Student materials (A copy of *Spending Time Alone with God*, a set of

Time Alone with God Notebook Inserts, and a 5½″ x 8½″ looseleaf notebook for each student)

THE MEETING

BUILDING THE GROUP *(20 minutes)*

As each person arrives, greet him warmly and ask him to write his name, address, and phone number on a 3″ x 5″ card (unless you already have this information from a previous Discipleship Family).

When everyone has arrived, ask each group member to think of three words that describe himself. Let each person share his three words with the rest of the group.

FOCUSING ON LIFE *(5 minutes)*

Discuss: **What factors in our lives help determine the kinds of persons we become?** (Parents, teachers, natural abilities, etc.) **By what means does God mold each of us into the person He wants us to be?** (Scripture, tests of faith, fellowship with other Christians, etc.) Write down the responses to this question to use later in "Considering the Choice."

EXPLORING THE CHALLENGE *(20 minutes)*

Have a volunteer read 1 Corinthians 12:12-20, 27. Share with the group that God has designed the body of Christ in such a way that Christians need each other. Through fellowship, the members of the body give each other insight, support, and encouragement. Emphasize that being part of a small group such as the Discipleship Family is an excellent way to grow as a part of the body of Christ.

Review the purpose of the Moving Toward Maturity Series and the function of the Discipleship Family (page 54 of this Leader's Guide). Let each student share something he learned or experienced from being in a previous Discipleship Family. Emphasize the necessity of commitment to God and to each other in order for the Discipleship Family to be effective.

Give everyone a copy of *Spending Time Alone with God.* Review the topics to be discussed, and read the group disciplines (page 11). (Also hand out the 5½″ x 8½″ notebooks and the *Time Alone with God Notebook Inserts,* but explain that they will not be used until next week's session.) Provide an opportunity for any questions concerning the commitment or the responsibilities that are included. (NOTE: Even though the group may want to continue as a Discipleship Family after studying *Spending Time Alone with God,* they are only being asked to consider a commitment for the next 10 weeks.)

Briefly review the length and number of meetings (one-and-a-quarter to two hours per week with the group, plus individual study time, for the next 10 weeks). Then have everyone consult their schedules and decide on a specific time and place to meet. Also schedule dates for your fun activity (see page 56) and half day of prayer (see page 95), but don't discuss specific plans at this time.

CONSIDERING THE CHOICE *(15 minutes)*

Review the list you compiled earlier of things God uses to influence our lives. Ask the group which of these ways God could use to give their lives direction through this Discipleship Family.

Challenge the group to think and pray about making another 10-week commitment to the Discipleship Family. Be sure they understand that this time they will be expected to have a daily time alone with God. Anyone who decides not to become a part of this particular Discipleship Family should let you know before the next meeting and return his unmarked set of materials. Those who choose to join should complete Bible study 1 in *Spending Time Alone with God* before the next meeting.

Encourage everyone to set aside a specific time each week to complete the Bible study to be discussed during the next Discipleship Family meeting. (NOTE: The *Assignment* section of each Bible study is not to be completed until *after* the Bible study material has been discussed in the Discipleship Family. For example, your assignment this week will be to complete Bible study 1 [ending with the *Making It Personal* section] in preparation for next week's Discipleship Family meeting. *After* the next meeting, students should complete the *Assignment* at the end of Bible study 1 as well as Bible study 2.)

Close with a prayer for wisdom as each person makes his decision about joining the Discipleship Family. Thank God for what He is going to do in all of your lives as you commit yourselves to Him and to each other.

Assignments for Next Week Give the following assignments to those who decide to join the Discipleship Family:

1. In *Spending Time Alone with God,* **read pages 5-10, study and sign the "Personal Commitment" sheet (page 11), complete Bible study 1 (down to the** *Assignment* **section), and put together the memory verse packet in the back of the book.** (Show the group your packet to demonstrate what it looks like put together.)

2. Memorize Mark 1:35, as indicated in the *Making It Personal* section of Bible study 1.

3. Bring a Bible, a pen or pencil, *Spending Time Alone with God,* **and your Time Alone with God Notebook to every meeting.**

Also remind the group to bring enough money next week to reimburse you for the student book, notebook, and inserts.

As students leave, try to talk with them individually. See if they have any questions or problems. Encourage them to join the group, and let them know you care about each of them and their concerns.

AFTER THE MEETING

1. Evaluate: Did each person become involved in sharing his ideas and feelings? How can you more effectively involve each person in next week's discussion? Review "Effective Meetings," page 57 of this Leader's Guide.

2. This week, and every week, begin preparing for the next session at least five days in advance. Complete Bible study 1 in *Spending Time Alone with God,* and read through the Leader's Guide suggestions.

Getting to Know Him
Bible Study 1

OVERVIEW

Key Concept   A daily time alone with God stimulates our spiritual growth.

Memory Verse   Mark 1:35

Goals   *Individual Growth:* To begin the lifetime discipline of spending time alone with God each day.
Group Life: To agree to support one another as a Discipleship Family for the next 10 weeks.

BEFORE THE MEETING

1. Pray for each person who came to the last meeting, asking God to give each one a deep desire to spend time alone with Him.
2. In *Spending Time Alone with God*, do Bible study 1, writing down your personal responses to each question. Each week, note in the margins other observations or personal experiences that relate to the lesson and bring them up during the group meeting.
3. Memorize Mark 1:35.
4. Telephone each group member, reminding him of the place and time for the meeting. Answer any questions students have. If someone has decided not to participate in the Discipleship Family, assure him that you still care for him, and express hope that he will be able to participate in a future group.
5. Make a list of the names, addresses, and phone numbers of all the group members (from the 3" x 5" cards filled out last week). Make enough copies for each person to have one.
6. Examine your own time alone with God. Pray for motivation and diligence to strengthen your personal devotional time.

7. Gather materials for the meeting:
   Bible
   Spending Time Alone with God
   List of group members' names and addresses
   Memory verse packet
   Time Alone with God notebook (3 ring binder that holds 5½" x 8½" paper and containing *Time Alone with God Notebook Inserts*)
   One sheet of 5½" x 8½" paper for each group member

THE MEETING

BUILDING THE GROUP *(15 minutes)*

Greet each person. Welcome him as an important member of the group.

Confirm that by each person's presence, he is saying, "Yes, I want to be a part of this Discipleship Family." Have everyone turn to the *Personal Commitment* sheet (page 11, *Spending Time Alone with God*). Read it aloud. Then ask anyone who hasn't already done so to sign his sheet. (Be sure to sign yours too!)

Have someone read Hebrews 10:24-25. Ask volunteers to share how they think these verses could apply to the Discipleship Family. Challenge group members to begin to encourage one another—in their time alone with God, in their Christian witness at school, and in their relationships with others. Take time for volunteers to offer short prayers asking God: (1) to strengthen each person's commitment to Christ and the Discipleship Family, and (2) to develop a closeness between the group members so they will begin to encourage each other.

FOCUSING ON LIFE *(15 minutes)*

Discuss: **Has there ever been someone you've really wanted to get to know? Why? How did you go about trying to get to know that person? What questions did you ask? What did you tell him about yourself?**

What has God done to encourage us to get to know Him? (Gave us the Bible; sent Jesus; provided Christian witnesses, etc.). **How can we respond to God's initiative?** (Receiving Christ as Savior; spending time with the Lord in prayer; reading the Bible, etc.).

Emphasize that spending time alone with God should not be considered a duty or a demand, but rather an opportunity to get to know the Lord of the universe in a more intimate way.

EXPLORING GOD'S WORD *(20 minutes)*

(NOTE: Each week this section is based on the work students have done in Spending Time Alone with God. The discussion questions are usually not identical to those in the study book, but they draw from the same Scriptures and assignments. This technique helps students think through what they've studied rather than just parroting written answers.)

Allow time for group members to review their answers and comments for Bible study 1 in *Spending Time Alone with God*. Let them ask questions and make observations. Then discuss these questions:

1. According to Hebrews 4:12, in what ways can God's Word penetrate our lives? What benefits will result from spending time in God's Word? (Our motivations become more clear; we see how our thoughts measure up to God's standard, etc.)

2. According to John 4:23 what kind of people does God want to worship Him? How **does He desire those people to worship Him?** (In spirit and truth.) **How does this verse apply to spending time alone with God?** (We should be wholeheartedly committed to God, willing to obey what He says, and open and honest with Him.)

3. Have someone read Hosea 6:6. **What makes God happy?** (Our knowledge of Him.) **How can your time alone with God please Him?**

To affirm each person's commitment to begin a daily time alone with God, quote the memory verse (Mark 1:35) together.

APPLYING GOD'S WORD *(20 minutes)*

Have group members recall any problems they have experienced in trying to pray, be obedient to God, or study the Bible. Ask volunteers to share some of their struggles. (Start with Sam's experience described on page 19 of *Spending Time Alone with God*, or share an example from your own life.) Then discuss how spending time alone with God each day can prevent such inconsistencies in the lives of your group members.

Ask each person to write on a 5½" x 8½" sheet of paper: (1) One thing he will do this week to make it easier to have his time alone with God. (Examples: Go to bed earlier; set two alarms; find a private place with no interruptions.) (2) One thing he will do this week to encourage another group member to have his time alone with God. (Examples: Check with him each day about his time alone with God; call at a set time in the morning to make sure he is up.)

Ask each group member to pray for the person on his right, that he would begin to have a regular time alone with God, resulting in greater consistency in his walk with the Lord. (If group members are shy about praying aloud, talk to them individually and challenge them to prepare this week to take part in future group prayers.)

Assignments for Next Week As you give the following assignments, be positive. Let the young people know that you have faith in them and their desire to learn.

1. Complete the *Assignment* **at the end of Bible study 1 in** *Spending Time Alone with God.* (Review this assignment with the group.)

2. Do Bible study 2. Don't forget to learn the memory verse and study the daily Scripture readings listed there.

3. Begin your Time Alone with God Notebook with the suggestions you wrote down during this Discipleship Family meeting. Put those ideas into practice this week, and be prepared to tell how they worked.

AFTER THE MEETING

1. Evaluate: Was the atmosphere relaxed? Did everyone take part? If not, jot down some things you can do to improve the next group meeting. If any student was particularly silent, you may want to spend time with him this week to get to know him better.
2. Familiarize yourself with the planned half day of prayer at the end of the 10-week study (see page 95). Begin to pray now for this special day. Remember it daily in your time alone with God.
3. Begin to plan a group outing (picnic, hike, swimming, etc.) to allow group members to fellowship outside the regular Discipleship Family meetings.
4. If possible, meet with several members of the group this week—separately, or two or three together—to build relationships.

Build the Relationship
Bible Study 2

OVERVIEW

Key Concept | Consistently spending time alone with God results in a deepening relationship with Him.

Memory Verse | 2 Timothy 3:16

Goals | *Individual Growth:* To discover and put into practice a specific plan for spending time alone with God daily.
Group Life: To encourage one another to be faithful in spending time alone with God.

BEFORE THE MEETING

1. Pray for each group member by name, asking God to make you aware of his particular needs.
2. In *Spending Time Alone with God*, complete Bible study 2 and the daily assignments from Bible study 1.
3. Memorize 2 Timothy 3:16.
4. Drop a postcard in the mail to each group member, reminding him of your prayers, and encouraging him to continue his daily time alone with God.
5. Gather materials for the meeting:
     Bible
     Spending Time Alone with God
     Memory verse packet
     Time Alone with God Notebook

THE MEETING

BUILDING THE GROUP *(15 minutes)*

Ask volunteers to share what they did this past week to (1) get motivated to have a time alone with God, and (2) encourage another group member to do the same.

Then discuss: **Have you ever been in love or thought you were?**

Did you let the other person know? How did you feel when you caught a glimpse of that person coming down the hall, and knew you were going to get a chance to talk? Do you think you could ever have the same kind of eager expectation and excitement about getting to talk to God? Why or why not?

FOCUSING ON LIFE *(20 minutes)*

Discuss: **Have you ever talked to someone and felt like he wasn't listening to you? How did that make you feel? How did you respond to him?**

How does God speak to us most of the time? (Through the Bible.) **Do you listen? Can you think of one time you** *did* **listen? What happened?** (Let volunteers respond.)

EXPLORING GOD'S WORD *(25 minutes)*

Allow time for group members to review their answers and comments for Bible study 2 in *Spending Time Alone with God*. Let them ask questions and make observations. Then discuss these questions:

1. **In Jeremiah 29:12-14, God says that He will listen to us and will let us find Him. However, there are things we have to do in order to receive that promise. What are they?** (Call upon Him; pray to Him; seek Him with all our heart.)

2. **What do you think it means to seek God with all your heart?** (To make Him the most important priority in your life.) **How does that relate to having a time alone with God and studying the Bible?**

3. **What does 2 Timothy 3:16 say about the Bible?** (All Scripture is God-breathed; it is useful for teaching; it rebukes; it corrects; it trains in righteousness.) **What are the benefits of allowing God to correct, rebuke, teach, and train us through Scripture?** (See 2 Timothy 3:17. We become equipped for every good work.)

Quote 2 Timothy 3:16 together as a group.

APPLYING GOD'S WORD *(10 minutes)*

Have group members discuss their first week of spending time alone with God. **Was it an awkward experience or a beneficial one** (or both)? **Was it hard to meet with God every day? Did anyone miss a day or two? What problems did group members face?**

Make a list of these problems, and then brainstorm ways to overcome them. Allow the group to give help in solving each other's problems as much as possible.

Divide into pairs and have partners pray for each other, asking God to help each one overcome specific obstacles that stand in the way of a successful time alone with Him.

(NOTE: *Not every session in this Leader's Guide will include a group discussion of individual times alone with God. However, the leader should regularly ask about the daily times with God to see if anyone is having difficulty or needs help. Try to spend a couple of minutes on this topic each week.*)

1. **Complete the** *Assignment* **at the end of Bible study 2 in** *Spending Time Alone with God*. (Review this assignment with the group. Make sure everyone understands how to fill out their Bible Response sheets. Then remind them to complete one every day during the next week.)

2. **Do Bible study 3. Don't forget to learn the memory verse.**

3. **Be ready to share the positive steps you've taken to overcome personal obstacles in spending time alone with God.**

AFTER THE MEETING

1. Evaluate: Is the group continuing to develop a closeness? Were group members relaxed and comfortable? Did everyone participate? If not, perhaps something as simple as having soft drinks or hot chocolate before the meeting would help. If there are new members in your group, make sure they are beginning to feel like they belong.

2. Are group members coming to the meetings with their assignments completed? Give encouragement as needed, with a phone call, postcard, or visit.

3. If anyone seems overwhelmed by beginning a time alone with God, call or visit him sometime this week.

4. Continue to plan a group outing for sometime during the next two weeks and the half day of prayer after session 11.

Learn the Word
Bible Study 3

OVERVIEW

Key Concept   Studying God's Word helps us get to know ourselves and Jesus better.

Memory Verse   Joshua 1:8

Goals   Individual Growth: To apply God's Word to specific problem situations.
Group Life: To encourage one another to begin a regular practice of Bible study.

BEFORE THE MEETING

1. Ask God to give each group member a deep trust in and love for His Word.
2. In Spending Time Alone with God, complete Bible study 3 and the daily assignments from Bible study 2.
3. Memorize Joshua 1:8.
4. Gather materials for the meeting:
   Bible
   Spending Time Alone with God
   Memory verse packet
   Time Alone with God Notebook
   Extra paper

THE MEETING

BUILDING THE GROUP (20 minutes)

Ask the group to imagine this situation: **You have fallen in love with someone. You know a lot about him (her), but this person barely knows you. And you've decided to write him (her) a love letter.**

Pass out extra paper to anyone who needs it. Allow three to five minutes for each group member to write this fictitious love letter. Then ask two or three volunteers to read their letters. As a group, discuss the contents of the letters. **What did these letter writers tell about themselves? In what ways is God's Word a love letter to us? What similarities does the Bible have to the love letters that were read to the group? What differences?**

FOCUSING ON LIFE *(15 minutes)*

Discuss: **Have you ever been confused about the question, "Who am I?"** Not in the sense of "I'm a boy, son of Mr. Smith, 5'8", good looking"; but rather, **"Who am I, deep down inside?"** Allow two or three volunteers to respond.

Then ask: **Have you ever been confused about what God is like, perhaps as a result of some seemingly senseless tragedy (a death, personal failure, etc.)?** Give an example from your own life or again ask for volunteers. Let the group members struggle with the questions for a while before continuing. Then have them look up Hebrews 4:12 and James 1:23-24. Ask: **What can we discover about ourselves from God's Word?** (Our true attitudes and our thoughts.) Point out that the Bible works as a mirror to show us who we really are.

What does the Bible reveal about God? (His character over the ages; His love for the world and the sending of His Son; His perfect qualities; how He has been involved with mankind throughout history.)

EXPLORING GOD'S WORD *(30 minutes)*

Allow time for group members to review their answers and comments for Bible study 3 in *Spending Time Alone with God.* Let them ask questions and make observations. Then discuss these questions:

1. **What are some results of spending time in God's Word?** (Getting to know yourself better; knowing Jesus better; growth as a Christian; a fruitful life; ability to handle temptation.)

2. **Define a "fruitful life."** (Refer to Psalm 1:1-3.)

3. **Psalm 1:3 refers to a "tree planted by streams of water." Jeremiah 17:8 further describes characteristics of a tree planted by water. How do these passages apply to a Christian's life?** (No fear when facing temptation and stress; no worry when circumstances look bad; able to produce "fruit.")

4. **What are some reasons, found in Bible study 3, why we can trust the Bible?** (The human authors were eyewitnesses of the events they wrote about—2 Peter 1:16 and 1 John 1:1-3; the writers investigated the facts before writing—Luke 1:1-4; the Bible is inspired by God—2 Timothy 3:16; the whole Bible, though written by many different human authors who lived hundreds of years apart, fits together as a single expression of God's truth—Psalm 119:160.)

Quote Joshua 1:8 together, making note of the *commands* as well as the *promises* that are included in the verse.

APPLYING GOD'S WORD *(10 minutes)*

Have a volunteer quote 2 Timothy 3:16 (last session's memory verse.) Then have each person make two columns in his Time Alone with

God Notebook with the headings, "Training in Righteousness" and "Areas Needing Correction." Any personal characteristics he feels he needs to acquire or develop should go in the first column. Any bad habits or attitudes that need correction should be listed in the second.

After completing his list, have each student select the one characteristic he most wants to acquire and the one attitude or habit he most wants to improve. Close with individual silent prayer that God will change those areas of each person's life.

Assignments for Next Week

1. Complete the *Assignment* **at the end of Bible study 3 in** *Spending Time Alone with God*. (Review this assignment with the group.)

2. Do Bible study 4. Don't forget to learn the memory verse.

AFTER THE MEETING ─────────────────────────────

1. Evaluate: Is any student dominating the group time? If so, tactfully suggest that he give the less vocal members an opportunity to share.
2. If anyone is still coming unprepared or is slack in his assignments, get together with him this week to see if you can help in any way.
3. Your special outing should take place this week or next. Plan it well, and use the time to strengthen relationships.
4. Continue to pray for the half day of prayer.

Hide the Word
Bible Study 4

OVERVIEW

Key Concept   Scripture memory equips us to handle life's demands.

Memory Verses   Psalm 119:9-11

Goals   *Individual Growth:* To discover the importance of carrying God's Word in the heart and mind, and to begin a lifelong discipline of Scripture memory.
Group Life: To develop a positive attitude toward Scripture memorization.

BEFORE THE MEETING

1. Pray that God will give each group member enjoyment and persistence in memorizing Scripture.
2. In *Spending Time Alone with God,* complete Bible study 4 and the daily assignments from Bible study 3.
3. Memorize Psalm 119:9-11.
4. Gather materials for the meeting:
   Bible
   Spending Time Alone with God
   Memory verse packet
   Time Alone with God Notebook
   Two road maps—one intact, and one with several holes cut in it
   Bible concordance

THE MEETING

BUILDING THE GROUP *(20 minutes)*

Divide into two groups. Give one group an intact road map. Give the second group an identical map, except with a few large holes in it. Ask both groups to chart the best route from one major city to another.

After five minutes, ask one person from each group to describe the route his group took. (The second group should describe a much more complicated route because of the detours forced by the holes.) Discuss: **In what way(s) is the Bible a road map for our lives? What happens when we try to plan our lives with an incomplete knowledge of God's Word?** (Our lives become unnecessarily complicated.)

FOCUSING ON LIFE (15 minutes)

Discuss the following questions:

Have you ever been faced with a tough decision when you didn't have any idea what to do? (Share a personal example or ask volunteers to do so.)

How did you finally make the decision? (Pressure from friends; advice from parents; flipped a coin; took no action; etc.)

What difference would it have made if you had known a Bible passage that related to the situation?

EXPLORING GOD'S WORD (25 minutes)

Allow time for group members to review their answers and comments for Bible study 4 in *Spending Time Alone with God.* Let them ask questions and make observations. Then discuss these questions:

1. **What are some positive things memorizing Scripture does for you?** (Makes the Bible come alive; keeps you spiritually strong in everyday situations; helps you prosper spiritually; helps you overcome temptation; helps you be a more effective witness for Christ; changes the way you think.)

2. **Which of those benefits means the most to you and why?**

3. **What are three reasons you can memorize Scripture?** (Your memory is good; a right attitude makes a difference; you have what you need.)

4. Ask volunteers to share how they completed the sentence, "I can memorize Scripture because . . . " on page 57 of this week's Bible study.

Have the group recite Psalm 119:9-11, and emphasize the reasons given in those verses for developing the discipline of Scripture memory.

APPLYING GOD'S WORD (15 minutes)

As a group, make a list of problems that young people frequently face. Select one that is common to most of your students. Use a Bible concordance to find Scripture passages that apply directly to the problem, having group members read each passage aloud. (Make sure everyone knows how to use a concordance.)

Encourage students to use this method whenever they face problems in the future. If their problem is recurring, challenge them to memorize the verse(s). Then whenever the same problem arises again, they will have God's Word with them to give them guidance.

Assignments for Next Week

1. Complete the *Assignment* **at the end of Bible study 4 in** *Spending Time Alone with God.* (Review this assignment with the group.)

2. Do Bible study 5 in *Spending Time Alone with God* **and be prepared to recite the assigned memory verse, John 15:7.**

AFTER THE MEETING ─────────────────────────

1. Evaluate: Are group members enthusiastic about Scripture memory? If anyone seems indifferent, set a time to talk with him and find out why.

2. Are you giving group members plenty of time to share, and not dominating the meeting yourself?

3. Try to spend some time with two or three group members this week, to get to know each other better.

4. Prepare to announce the half day of prayer at the next meeting.

Talk with God
Bible Study 5

OVERVIEW

Key Concept Talking to God in prayer is a privilege that allows us to know Him better.

Memory Verse John 15:7

Goals *Individual Growth:* To begin knowing God better by spending time with Him in prayer.
Group Life: To recognize the importance of prayer as a means for ministering to each other.

BEFORE THE MEETING

1. Spend some time in prayer, asking God to make your own time alone with Him such a vital part of your life that the group members can tell how important it is to you.
2. In *Spending Time Alone with God*, complete Bible study 5 and the daily assignments from Bible study 4.
3. Memorize John 15:7.
4. Gather materials for the meeting:
   Bible
   Spending Time Alone with God
   Memory verse packet
   Time Alone with God Notebook

THE MEETING

BUILDING THE GROUP *(25 minutes)*

Ask volunteers to recite John 15:7. Have each volunteer share ways God has applied the verse to specific situations they have faced this week.

Since this is the halfway point of your Discipleship Family meetings, ask group members to evaluate the meetings so far: what they have liked best, what they have liked least, etc.

Review the main points of the past four weeks with the following questions:

(1) **What is the purpose of having a time alone with God?** (See Bible study 1.)

(2) **What are some actions or attitudes you need in order to build a relationship with God?** (See Bible study 2.)

(3) **What are the results of spending time in God's Word?** (See Bible study 3.)

(4) **What are the benefits of memorizing Scripture?** (See Bible study 4.)

Recite together the memory verses from the first four Bible studies.

Ask group members to pray sentence prayers, renewing their commitments to God and to each other for the next five weeks. Close the prayer, asking God to continue to lead each student into a life of committed discipleship.

FOCUSING ON LIFE *(15 minutes)*

Discuss: **Have you ever had someone make and then break a promise to you? How did you feel? What was your response? How did you react to that person's promises later on?**

When God makes a promise, what can we expect to happen? (Have volunteers give personal examples of how God has kept His promises.)

Does experiencing God's faithfulness in the past make you trust Him more?

Explain to the group that God is the only One who is *completely* trustworthy. He will *never* fail us. He may not give the answer we expect, or do exactly what we want, but He will never break His promises or forsake us.

EXPLORING GOD'S WORD *(25 minutes)*

Allow time for group members to review their answers and comments for Bible study 5 in *Spending Time Alone with God.* Let them ask questions and make observations. Then discuss these questions:

1. **What are the purposes of prayer?**

2. Have someone read 2 Peter 3:18. **What was Peter's prayer for the people he wrote to? How do you think we go about "growing in the grace and knowledge of our Lord and Savior"?** (Primarily through prayer and Bible study.)

3. **What answers may God give us when we pray? Why does He answer in each of those ways?**

4. Jesus says that one goal of prayer is to "remain in Me and My words remain in you" (John 15:7). **What does it mean to remain (or** *abide***) in Christ?** (Refer to John 15:4, 5, 10.) **How can spending time with God in prayer help us remain in Him?**

Recite John 15:7 together and note the result of remaining in Christ.

APPLYING GOD'S WORD *(10 minutes)*

Have each person list in his Time Alone with God Notebook the concerns in his life that he normally takes to the Lord in prayer. Let a few students share the prayer requests they have listed. Point out common, everyday things not on the list that perhaps they take for granted (daily food, good clothes, loving parents, etc.). Remind group members that prayer is important in every detail of their lives, and challenge them to pray this week about all the items they listed in their notebooks.

Assignments for Next Week

1. Complete the *Assignment* at the end of Bible study 5 in *Spending Time Alone with God*. (Review this assignment with the group.)

2. Do Bible study 6. Don't forget to learn the memory verse.

3. Focus on prayer during your time alone with God this week, remembering to pray for the little things, as well as the "major" concerns of your life.

(At this time you should also announce the half day of prayer at the end of your study of *Spending Time Alone with God*. Briefly describe the events to take place, and make sure the date you have set is still a good one for each group member.)

AFTER THE MEETING

Evaluate: How did your group members seem to respond to this session on prayer? Do they seem to have a positive attitude, or do they see prayer as a chore? Are they comfortable when asked to pray aloud? If not, encourage them to participate in sentence prayers from time to time. Try to provide opportunities for them to pray in a group with as little pressure as possible. Teach them by example. If your prayers are usually long and eloquent, students may be intimidated when they are asked to pray.

Praise the Lord!
Bible Study 6

OVERVIEW

Key Concept   Praise should be an integral part of the disciple's daily life, and a key element of his time alone with God.

Memory Verses   Psalm 146:1-2

Goals   *Individual Growth:* To discover the importance of giving praise to God on a daily basis, and to develop an attitude of praise that permeates life.
Group Life: To practice praise as a Discipleship Family, so it will become more natural on an individual level.

BEFORE THE MEETING

1. Pray for the individual needs of group members. Ask God to give each person an attitude of praise that results from an understanding of His character.
2. In *Spending Time Alone with God*, complete Bible study 6 and the daily assignments from Bible study 5.
3. Memorize Psalm 146:1-2.
4. Focus on praise during your personal prayer and Bible study times this week.
5. Gather materials for the meeting:
   Bible
   Spending Time Alone with God
   Memory verse packet
   Time Alone with God Notebook
   Refreshments
6. Optional: Obtain a copy of the book, *Tracks of a Fellow Struggler* (John Claypool, Word Books). Chapter 3 should provide much insight into the importance of praise (this week's topic) and thanksgiving (next week's topic).

THE MEETING

BUILDING THE GROUP *(20 minutes)*

Greet each person as he arrives. Serve refreshments, and begin with about five minutes of informal fellowship. Then begin the meeting by asking volunteers to share any insights from prayer they received during the past week and/or any steps they took to encourage fellow group members to improve their time alone with God.

Then ask each group member to point out one positive characteristic of the person on his left. After everyone has had a turn, ask: **How did you feel when you were praised for your good qualities? What are some of the characteristics of God that are worthy of praise?** (After group members respond, ask a volunteer to read Revelation 4:11.)

FOCUSING ON LIFE *(10 minutes)*

Discuss the following questions:

1. When did you feel the best this past week? At that point, how did you respond to God, and to others around you?

2. When did you feel worst this past week? What made you feel that way? At that point, how did you respond to God and to others? Is it hard for you to praise God when things don't go your way?

Explain that even though God may not have directly caused the unpleasant situations, He can use them for our good. The secret of being able to praise God at all times is realizing who He is. He is always faithful and His character never changes, so He will never fail us.

EXPLORING GOD'S WORD *(35 minutes)*

Allow time for group members to review their answers and comments for Bible study 6 in *Spending Time Alone with God.* Let them ask questions and make observations. Then discuss these questions:

1. How can praise affect how we handle problems? (Refer to the "gaze/glance" sections of this week's study.)

2. What are some elements of praise found in Psalm 105:1-4? (Refer to subhead, "Praise: How to Do It.") **Which of these elements is the most meaningful to you? Why?**

3. One thing that can help us praise God when we're in difficult situations is remembering how He has worked in our lives in the past. What are some ways God has come through for you during difficult times?

Recite the memory verses (Psalm 146:1-2) together as a commitment to live with an attitude of gratitude and praise toward God.

APPLYING GOD'S WORD *(10 minutes)*

Have each group member list in his notebook the good things God has done for him during the past month. Then have him write out a personal prayer of praise to the Lord. (In Bible study 7 the group members will discover that *praise* is directed toward God's character, and *thanksgiving* toward His actions. These written prayers should focus on the character of God.)

When everyone has finished writing out their prayers, have members list one bad thing that has happened to them during the past month. Can they pray the prayer they just wrote in relation to their *bad* experience? God's character doesn't change. Challenge each student to praise God for *every* circumstance in his life, because it is usually the negative events that lead to spiritual growth (James 1:2-4; 2 Corinthians 12:7-10).

Close with sentence prayers of praise, thanking God for who He is.

Assignments for Next Week

1. Complete the *Assignment* **at the end of Bible study 6 in** *Spending Time Alone with God.* (Review this assignment with the group.)

2. Do Bible study 7. Don't forget to learn the memory verse.

3. *(Optional)* Ask a volunteer to read and report on chapters 13 and 14 of *The Hiding Place* (Corrie ten Boom, Bantam). Have him relate the story about the fleas, and any other reasons for thanksgiving he finds in the chapters.

AFTER THE MEETING ─────────────────────────

1. Evaluate: Are the group members answering honestly, or do they give "pat" answers to questions? If you detect that they are giving the answers they know to be "right," challenge them at the next meeting to be honest with the group, and with themselves.
2. If any students are not participating, or have a negative attitude, meet with them individually this week.

Give Thanks
Bible Study 7

OVERVIEW

Key Concept A thankful attitude for God's gifts reflects spiritual maturity.

Memory Verse 1 Thessalonians 5:18

Goals *Individual Growth:* To develop an attitude of thankfulness for the gifts and actions of God.
Group Life: To express thankfulness to God for the Discipleship Family members.

BEFORE THE MEETING

1. Pray for each group member, thanking God for the positive qualities He is building in each person's life. Ask Him to give you wisdom to help each one develop a thankful heart.
2. In *Spending Time Alone with God,* complete Bible study 7 and the daily assignments from Bible study 6.
3. Memorize 1 Thessalonians 5:18.
4. Gather materials for the meeting:
   Bible
   Spending Time Alone with God
   Memory verse packet
   Paper
   Time Alone with God Notebook
5. *Optional:* Call to remind your volunteer that he is to report on *The Hiding Place.* Offer to loan him a copy of the book if he hasn't found one yet.

THE MEETING

BUILDING THE GROUP *(20 minutes)*

Discuss the similarities and differences between praise and thanksgiving. Explain that the terms are often used interchangeably, but we are making a distinction between God's characteristics (for which He should be praised) and His gifts and actions (for which He should be thanked).

As a group, make a list of God's attributes that you should praise Him for. Then for each attribute, go back and make a list of gifts the Lord gives as a result of each particular characteristic. Have the group offer sentence prayers, thanking God for specific gifts He has given them.

FOCUSING ON LIFE *(10 minutes)*

Discuss: **Think about one person you see every day at school or work. Does he tend to be thankful? Explain your answer. Do you consider yourself a thankful person? How has this week's study helped you become a more thankful person?**

EXPLORING GOD'S WORD *(30 minutes)*

Allow time for group members to review their answers and comments for Bible study 7 in *Spending Time Alone with God*. Let them ask questions and make observations. Then discuss these questions:

1. **What are some things that we can always be thankful for?** (Refer to the section heading in Bible study 7, "Giving Thanks: Working It Out.")

2. **What was Job's response when his friends tried to get him to repent for sins he had not committed?** (Job 13:15) **What word in verse 15 describes Job's attitude toward God?** (Hope or trust.) **Does that mean Job never questioned what happened to him?**

Explain that even though tragedy had struck Job, he was still thankful to God. Job knew that no matter how bad circumstances looked, he could trust in the God whose character never changes. However, Job didn't always understand God's actions and was not afraid to ask, "Why?" Explain that God desires our honesty and we can question Him if we don't understand our circumstances.

As a commitment to maintain a thankful attitude in all areas of life, quote the memory verse, 1 Thessalonians 5:18, together.

APPLYING GOD'S WORD *(15 minutes)*

Option 1: Ask each group member to write in his Time Alone with God Notebook: (1) One thing he is particularly thankful for this week and one thing he has had problems being thankful for (an unpleasant person, a physical characteristic, etc.). Encourage each group member to commit himself to thank God for both of those things every day this week. (2) One thing he will do to demonstrate his thankfulness for another member of the Discipleship Family. (Examples: send a note or tell that person why he appreciates him, thank him for something he has done, etc.)

Option 2: Call on your volunteer to report on chapters 13 and 14 of *The Hiding Place* (Corrie ten Boom, Bantam). The author and her sister were placed in Ravensbruck, the notorious German concentration camp, during World War II. Yet even under those horrible conditions, they learned to thank God for every circumstance—even the fleas that infested their living quarters. And later, God allowed the women to discover His purpose for those fleas, and how He had used them to accomplish His will in the midst of a hate-filled camp.

After the report, have each person make a list of things he finds it hard to thank God for. Challenge everyone to begin thanking Him anyway for those things during time alone with God this week.

Assignments for Next Week

1. Complete the *Assignment* at the end of Bible study 7 in *Spending Time Alone with God*. (Review this assignment with the group.)

2. Do Bible study 8 and learn the memory verse.

3. Begin to pray for the half day of prayer during your times alone with God.

AFTER THE MEETING

1. Evaluate: Is there a group member who tends to be a loner? If so, do something this week to let him know you are thankful for him. Also ask one of your more mature group members to get together with him this week and plan an activity that will begin building a stronger relationship.

2. Try to meet with two or three group members this week on an individual basis.

Live Clean
Bible Study 8

OVERVIEW

Key Concept   Confession of sins leads to forgiveness and freedom.

Memory Verse   1 John 1:9

Goals   *Individual Growth:* To experience the freedom that comes from staying current with confession of any known sins.
Group Life: To learn to forgive each other, as Christ forgave us.

BEFORE THE MEETING

1. Pray that group members will grasp the concept of God's forgiveness in a way they can apply to their daily lives.
2. In *Spending Time Alone with God,* complete Bible study 8 and the daily assignments from Bible study 7.
3. Memorize 1 John 1:9.
4. Examine your own life for any unconfessed sin. Is there anyone you need to forgive? Is there anything you feel that God has not forgiven you for? If so, claim 1 John 1:9 for yourself before the next group meeting.
5. Gather materials for the meeting:
   Bible
   Spending Time Alone with God
   Memory verse packet
   Time Alone with God Notebook
   A large nail or spike
   Matches
   Fireproof receptacle, such as a metal trash can or ash tray

THE MEETING

BUILDING THE GROUP (15 minutes)

Begin by asking if last session's discussion on thanksgiving had a positive influence on group members' relationships with the Lord. Spend a few minutes reviewing the major ideas from last week. Then discuss: **Have you ever had a "feud" with a friend, in which both of you were so mad you wouldn't speak to each other? How did you feel after a day or two? What did it take to resolve the situation?**

Ask: **Have you ever done something that really hurt someone close to you, and even after you apologized, things just weren't the same? Did you ever regain the other person's trust? How?**

FOCUSING ON LIFE (30 minutes)

Discuss: **Have you ever felt as if you had really hurt God? How? What did you do to make things right? How did God respond? Would most people have responded in the same manner?**

Hold up a large nail or spike as you read aloud Isaiah 53:3-6. (Use a contemporary-speech version such as *The Living Bible*.) Then tell each group member to find a spot by himself, and for a few minutes meditate on the price Jesus had to pay in order to forgive his sins. Also ask everyone to read Psalm 103:10-12, and think about the completeness of God's forgiveness.

Reassemble the group and discuss these questions: (1) **What price did Christ pay for us to be forgiven? Was the price He paid sufficient to cover all our sins?** (2) **What does Psalm 103:10-12 say about the removal of our sins? Do you tend to remember your sins and feel guilty long after God has forgiven you?**

Explain that God has promised us forgiveness, and if we confess our sins, *we are forgiven!*

EXPLORING GOD'S WORD (20 minutes)

Allow time for group members to review their answers and comments for Bible study 8 in *Spending Time Alone with God*. Let them ask questions and make observations. Then discuss these questions:

1. **What does it mean to** *confess* **your sins?** (Refer to Bible study 8 subhead, "How Do You Confess Your Sins?")
2. **What attitude did David have when he confessed his sin (Psalm 51:17)?** (His heart was yielded to God.)
3. **Psalm 51 is King David's confession. He asked God for some specific things to happen as a result of being forgiven. What are some of those requests?** (Refer to Bible study 8 subhead, "Accept Forgiveness.") **In your Time Alone with God Notebook, paraphrase David's prayer in your own words. If you are aware of any un-**

confessed sin in your life, make this paraphrase your personal confession.

When group members are finished, quote 1 John 1:9 together.

APPLYING GOD'S WORD *(10 minutes)*

Ask each group member to write, on a separate sheet of paper, any sin(s) he has committed for which he still feels guilty. Explain that this list will remain confidential. When everyone is finished writing, have students fold their papers to keep them private. Then put all the lists into a metal wastebasket or large ashtray and burn the lists. (Make sure you can *safely* conduct this activity. You may even want to go outside for this part of the meeting.)

As the written confessions are burning, ask group members to silently confess their sins to God. Explain that God has forgiven every sin that has been confessed. However, if some of the sins involved other people, group members may need to make things right with these persons. If the sin was against another group member, encourage those involved to settle the issue before leaving the meeting.

Assignments for Next Week

1. Complete the *Assignment* at the end of Bible study 8 in *Spending Time Alone with God*. (Review this assignment with the group.)

2. Do Bible study 9 and learn the memory verses.

3. Continue to remember the upcoming half day of prayer during your daily times alone with God.

AFTER THE MEETING

1. Evaluate: Do you detect any cliques among the members of your Discipleship Family? If so, try to pair different people before and after the meetings to strengthen your weaker relationships.

2. Are all group members keeping up with their daily time alone with God, weekly assignments, and memory verses? As you see different group members this week, talk to them about previous material to make sure they are retaining what they learn.

3. Begin to plan specific details for your half day of prayer (location, materials needed, transportation, etc.). Be ready to delegate specific assignments to any group members who are willing to help.

Pray for Yourself
Bible Study 9

OVERVIEW

Key Concept God is a loving Father who will provide what we need as we bring our petitions to Him in prayer.

Memory Verses Matthew 7:7-8

Goals *Individual Growth:* To discover the privilege of making personal needs known to God and receiving His provision for them.
Group Life: To practice petition as a group by praying for God's blessings on the Discipleship Family.

BEFORE THE MEETING

1. Pray that each group member will understand the importance of petition and the privilege of approaching God as a loving Father who wants to meet our needs.
2. In *Spending Time Alone with God*, complete Bible study 9 and the daily assignments from Bible study 8.
3. Memorize Matthew 7:7-8.
4. Gather materials for the meeting:
   Bible
   Spending Time Alone with God
   Memory verse packet
   Time Alone with God Notebook

THE MEETING

BUILDING THE GROUP (15 minutes)

Discuss the following:
   Describe how you viewed God when you were young. What character qualities did He have? What physical qualities? Did he ever seem like an invisible Santa Claus?
   What kinds of prayers did you pray to God at that age?

Have your prayers changed since then? How?
How has your mental image of God changed as you have grown older?

FOCUSING ON LIFE (15 minutes)

When you were a small child, who took care of your daily needs? (Parents or guardians.) **Did they ever intentionally keep you from having anything you really needed? Does that mean you never had to ask them for anything?** (Even though loving parents want to provide for their children, sometimes they don't know what the children want. Other times they wait for the child to ask, because it makes the child aware of his needs.)

Since God already knows what we need, why is it still important to ask Him for those things in prayer? (Petition shows God that we trust Him to take care of us, and it reminds us that we are not self-sufficient.)

EXPLORING GOD'S WORD (35 minutes)

Allow time for group members to review their answers and comments for Bible study 9 in *Spending Time Alone with God*. Let them ask questions and make observations. Then discuss these questions:

1. **How would you define** *petition* **in your own words?**
2. **What conditions must be met in order for our prayers to be answered?** (Belief that God will hear us; prayer in Jesus' name; remaining in Christ.)
3. **Why does God refuse our requests at times?** (Wrong motives, unbelief, prayers that don't agree with His character and purposes. See Bible study 5.)
4. **What does it mean to ask "in Jesus' name"?** (See text subhead, "Petition: Asking.") **Will praying in Jesus' name change the way you've prayed in the past? Why or why not?**
5. **The Bible contains thousands of promises that you can ask God to apply to your life. What are some promises in Scripture that you want to ask God to fulfill in the weeks to come?**

APPLYING GOD'S WORD (10 minutes)

Close with silent prayers of petition. Ask each group member to pray that God will supply his specific needs. Then encourage everyone to pray for the Discipleship Family as a whole. List some group needs together before you pray. Complete your time of prayer by quoting the memory verses, Matthew 7:7-8, together.

Before dismissing, remind your group members of the half day of prayer (which should take place soon after your next meeting).

Assign specific responsibilities to willing students (planning transportation, bringing needed materials, etc.).

Assignments for Next Week

1. Complete the *Assignment* **at the end of Bible study 9 in** *Spending Time Alone with God.* (Review this assignment with the group.)

2. Do Bible study 10 and learn the memory verses.

3. Review the material already covered in *Spending Time Alone with God* **and all the memory verses. Write down any questions you have.**

AFTER THE MEETING

1. Evaluate: Can you see a difference in the group members as they have committed themselves to the disciplines of prayer, Bible study, and Scripture memory during the past nine weeks? If you have noticed that any topics might not be clear to the group, be prepared to discuss them during the next meeting.

2. If you are aware that any group member is struggling with an issue raised during the study of *Spending Time Alone with God,* talk to him this week about his concern.

3. Send all group members a postcard, reminding them that next week is the last meeting and to review all memory verses. Assure members of your prayers, your friendship, and your willingness to help them any way you can.

4. Finalize your plans for the half day of prayer.

Pray for Others
Bible Study 10

OVERVIEW

Key Concept Intercessory prayer is the greatest weapon believers have for influencing the lives of others.

Memory Verses 2 Corinthians 10:4-5

Goals *Individual Growth:* To experience the joy of seeing God minister to other people as a result of intercessory prayer.
Group Life: To select group members for which to intercede in the weeks following this last Discipleship Family meeting.

BEFORE THE MEETING

1. Pray for each group member by name, asking God to give each one the desire and discipline to pray for others.
2. In *Spending Time Alone with God*, complete Bible study 10 and the daily assignments from Bible study 9.
3. Memorize 2 Corinthians 10:4-5.
4. Gather materials for the meeting:
   Bible
   Spending Time Alone with God
   Memory verse packet
   Time Alone with God Notebook

THE MEETING

BUILDING THE GROUP *(15 minutes)*

When the class assembles, have volunteers share any results from their prayers of petition during the week. What did they pray for? What promise did they claim? Were any prayers answered? (Keep in mind that *no* and *wait* are valid answers to prayer.)

After you have answered any questions concerning petition, ask a volunteer to read the introduction to Bible study 10, down to the heading, "How Intercession Works." Ask your group members: **Have you ever had experiences such as these, where you were asked for help, but didn't know what to do? What *did* you do?**

Spend a few minutes discussing students' experiences. Perhaps prayer was a natural response for some of them. If so, ask if they prayed in confidence that God would take action, or if their prayer was more from desperation and lack of knowing what else to do.

Make sure all examples discussed at this time are from the *past*. The next section will cover *current* problems.

FOCUSING ON LIFE *(10 minutes)*

Discuss the following questions:

Do you know anyone whose life you would like to see changed in a positive way? (Ask them to think about someone *outside* the group.) **What change would you like to see?** (Give up a sinful habit, become a Christian, start going to church, etc.)

Have you tried to do anything to make that person change? What have you done? What were the results?

After completing this week's study, did you pray for that person?

EXPLORING GOD'S WORD *(20 minutes)*

Allow time for group members to review their answers and comments for Bible study 10 in *Spending Time Alone with God.* Let members ask questions and make observations. Then discuss these questions:

1. **Why are your prayers important in God's process of touching other people's lives?** (Even if the other person doesn't pray, God will hear our intercessory prayers.)

2. **What is the Holy Spirit's function in intercessory prayer?** (He penetrates the life of the other person when our personal effort fails.)

3. **How many times should you pray for someone?** (See 1 Samuel 12:23.)

4. **Why is it good for several people to pray for the same thing?** (See Matthew 18:18-20.)

5. **What are some steps to effective intercessory prayer?** (Refer to Bible study 10 subhead, "Steps to Effective Intercessory Prayer.")

Recite the memory verses (2 Corinthians 10:4-5) together. Remind the group members that any stronghold of resistance can be destroyed if they continue to practice intercessory prayer.

APPLYING GOD'S WORD *(30 minutes)*

Ask each group member to write in his notebook the name of the person outside the group that he would like to pray for. Then divide the group into pairs, and have each person add to his notebook (1) his partner's name, and (2) the name of the person who is his partner's prayer concern. Each person should then have a total of three names. Ask everyone to pray for the three names on their lists for the next 30 days. Encourage prayer partners to check with each other at least once a week for progress reports.

Then spend a few minutes to review the material covered in the *Spending Time Alone with God* book. Use the following questions as guidelines:

(1) **How has your daily time alone with God affected your life over the past 10 weeks?**

(2) **What have you learned from spending time in God's Word?**

(3) **Has the Scripture you have memorized so far helped you overcome any hard-to-handle situations?**

(4) **Has God answered yes to any of your recent prayers?**

(5) **Has He answered no, or wait? Can you understand why?**

(6) **Why should you praise God? What does praise have to do with how you handle problems in life.?**

(7) **Have you begun to confess your sins regularly? What is God's promise when you do?**

(8) **What is the difference between praise and thanksgiving? Why can we still be thankful even if we're in the midst of a struggle or tragedy?**

Next, if time permits, review the 10 memory verses from *Spending Time Alone with God.*

Ask group members to pray sentence prayers, thanking God for what they have learned so far, and asking God to continue to teach them. As you close the prayers, ask God to direct each student into a life of committed discipleship.

Before dismissing, issue a challenge to your group members. Explain that even though they have completed *Spending Time Alone with God,* their daily devotional times of prayer, Bible study, and Scripture memory should continue. (The *Assignment* section of Bible study 10 contains the rest of the breakdown of the Gospel of John.) Now that they have fulfilled their 10-week commitment, encourage them to make a lifelong commitment to spend time alone with the Lord each day.

One of the best ways to keep individual commitment strong is to back it up with group support. Display and describe *Making Jesus Lord,* the next book in the Moving Toward Maturity series. Set up a meeting to organize a new Discipleship Family, and encourage each person to attend and renew his commitment to the group.

Make sure everyone is sure of the time and place for the half day of prayer, and knows what to bring. Answer any final questions students might have.

No Assignment

AFTER THE MEETING

1. Evaluate: Remove page 97 from this Leader's Guide and evaluate your 10-week experience with your Discipleship Family. Mail your comments to us right away. Your input is important.
2. Contact each member of the group a week or so before your organizational meeting for the *Making Jesus Lord* Discipleship Family. Encourage every person to continue his commitment to the group.

PLANNING A HALF DAY OF PRAYER

After students complete their 10-week study of *Spending Time Alone with God*, an organized half day of prayer can be a special learning experience as they are given the opportunity to apply everything they have covered. Set a date for this event early in the study, but don't say too much about it until you get to session 6 (the session on prayer).

Structure this activity to meet the needs of your specific group, but the outline below should get you started in the right direction. Your attitude is likely to influence the group. The more enthusiasm you show for this activity, the more excited your students will become.

Step #1: Orientation (10 minutes)
Meet together to discuss the schedule, hand out any materials you have prepared, and answer questions.

Step #2: Individual prayer (3 hours and 20 minutes)
Have your students go to an area where they can be by themselves to spend individual time alone with God. They should gauge their time in order to cover three major areas:
- •Waiting on the Lord—Realizing His presence, being cleansed, and worshiping Him
- •Prayer for Others—Making specific intercession and asking for others what they usually ask for themselves.
- •Prayer for Themselves—Petitioning God openly and honestly about their own needs.

Students should vary their activities during each of these areas. They can pray a while (both aloud and silently), read the Scriptures, plan and organize, or whatever else is relevant to this special time alone with God. They should list the requests they take to God, so they can follow up on them in future prayer times.

Step #3—Response (30 minutes)
Reassemble as a group and let each person share what he learned or observed about himself or God through this experience.

MATERIALS NEEDED:

Essential	**Helpful**	**Other Options**
Bible	Missionary prayer	Calendar for the
Time Alone with	letters	year ahead
God Notebook	Sack lunch/beverage	List of personal
Pen	Memory Cards	goals/objectives
Clock or watch	Devotional/Prayer	List of personal
	books	decisions to be made
		Songbook

NOTES

Dear Discipleship Family Leader,

After completing your group study of *Spending Time Alone With God*, please fill out and mail this evaluation sheet to the editor. Thanks for your input!

1. Did you and your young people enjoy this study? _____

Why? _____

_____

2. How many people were in your Discipleship Family group? _____

3. How many had been in a previous Discipleship Family? _____

4. What benefits and problems did you experience as a Discipleship Family?

Benefits: _____

_____

Problems: _____

_____

5. Do you plan to continue the series as a Discipleship Family? _____

Why? _____

_____

6. What did group members like best and least about the student book?

Best: _____

_____

Least: _____

_____

7. What are the strengths and weaknesses of this Leader's Guide?

Strengths: _____

_____

Weaknesses: _____

8. Were the *Time Alone with God Notebook Inserts* helpful? _____

How might they be improved? _____

_____

Additional comments: _____

_____

_____

_____

_____

_____

_____

Place
Stamp
Here

Mail this page to:

SonPower Youth Sources Editor
1825 College Avenue
Wheaton, Illinois 60187

MAKING JESUS LORD

Leader's Guide
prepared by
Sandy Larsen

Introduction

Moving Toward Maturity is a five-part discipleship training series for young people. It is designed to help them become so independently dependent on Jesus Christ that they can teach others to do the same. This series has three main purposes:

1. To train students in the "how to's" of Christian living.
2. To help students develop strong, Christlike characters.
3. To move students from the point of getting to know Jesus Christ to the point of sharing Him with others.

Making Jesus Lord, the third book in the series, will challenge students to yield their lives completely to the lordship of Jesus Christ. Your group members will take a realistic look at Jesus' credentials for lordship, weigh the costs and benefits of discipleship, and examine their lives to detect areas not yet under the lordship of Christ.

The other four study books in the series, and related materials, are described on the outside back cover of this Leader's Guide.

Discipleship Family

Commitment is the key to a successful group study of Making Jesus Lord. So limit the study group to those young people who will commit themselves to study the book and Bible on their own and will faithfully take part in every group meeting. This group of committed young people and their leader are referred to as a Discipleship Family. (Turn to page 11 in Making Jesus Lord and read the commitments required of each person.)

By making and keeping these commitments, each Discipleship Family member will:

1. Learn to depend on Jesus Christ.
2. Develop personal discipline in Bible study, prayer, and Scripture memory.
3. Experience the rich fellowship and love of a committed, caring Christian community.

The young people and leaders who commit themselves to this discipleship training will move toward Christ's goal for the church: "His gifts were made that Christians might be properly equipped for their service, that the whole body might be built up until the time comes when, in the unity of common faith and common knowledge of the Son of God, we arrive at real maturity—that measure of development which is meant by 'the fullness of Christ' " (Eph. 4:12-13).*

---

*Quoted from The New Testament in Modern English, © 1972 by J. B. Phillips, published by The MacMillan Company. Used by permission.

You, the Leader

Being a leader of a Discipleship Family will require more time and personal involvement than most Bible studies or Sunday School classes you may have taught in the past. As a member of the group (not just its leader) you should take part in all the commitments, activities, and assignments of the Discipleship Family. To get started, here are some things you will need to do.

1. Get familiar with the Moving Toward Maturity series (see back cover) **and your role as a Discipleship Family leader.** Besides the introduction of this Leader's Guide, two other resources by Barry St. Clair can clarify your role: the book *Building Leaders for Strategic Youth Ministry* and the six-part video "The Youth Ministry Puzzle." Both are available in Christian bookstores or from Victor Books or Reach Out Ministries.

2. Read through *Making Jesus Lord* **and this Leader's Guide.** Call each person from your previous Discipleship Family, describe to him the purpose of Book 3, and ask him if he is planning to continue with the Moving Toward Maturity series. Explain the need for him to renew his commitment for the next 10 weeks.

3. Organize your Discipleship Family. Pray that the Lord will cause those who need to continue the series to make that commitment. If some students have gone through Books 1 and 2 on their own, or have been members of another Discipleship Family, allow them an opportunity to join your group if there is room. Your group will be most effective with 4 to 8 members, and should not exceed 12. If more people are interested, a second group should be formed.

4. Purchase the materials you will need well in advance of the first meeting. Everyone who is leading a Discipleship Family group should have his own copy of the Leader's Guide. Each Discipleship Family member (including yourself) should have his own copy of *Making Jesus Lord,* a Bible, a 5½" x 8½" looseleaf notebook, a set of *Time Alone with God Notebook Inserts* (you can photocopy them from pages 249-264 of this Leader's Guide), and a supply of paper. Provide these materials for everyone at the first meeting.

5. Decide the best time and place to meet. Have everyone bring their school and work schedules to the first meeting so they can decide as a group when and where to meet for the next 10 sessions. If possible, plan to hold the meetings in your home or the home of one of the group members. Meeting in the informal atmosphere of a living room or around a dining room table will help people open up and join in discussions.

6. Allow up to two hours for each meeting. Suggested time allotments for each part of the meeting are given in this Leader's Guide. A total of 60 minutes is suggested for the introductory meeting (session 1); 75 minutes are suggested for sessions 2-11. Since these are not instructional classes, but meetings designed to build relationships and share insights, they should be open-ended. If you finish a session in 75 minutes, fine. But you should have the freedom to meet for two hours if necessary (never longer).

7. Get the group together for a fun activity. Before or after session 1, plan a fun get-acquainted activity (softball game, bike hike, retreat, pizza party, picnic) for the participants of the Discipleship Family. This will help them renew the relationships they have developed with one another.

Building relationships

Your role in the Discipleship Family is that of leader, not teacher. By explaining that you and all members of the group are in the process of becoming more mature disciples of Christ, you will begin to establish yourself as one of the group rather than as the "instructor." But because you are more mature in years and in experience than the young people in your Discipleship Family, they will look to you for organization, guidance, and example.

1. Meet with each group member. Schedule an appointment with each member of your Discipleship Family during the first week or two. Strengthen your relationship with each person. Check on his needs, interests, concerns, and any goals he set as a result of previous studies. Share those things about yourself as well. This will help you see one another as unique, important individuals with feelings and ideas. It will also result in more meaningful discussions during your group meetings.

2. Keep your own Time Alone with God Notebook during this 10-week study. In addition to the student notebook assignments, also write your observations about members of your Discipleship Family. Regularly pray for each one by name. Keep track of individual needs and achievements. If someone misses a session, contact him personally. Help him when he has trouble understanding something from Scripture. Talk with him if he seems to be breaking his commitments. Call on him for his opinions during meetings. Build him up so he will be valued and appreciated by the group. You can also use your notebook for writing your evaluation of each session as well as what you plan to do to improve as a leader.

3. Keep your pastor and church informed. While you're building relationships in your Discipleship Family, continue to build relationships within the church as well. Keep your pastor informed as to what is happening in your group. Encourage group members to be involved in the church and to strengthen their relationships with other believers—particularly other young people who are not a part of a Discipleship Family. Group members should continue in the strong relationships they have built with one another, but they should avoid becoming a "clique."

4. Limit group membership. The people who are a part of this group should come from those who have studied Books 1 and 2 with you, and possibly others who have finished those books and want to join the group. Because your Discipleship Family will be building trust based on shared experiences, don't take in any new members once the group has been established. You should also make sure that everyone who plans to join this group has completed all previous group commitments. Anyone who has dropped out of a prior group should not move on until he finishes his work on that book. After completing the study of *Making Jesus Lord*, challenge each person to renew his commitment and to continue with the group in the study of *Giving Away Your Faith* (Book 4 in the Moving Toward Maturity series).

Effective meetings

The Discipleship Family's meetings are based on biblical principles of discipleship. Each session has at least one *Group Life* and one *Individual Growth* goal. It's important that you work toward accomplishing both.

1. Be prepared. Begin your preparation for each session at least five days in advance. Do the Bible study, answering the questions for yourself, not as you think the students might answer. Then skim through the Leader's Guide suggestions to see if there is anything you need to do right away. Later in the week (one or two days before the meeting) finalize your preparation: Review the material, and study the Leader's Guide suggestions, adapting activities according to the particular needs of your group.

2. Start on time. Since Discipleship Family meetings can last up to two hours, ask everyone to come on time, or even a few minutes early. (Those who arrive early can use the time to share with other group members or review Bible memory verses.)

3. Help students keep their commitments. Students are to complete each week's Bible study **before** each session so the meeting can be devoted to building on what the students are learning on their own. For that reason, the "Exploring God's Word" section of each session does not contain a verbatim review of the Bible study material. Instead students are given an opportunity to quickly look over the Bible study content and their written responses. Then the discussion that follows builds on and reinforces what students have learned during the week prior to the meeting. Group members should also have a regular time each week to share results of their personal times with God.

Be sensitive to group members who may lack self-discipline and need extra encouragement and motivation to keep their commitments. Be positive. Recall how Christ loved, encouraged, and disciplined the early disciples; then follow His example in helping His new disciples along.

4. Continue to develop skill in leading discussions. Here are a few ways to keep your Discipleship Family discussions on track so each member can contribute and learn during each session:

▶*State questions clearly and concisely.* You're more likely to get specific answers if you ask specific questions.

After you ask a question, allow time for the group to think. Don't be afraid of short periods of silence. And don't jump in with your own answers or opinions. Don't make a contribution to the discussion that someone else in the group can make.

►*Respect each person's comments.* Encourage each one to say what he thinks, not just what he thinks he should say. Ask additional questions to help him amplify his thoughts and move from ideas to applications.

►*Stay close to Scripture.* The Bible is the authority for this study and for your group discussions. Encourage group members to base their ideas on biblical principles.

►*Challenge trite or superficial answers.* Don't let group members get away with simply rattling off a cliché or a Bible verse. Ask them to explain what they mean or give an illustration.

►*Ask review questions when appropriate to help the group think through things they've studied up to that point.* Use this time for members to raise previously-discussed issues with which they're still having problems.

►*If some group members are hesitant to take part in the discussions, ask them direct questions relating to their personal opinions or experiences.* Let them know that you care about them and what they think.

►*If some members answer all the questions, begin addressing your questions to others by name so everyone may be heard.* If a member continues to monopolize the discussions, you may want to talk with him privately after the meeting. Let him know you appreciate him and his contributions, but ask him to give others more opportunity to take part.

5. Evaluate each session. Within 24 hours of each meeting, evaluate how the session went and note the emerging needs of group members. The "After the Meeting" section of each session in this Leader's Guide will help you do this.

As you prepare to lead each meeting, pray that God will help you model the life of a true disciple—especially when it comes to having your own time alone with God. Be enthusiastic about growing spiritually, helping others grow, and sharing your faith with non-Christians. Your spirit can be contagious.

If group meetings are enjoyable and helpful to a Discipleship Family member, he will not only grow in his relationships with Christ and the rest of the group, but will probably be eager to commit himself to the Discipleship Family until all five books in the Moving Toward Maturity series have been completed. □

Continuing Your Discipleship Family

OVERVIEW

Key Concept
To benefit most from a group study of *Making Jesus Lord*, we must commit ourselves to the disciplines of a Discipleship Family.

Goals
Individual Growth: To accept the responsibilities and commitments of a Discipleship Family for another 10-week period.
Group Life: To continue the strong fellowship ties within the group established during previous Discipleship Families.

BEFORE THE MEETING

1. Study pages 100-104 of this Leader's Guide for important background information.
2. In *Making Jesus Lord*, study pages 5-11, and put together the memory verse packet located in the back of the book.
3. Call each person who said he'd come to the first meeting. Your group should consist of members who have been through *Following Jesus* and *Spending Time Alone with God* Discipleship Families or who have completed those books on their own. Ask everyone to bring their school and work schedules.
4. Be prepared to present the purpose and format of the Moving Toward Maturity series to the group. Place special emphasis on the content of *Making Jesus Lord*.
5. Gather materials for the meeting:
   Bible
   Making Jesus Lord
   3" x 5" cards
   Sheets of 8½" x 11" paper, preferably in colors
   Pencils

Bible memory packet
Student materials (a copy of *Making Jesus Lord* and a set of *Time Alone with God Notebook Inserts* for each person)

THE MEETING

BUILDING THE GROUP *(20 minutes)*

As each person arrives, greet him warmly and ask him to write his name, address, and phone number on a 3" x 5" card (unless you already have this information from a previous Discipleship Family).

When everyone has arrived, give each group member a sheet of 8½" x 11" paper and ask him to draw, or write a paragraph about, something in his life which is very important to him. It may be a possession, another person, a life goal, a hobby or activity, anything at all—including his relationship with the Lord. (Take part in this activity yourself.) Let each person share what he has drawn or written. (You go first.)

FOCUSING ON LIFE *(5 minutes)*

Discuss: **What person has had the most influence on you? How and why?** (Let a few group members respond briefly.) **What difference does it make what kind of people influence us?** (We'll tend to become like the people who influence us, taking on their values and ways of looking at life, even their behavior.) Record the responses of your group members to use later in "Considering the Choice."

EXPLORING THE CHALLENGE *(20 minutes)*

Have a volunteer read Colossians 2:6-10. Emphasize to the group that just as they have begun their lives with Christ by faith, they must continue to live with Him by faith, trusting more and more of their lives to Him.

Review the purpose of the Moving Toward Maturity series and the function of the Discipleship Family (page 100 of this Leader's Guide). Let each student share something he learned or experienced from being in a previous Discipleship Family. Stress the necessity of commitment to God and to each other in order for the Discipleship Family to be effective.

Give everyone a copy of *Making Jesus Lord*. Review the topics to be discussed, and read the group disciplines (page 11). Discuss any questions students have about the commitments they are expected to make.

Also hand out copies of the *Time Alone with God Notebook Inserts*. Explain that group members will be expected to continue their daily times alone with God as they learn to make Jesus Lord of their lives. Challenge them to learn as much as they can on their own as they read through the Gospel of Mark.

Briefly discuss the length and number of meetings (one-and-a-quarter to two hours per week with the group, plus individual study time, for the next 10 weeks). Then have everyone consult their schedules and decide on a specific time and place to meet.

CONSIDERING THE CHOICE *(15 minutes)*

Review the list you compiled earlier of people who have strongly influenced your group members, and why. Ask the group to silently consider whether they really want Jesus Christ to be the top influence in their lives.

Challenge them to think and pray about making another 10-week commitment to the Discipleship Family. Anyone who decides not to become a part of this particular Discipleship Family should let you know before the next meeting and return his unmarked copy of *Making Jesus Lord* and notebook inserts. Those who choose to join should complete Bible study 1 in *Making Jesus Lord* before the next meeting.

Encourage everyone to set aside a specific time each week to complete the Bible study to be discussed during the next Discipleship Family meeting. (NOTE: The *Assignment* section of each Bible study is not to be completed until *after* the Bible study material has been discussed in the Discipleship Family. For example, your assignment this week will be to complete Bible study 1 [ending with the *Making It Personal* section] in preparation for next week's Discipleship Family meeting. *After* the next meeting, students should complete the *Assignment* at the end of Bible study 1 as well as Bible study 2.)

Close by praying for each person by name. Thank God for your group members and ask Him to give each one of you the willingness to make Jesus Lord of your lives.

Assignments for Next Week Give the following assignments to those who decide to be a part of the Discipleship Family:

1. In *Making Jesus Lord*, **read pages 5-11, study and sign the "Personal Commitment" sheet (page 11), complete Bible study 1 (down to the** *Assignment* **section), and put together the memory verse packet in the back of the book.** (Show the group your packet to demonstrate what it looks like put together.) Remind everyone to memorize Psalm 63:1 as part of Bible study 1.

2. Bring a Bible, a pen or pencil, and *Making Jesus Lord* **to every meeting.**

Also remind the group to bring enough money next week to reimburse you for the student books and notebook inserts.

Before students leave this first meeting, try to talk with them individually. See if they have any questions or problems. Encourage them to join the group, and let them know you care about each of them and their concerns.

AFTER THE MEETING

1. Evaluate: Did each person become involved in sharing his ideas and feelings? Are there people who especially need to be drawn out to participate more freely? Review "Effective Meetings," page 103 of this Leader's Guide.

2. This week, and every week, begin preparing for the next session at least five days in advance. Complete Bible study 1 in *Making Jesus Lord*, and read through the Leader's Guide suggestions.

Get Ready . . . Get Set!
Bible Study 1

OVERVIEW

Key Concept	Jesus Christ is qualified to be your Lord.
Memory Verse	Psalm 63:1
Goals	*Individual Growth:* To make a commitment to begin making Jesus Lord.
	Group Life: To agree to support one another as a Discipleship Family for the next 10 weeks.

BEFORE THE MEETING

1. Pray for each person who came to the last meeting, asking God to give each one the willingness to yield himself to the lordship of Jesus.
2. In *Making Jesus Lord*, do Bible study 1, writing your personal responses to each question. This week and every week, note in the margins other observations or personal experiences that relate to the lesson, and bring them up during the group meeting.
3. Memorize Psalm 63:1.
4. Contact each person who attended the last session. Remind him of the meeting time and place and answer any questions he may have. If someone has decided not to participate in this Discipleship Family, assure him that you still care for him, and express your hope that he will be able to participate in a future group.
5. Make a list of the names, addresses, and phone numbers of all the group members from the 3″ x 5″ cards filled out last week. Make enough copies for each group member to have one.
6. Begin to consider areas of your life which still need to be brought under the lordship of

Jesus Christ. It helps to remain aware that even as the leader of this Discipleship Family you have not "arrived" spiritually.
7. Gather materials for the meeting:
Bible
Making Jesus Lord
Copies of group members' names, addresses, and phone numbers (one per student)
Bible memory packet

THE MEETING

BUILDING THE GROUP *(15 minutes)*

Greet each person warmly. Welcome him as an important member of the group.

Confirm that by each person's presence, he is saying, "Yes, I want to be a part of this Discipleship Family." Have everyone turn to the *Personal Commitment* sheet (page 11 in *Making Jesus Lord*). Read it together. Then ask anyone who hasn't already done so to sign his sheet. (Be sure to sign yours too!)

Ask volunteers who have been through the first two Discipleship Families (*Following Jesus* and *Spending Time Alone with God*) to recall how they felt at first about signing *Personal Commitment* sheets. (Scared? Excited? Hopeful? Doubtful?) Ask them to tell a little about how God helped them stay faithful to their Discipleship Family commitments, and/or how He picked them up when they failed. Join in with your own personal experiences.

Assure your young people that you are available to help them keep their commitments to this Discipleship Family. Take time for volunteers to offer short prayers: (1) for wisdom to understand what it means to make Jesus Lord of their lives; and (2) for courage to make Him Lord in every area of life.

FOCUSING ON LIFE *(15 minutes)*

Discuss: **If someone asked you to prove that you know how to drive a car, how would you do it?** (Show him your driver's license; invite him to take a drive with you; get your parents or friends to vouch for your driving ability; show him your report card proving you passed Driver's Ed; etc. Those things are all "credentials" that you can drive a car.) **What are some other things for which we like to see people's credentials?** (You want to be sure that the doctor who's going to operate on you is a qualified M.D.; that the dentist who's going to pull your tooth really did graduate from dental school; that your

English teacher knows how to write a sentence properly; that your preacher knows his Bible; etc.) **What sort of credentials could you expect from those people?** (Diplomas; other people's recommendations; your personal experience with those people's expertise.)

Explain that when Jesus claims the right to be Lord of our lives, He shows us His credentials and proves His ability to become Lord.

EXPLORING GOD'S WORD *(30 minutes)*

(NOTE: Each week this section is based on the work students have done in Making Jesus Lord. The discussion questions are usually not identical to those in the study book, but they draw from the same Scriptures and assignments. This technique helps students think through what they've studied rather than just parroting written answers.)

Allow time for group members to review their written responses for Bible study 1 in *Making Jesus Lord*. Let them ask questions and make observations. Then discuss:

1. **Did it surprise you to read that Jesus Christ was in on the creation of the world, and your creation in particular? How does that help you understand more about Him?** (It shows He is God; that He existed before the world, and still exists in our lifetime; that He is intimately concerned with our lives.)

2. **According to Hebrews 4:15, Jesus struggled with all the temptations that we struggle with. What temptations is it hard to imagine Jesus struggling with?** (Since Jesus was perfect, we may find it hard to believe he struggled with sexual temptations, the temptation to get rich quick, the temptation to harbor bitterness and resentment. Perhaps it's hardest to imagine Him struggling with the very thing that trips us up most often.) **What difference does it make that He underwent all those temptations?** (He understands us; He doesn't look down on us for being tempted; we don't have to be afraid to tell Him about our shortcomings.)

3. **What do we have as a result of Jesus redeeming or rescuing us?** (Access to God without the barrier of sin; the assurance of His love for us; the assurance of His forgiveness for our future failures; the right to call ourselves God's children; etc.)

4. **What are some areas of life in which we need Christ's power?** (Just about everything! Honesty, keeping relationships pure, resisting temptations, correcting bad attitudes, coping with fears, etc.) **When Jesus is truly Lord of our lives, He'll be Lord over each of those areas and His power will flow through us. But it won't be power for us to use as we want; instead, He will take charge of those things in our lives.**

Invite group members to share their definitions of "Lord" (under subhead, "Jesus' Responsibilities as Lord" in *Making Jesus Lord*). Use the best sections from different people's definitions and create a definition as a group. Affirm everyone's efforts as they contribute.

Point out the list of specific areas where you'll be considering Jesus' lordship ("Making It Personal," Bible study 1) and suggest that group members circle the area or areas where they expect to have the most trouble submitting to the Lordship of Christ.

APPLYING GOD'S WORD *(10 minutes)*

Have group members silently reread their answers under "Desire" in "Making It Personal." Give them the opportunity to change or add to any of their answers. Read aloud the prayer *you* wrote asking God to give you the desire to make Jesus your Lord.

Encourage any group members who could *not* sign the statement under "Decide" to consider it again and sign now if they wish to. Assure them that you will be glad to talk and pray with them if they need help making this decision. Emphasize that their decisions should be reached by faith (not by feelings). Assure your youth that even if they have not yet signed the statement, God will be working with them as they continue in this Discipleship Family, and His Spirit will help them. It is better for them to make a carefully thought-out, slowly reached decision than to dash off a signature and not mean it!

Assignments for Next Week As you give the following assignments, be positive. Let your young people know that you have faith in them and their desire to have Christ as the Lord of their lives.

1. Have a time alone with God each day this week, using the Bible readings at the end of Bible study 1 and the helps under "How to Have a Time Alone with God" (page 251 of the *Time Alone with God Notebook Inserts* at the end of this Leader's Guide).

2. Complete Bible study 2 in *Making Jesus Lord*. Don't forget to learn the memory verse.

3. As you have more thoughts on what it means to make Jesus Lord of your life, note them in your Time Alone with God Notebook.

AFTER THE MEETING

1. Evaluate the meeting: Were students relaxed, or was the atmosphere uncomfortable? Did everyone seem to feel free to take part? If the atmosphere was not as you wished, jot down some possible causes and things you can do to improve the situation next week.

2. If any group member expressed special questions or problems, meet with or call him this week.

No Pain, No Gain
Bible Study 2

OVERVIEW

Key Concept Having Jesus as your Lord is often costly, but the rewards are greater than the costs.

Memory Verse Matthew 16:24

Goals *Individual Growth:* To identify the personal costs of making Jesus Lord, particularly in the area of material possessions, and to appreciate the great benefits of making Him Lord.
Group Life: To encourage one another to go ahead with Christ in faith despite the cost.

BEFORE THE MEETING

1. Pray for all your group members by name, asking God to help them think clearly about the costs and the rewards of following Jesus.
2. Complete Bible study 2 in *Making Jesus Lord*. Remember, as a member (not just the leader) of this Discipleship Family, take part in all group activities and discussions, but be careful not to dominate.
3. Memorize Matthew 16:24.
4. Gather materials for the meeting:
   Bible
   Making Jesus Lord
   two objects (such as two wrist-watches, two radios, two calculators)—one very cheap, the other noticeably more expensive
   Bible memory packet

THE MEETING

BUILDING THE GROUP *(15 minutes)*

Greet each person warmly, particularly any who are newer to the group or with whom you don't yet have good rapport.

Ask for volunteers to share any new thoughts they've had on what it means to make Jesus their Lord.

Discuss: **What are some other "lords" that people have, besides Jesus?** (Money, fame, popularity, achievement in sports or school, etc.) **Why are those "lords" not as good as having Jesus for your Lord?** (They won't last, don't really satisfy, can't help when your time comes to die, etc.) **What can you do when you realize that the false "lord" you've been following isn't worth your devotion?** (Turn away from that false god and turn to Jesus in faith—He is always willing to receive you.)

FOCUSING ON LIFE *(10 minutes)*

Show the group the two objects you brought (one cheap, the other expensive). Ask: **Which one of these is worth more?** (Let students respond.) **What makes you think so?** (Usually we assume that if something costs more, it is better than something costing less. The higher cost reflects better workmanship, better materials, a better guarantee. While it's true that many good things in life are free, and some expensive things are a rip-off, in general a higher price indicates higher quality.) **What might this have to do with the Bible study you did this week in** *Making Jesus Lord?* (Making Jesus Lord has a high price, but that's because the quality of the relationship is so great.)

EXPLORING GOD'S WORD *(30 minutes)*

Allow time for group members to review their answers for Bible study 2 in *Making Jesus Lord.* Let them ask questions and make observations. Then discuss these questions:

1. **Did this chapter make you feel a little uneasy about having Jesus Christ as your Lord?** (It's likely it made many in the group uneasy because the price of following Jesus is high. Encourage any group members who express genuine reluctance or second thoughts.)

2. **What makes us not want to pay the price of having Jesus our Lord?** (Fear; desire to hang on to personal ambitions; doubt that the Lord will take care of us if we give up all rights to ourselves; reluctance to look like a "religious fanatic.")

3. **In your Bible study you read Philippians 2:5-11. What comfort can you find in that passage concerning the cost of following**

Christ? (Take time to turn to Philippians 2:5-11 and read through it. Jesus has already paid more of a price than any of us will have to pay: God Himself became a human being, served sinful people, and was humiliated and killed as the lowest kind of criminal.)

4. What further comfort and help can you find in Galatians 2:20? (Being "crucified with Christ" is not the end: Jesus then lives His life in us. Just as His crucifixion wasn't the end, but was followed by His resurrection, we receive new life—IIis life—when we die to ourselves.)

5. The Bible study named five "Good Deals" that you receive when Jesus is Lord of your life. Which ones have you already experienced at some time during your walk with the Lord? (After group members have had a chance to respond, answer from your own experience.) **Which ones would you like to see more of in your life, and why?** (A person facing difficult decisions might feel a special need for "Good Deal #1." A person defeated by a sinful habit might need "Good Deal #3." Again, share a response from your own life.)

APPLYING GOD'S WORD *(15 minutes)*

Say: **You have already seen that because Christ was obedient to death, God exalted Him** (Philippians 2:5-11). **Are you willing to suffer the cost of Christ's lordship in order to gain the value of being exalted as Jesus was exalted? Why or why not?** (Emphasize that the final decision comes down to our own individual wills. We decide who's going to be in control of our lives. Jesus will not force His lordship on us. This is a good time for you, as the leader, to briefly talk about some particular struggle you've had with making Jesus your Lord.)

Under the "Making It Personal" section of Bible study 2, students zeroed in on the issue of material possessions. Give them opportunities to share some responses from their Life Change sheets. But don't force them to share, because the Life Change sheets can be very personal, and students must remain free to write honest answers.

Ask for volunteers to pray, thanking God for giving us a Saviour who is worth the price of anything we might have to give up for Him.

Assignments for Next Week   Give the following assignments:

1. Complete Bible study 3 in *Making Jesus Lord.*

2. Continue to use the suggested Bible readings for your daily time alone with God.

3. Make sure you memorize 1 Peter 1:15-16. Review Psalm 63:1 and Matthew 16:24.

AFTER THE MEETING

1. Evaluate the meeting: Did students fully understand both the possible consequences of following Jesus, and the certainty of the rewards?
2. Is there someone who is shying away from fully making Jesus his Lord? Make the effort to spend some time encouraging that person this week, either over the phone or in a casual get-together.

What's the Difference?
Bible Study 3

OVERVIEW

Key Concept | Jesus is actually God, and He is worthy of our highest commitment and devotion.

Memory Verses | 1 Peter 1:15-16

Goals | *Individual Growth:* To realize that Jesus, because He is God, deserves our total commitment.
Group Life: To agree together to establish God's standards in the areas of dating and sexual relationships.

BEFORE THE MEETING

1. Pray for each group member, particularly about their temptations and problems in the areas of sexuality and dating.
2. Complete Bible study 3 in *Making Jesus Lord*. Even if you have been married for many years and "dating" may seem like a dead issue, don't skip doing the Life Change sheet for yourself.
3. Memorize 1 Peter 1:15-16 and review the preceding memory verses.
4. Gather materials for the meeting:
   Bible
   Making Jesus Lord
   Bible memory packet

THE MEETING

BUILDING THE GROUP *(10 minutes)*

Welcome each person warmly. If you know of something specific that happened in that person's life this week, mention it (a test, an

award, a sports event, an illness in the family).
Let other group members share events in their lives as well.

FOCUSING ON LIFE (15 minutes)

Ask: **What is something you own that is really special to you?** (Let students respond.) **Why is it special?** (Because it's unique in some way, because of who gave it to you, because of how you acquired it, etc.) **Who is a really special person in your life? Why is that person special?** (The example that person sets, special help the person has given in the past, something you have in common, etc.)

EXPLORING GOD'S WORD (35 minutes)

Have each person review Bible study 3 in Making Jesus Lord. Ask for questions or observations about the study. Then discuss:

1. **What difference does it make in your life to know that God is great? Or does God's greatness seem like a far-off concept that doesn't have much to do with everyday life?** (God is greater than any problem; He knows everything and can do anything, so He is aware of every detail of our lives and can help us with all of it.)

2. **Have you ever trusted something or someone that failed you? What were the results and how did you feel? How do you know that God is trustworthy?** (His Word, the promises He has kept, His faithfulness in the lives of older Christians who have trusted Him for many years.)

3. **Why does calling somebody "holy" or a "Holy Joe" sound like an insult?** (It implies that person thinks he's better than anybody else.) **What does it really mean to be holy?** (Set apart and separated; pure; special.) **The Bible says that God is holy** (for example, Isaiah 6:3) **and that we should also be holy** (for example, this week's memory verses, 1 Peter 1:15-16). **What is the difference between God's holiness and our holiness?** (God is holy in and of Himself. Read the A.W. Tozer quote under Making Jesus Lord subhead, "What is God Like?" (Quality #3). Then read Hebrews 10:10. Ask: **What does Jesus have to do with our holiness?** (Jesus died to bring us back to God. Without Him, we would still be devoted to our own selfish ways. He makes it possible for us to belong to God and be set apart for God.)

Point out that Jesus has made us holy by dealing with our sin on the cross. Our holiness is not a fuzzy, abstract ideal. Our holiness works itself out and shows itself in specific areas of our lives. The chart under Bible study 3 subtitle, "Being Set Apart" shows several ways that holiness can be seen in the lives of your group members. Notice that each way involves "putting off" something and "putting on" something else. And notice that God gives a reason in each case why the change is necessary.

4. Why would "foolish talk" or "unwholesome words" be just as bad as "sexual immorality" or "stealing"? (They all display a lack of holiness—a life set apart for self rather than set apart for God.) **In the same way, some signs of holiness may seem "big" to us while others seem "little," but they all show we're set apart for God.**

APPLYING GOD'S WORD *(15 minutes)*

Say: **God is somebody special, the most special Person of all. And we're special to Him, so special that He gave His Son for us and set us apart. Because we're "set apart" for Him, He cares how we live. He wants to change us in those areas of our lives that don't conform to His holy standards. Our Life Change sheet this week concentrates on the area of sex and dating. You don't have to share anything you don't want to, but as you studied the two Scripture passages, what did you discover?** (Let students respond.) Read 2 Corinthians 6:14—7:1 and discuss the issue of dating non-Christians. (God wants both partners in a marriage to be Christians so they can together accomplish His goals for their lives. He wants our physical and spiritual relationships to be pure.) Then read 1 Thessalonians 4:3-8. Summarize: **God has designed sex to be good. He wants your sexual life to be the best. This passage tells us God's plan for how it can be the best. The answer is really simple: wait until marriage. God's very best for your dating and sex life is that you don't cheat yourself or others** (v. 6). **What do you need to do in order to be in line with God's very best for your dating and sex life?**

(NOTE: If you have a mixed group of guys and girls, you may want to separate the sexes for the purpose of keeping the conversation as open and honest as possible.)

Be sensitive to the mood of your Discipleship Family members at this point. Are they open to a lively discussion on the topic of sex and dating, or are they becoming withdrawn and uncomfortable? Continue the discussion as long as they are open, but leave time to pray for God's strength and guidance in this important area of their lives.

Assignments for Next Week   Give the following assignments:
1. Complete Bible study 4 in *Making Jesus Lord.*

2. Memorize Hebrews 11:1. If you are having trouble memorizing the Scripture verses, find someone else in the group and work together on memorization. You can check on and help each other.

3. Spend at least 15 minutes each day for your time alone with God, using the Bible readings suggested at the end of Bible study 3.

AFTER THE MEETING

1. Evaluate the meeting: Were students relatively comfortable as you were discussing issues like the sex/dating issue in this study? Are they comfortable with each other?

2. If someone in the group is seriously involved with a non-Christian, look for a natural opening to discuss that relationship with him/her—without forcing the issue.

Total Confidence
Bible Study 4

OVERVIEW

Key Concept Because God is faithful, we can put our faith in Him.

Memory Verse Hebrews 11:1

Goals *Individual Growth:* To surrender our lives to God in faith.
Group Life: To encourage one another to put our faith into action.

BEFORE THE MEETING

1. Pray for each of your group members and for your own sensitivity to their needs and struggles as they make Jesus Lord of their lives.
2. Complete Bible study 4 in *Making Jesus Lord*.
3. Think of a time when you deliberately put your faith into action, even if you felt it was a small amount of faith. Be prepared to tell your group about your experience.
4. Contact any group member who might need your special attention this week.
5. Memorize Hebrews 11:1.
6. Gather materials for the meeting:
   Bible
   Making Jesus Lord
   Bible memory packet

THE MEETING

BUILDING THE GROUP *(10 minutes)*

Ask: **What are some things you used to believe in but found out weren't true?** (Santa Claus, the tooth fairy, the Easter bunny, etc.)

How did you find out you were wrong? (Most likely someone's belief was put to the test and it failed. For example, a group member may have spied on Santa Claus and discovered his dad to be behind the myth.)

FOCUSING ON LIFE *(10 minutes)*

Select two volunteers—one large, strong person and a smaller one. Have the smaller person stand about three or four feet in front of the larger one (facing the same direction). On your signal, the front (smaller) person should close his eyes and fall backward *if* he has faith that the other person will catch him.

After the person has fallen back (or perhaps chosen not to fall backward), discuss the parallels of this simple exercise with your group members' faith in God. (The smaller volunteer couldn't *see* the larger person who would keep him from falling; he had to believe that the other person physically *could* catch him; he had to believe that the other person *would* catch him; etc.)

Summarize: (Name of smaller student) **could have verbally expressed his faith in** (name of larger student) **all day long. But he couldn't** *prove* **his faith until he fell backward and allowed himself to be caught.**

EXPLORING GOD'S WORD *(35 minutes)*

Have students turn to Bible study 4 in *Making Jesus Lord* and review their written responses. Let them ask questions or make comments. Then discuss:

1. **Some people say it doesn't matter what you believe, as long as you have something to believe in. But what if you believed in God and He weren't really there? What effect would it have on your life?** (People would trust Him to do things and they would never happen. Their lives would be built on self-deception. No hope would exist for life after death.)

2. **But because God really is there and is dependable, what can we do?** (We can fully trust Him.) **Is there a time you deliberately decided to trust God, and you put your faith into action, even if you didn't feel like it or were scared?** (Let students share examples. Relate an example of your own, as well.)

3. Read Luke 16:10. Ask: **What does the verse reveal about trusting God in big and small situations?** (The way we act in life's

small situations is also how we'll act in complex ones.) **What's an example of a small situation where it's easy** *not* **to trust God?** (Covering up a small bit of bad behavior with a little lie; taking advantage of a teacher's grading error; sneaking around a parental rule now and then; etc.)

4. Hebrews 13:7 encourages us to look up to our leaders and imitate their faith. Think of a person you know whose faith you admire. What do you see in that person's faith that you would most like to have as your own? (Perseverance; inner peace under pressure; ability to forgive and leave things in the hands of God; etc.) **If possible, make plans to talk with the person you named about how (s)he has grown in his/her faith. But don't be surprised to learn that the person is not perfect and still has struggles!**

APPLYING GOD'S WORD *(15 minutes)*

Ask: **In what area of your life do you have the biggest struggle trusting God completely?** (Let students privately write down their answers.) **What is one small step you can take to begin to trust God in that area? Remember Luke 16:10—if you're faithful in small things, you'll be faithful in the big things.** (Give students time to consider and write answers.)

Have a time of prayer—much of it can be silent—committing these difficult areas to the Lord.

To close, break into pairs and have each student discuss his Life Change sheet on "Friendship" with his partner.

Assignments for Next Week As you give the following assignments, point out that this week's Bible study is #5, which means you'll be halfway through this Discipleship Family!

1. Complete Bible study 5 in *Making Jesus Lord*, **memorize John 14:21, and continue the daily Bible readings.**

2. Think about the progress you've made in this first half of the Discipleship Family. What changes have occurred in your life? (Any positive change, no matter how small, is OK.)

AFTER THE MEETING ——————————————————

1. Evaluate the meeting: Are group members comfortable praying out loud? Do you dominate the prayertime too much, or do you give them a chance? Don't be afraid of times of silence during prayer.

2. Are you still happy with the environment of your meeting room? What improvements can you make before the next meeting?

For Real
Bible Study 5

OVERVIEW

Key Concept | Jesus is who He says He is, and just as He obeyed His Father, we should obey Him.

Memory Verse | John 14:21

Goals | *Individual Growth:* To recognize that obedience is the key to letting Jesus be Lord of your life. *Group Life:* To encourage one another to obey Christ in the tough areas of life, and not look down on one another for failing.

BEFORE THE MEETING

1. Pray that God will increase the desire of your group members to obey Him in everything they do.
2. Complete Bible study 5 in *Making Jesus Lord.*
3. Memorize John 14:21.
4. Evaluate the progress of your group during the first half of this Discipleship Family. Note changes in your own attitudes or actions, new challenges God has shown you, areas of spiritual struggle He has revealed to you.
5. Gather materials for the meeting:
   Bible
   Making Jesus Lord
   Bible memory packet

THE MEETING

BUILDING THE GROUP *(10 minutes)*

As group members arrive, have them get in groups of three or four and plan a short skit that will demonstrate the negative results of a rumor. Encourage them to come up with an idea on their own. But if they can't think of anything, the following situations should get them started. (Each skit should include an encounter with the person being talked about.)

- One student tells another student that their history teacher is a Communist.
- The word spreads in the locker room that the football quarterback is taking Valium.
- A jealous girl tries to convince everyone at the lunch table that the homecoming queen works as a waitress at a sleazy bar outside of town (not realizing that she is listening at the next table).
- After an unpopular guy scores high on his SAT, several other students decide to tell everyone he cheated.

As group members present their skits, look for motives that cause rumors to get started. Also watch for reactions of the "rumorees" when they hear what is being said about them.

FOCUSING ON LIFE *(10 minutes)*

Ask: **Have you ever been the subject of someone's rumor?** (Let volunteers respond.) **How did you feel when you realized people were spreading untrue statements about you?** (Response.)

Some people say that Jesus Christ wasn't really who He said He was. What other ideas do they have about who He might have been? (A great teacher, but not the Son of God; a fake and a phony who tricked a lot of people; an ordinary religious person whose followers exaggerated His deeds; etc.)

EXPLORING GOD'S WORD *(35 minutes)*

Ask students to look over Bible study 5 in *Making Jesus Lord* and ask questions or make responses if they wish to. Discuss:

1. **Which of the fulfilled prophecies under "Proof #1" is most impressive to you, and why?**

2. **Why is it impossible to say that Jesus was a great moral teacher, but not the Son of God?** (He claimed to be the Son of God, able to forgive sins, do miracles, and rise from the dead. So if He couldn't do those things, He's the world's biggest liar—hardly a great moral teacher of goodness!)

3. **Do you find Jesus' resurrection difficult or easy to believe? Why?** (Though many have heard it taught all their lives, the resurrection is actually an amazing and revolutionary fact. We don't always grasp how amazing it really is.)

4. **Jesus is the greatest person who ever lived. Yet He was a perfect example of humility in His obedience to His heavenly Father.** Have volunteers read John 6:38 and Matthew 26:36-46. Then have students share their definitions of obedience (Bible study 5 subhead, "Trust and Obey").

5. **What are some results of being obedient to God?** (Some are listed in Bible study 5. Let students suggest others.)

6. **As you read the story of Barry St. Clair's struggle with whether basketball or God was going to come first in his life, what questions do you think were in his mind as he wrestled with the decision?** (Possibilities: Is putting God first really worth it? Have I made a big mistake by becoming a Christian? Can I be happy not playing basketball? Does God really love me if He's going to take basketball away from me? Will He give basketball back to me if I give it up?) **Have you ever asked similar questions when deciding whether to obey God?** (Let students share, and share from your own experience also.)

Summarize: **In the case of the author, God did give basketball back to him by letting him play on a team that witnessed for Jesus Christ. We have no guarantee that when we give up something for God, He will give it back to us. Yet we know He will reward obedience in some way.**

While you are discussing obedience, have your group members share responses from this week's Life Change sheet on the topic of "Obedience to Parents." Discuss the similarities between obeying Christ and obeying parents.

APPLYING GOD'S WORD *(15 minutes)*

You have two options for this part of your Discipleship Family meeting time. If you have time, do both options.

Option #1: Discuss and pray about students' answers to, "Name one area of your life where it is really tough for you to be obedient to Jesus Christ."

Option #2: Since you are now halfway through this Discipleship Family, spend some time reflecting on progress you've made and what you have learned together so far. Thank and praise God for the good things that have happened, and pray for the strength to continue the disciplines of the next five weeks.

Assignments for Next Week   Give the following assignments:
   1. **Complete Bible study 6 in** *Making Jesus Lord.*

2. Memorize Philippians 2:5.
3. Continue to have your daily time alone with God.

AFTER THE MEETING

1. Evaluate the meeting: Do students understand that obedience may be costly, but will bring rewards?
2. Are some students lagging in their preparation of the Bible studies or in other disciplines of the Discipleship Family? Give special encouragement to any who need it.
3. If student enthusiasm seems to be below average, analyze your meetings. Are you feeling a little burned out? Are your students feeling overcommitted? Are you spending personal time with students outside the group? Perhaps you need to add something to the meetings that will provide variety. List some possible suggestions that might increase motivation (an outing, an activity, a different place to meet, refreshments, a change in the format, etc.).

Go for It!
Bible Study 6

OVERVIEW

Key Concept — Jesus had the attitude of a servant and willingly gave up all His "rights."

Memory Verse — Philippians 2:5

Goals — *Individual Growth:* To compare our attitudes to the servant attitude of Jesus and, as a result, become better servants.
Group Life: To learn how to serve the other members of the Discipleship Family.

BEFORE THE MEETING

1. Pray for each group member by name. Ask God to give you an opportunity to serve each young person in some special way.
2. Complete Bible study 6 in *Making Jesus Lord.*
3. Memorize Philippians 2:5.
4. Gather materials for the meeting:
   Bible
   Making Jesus Lord
   Bible memory packet
   3" x 5" index cards

THE MEETING

BUILDING THE GROUP [15 minutes]

Ask: **What's the kindest thing anybody ever did for you?** (Let students respond.) **In what way was that person a servant to you?** (Met your need; helped you; put your needs above his own; considered you more important than he was; etc.)

FOCUSING ON LIFE *(10 minutes)*

Ask: **What's the kindest thing you've ever done for somebody?**
(Students may be slower to respond to this one.) **Does it feel good to
be a servant?** (Not always; it means giving up personal convenience
and desires to put somebody else first. But it also provides a sense of
satisfaction at doing the right thing, especially if the other person is
grateful.) **Would you rather be a servant or a master?** (Encourage
students to respond honestly, and don't criticize at this point.)

EXPLORING GOD'S WORD *(30 minutes)*

Ask students to look over Bible study 6. Let them ask questions or
make comments. Discuss:

1. **Are our attitudes under our control, or are we powerless about
what attitudes we have?** (Some basic attitudes may have been in-
stilled in us through our upbringing and events while we were growing up. But ultimately we determine our attitudes.) **How do you
know?** (Everyone has probably experienced some willful change of
attitude; and God wouldn't tell us what attitudes to have unless we
could decide to have them.)

2. **Even though Jesus was God, He was still a human being. What
selfish attitudes might He have chosen as He lived on earth?** (Pride
about the miracles He could do; self-rightcousness because He was
sinless; snobbishness because He was special; ambition at wanting
to be the world's greatest religious leader; etc.) **What attitude *did* He
choose?** (The attitude of a servant.)

3. **This week's Bible study said that having Jesus' attitude would
mean giving up your selfish ambitions and your rights. How did you
react to that possibility?** (Let students respond.)

4. **What help does Philippians 2:1-11 provide in your decision to
become a servant?** (Jesus, as God, chose to serve. We should choose
to serve each other.)

5. **From your knowledge of Jesus' life, what are some examples of
how He served people?** (Feeding them, healing them, teaching
them—often when He was exhausted and wanted to get away from
the crowds, etc.) **Did He show preference for serving a certain kind
of person—rich people or nice people, for example?** (No. He served
lepers and synagogue rulers, wealthy people and poor people, people of all ages, Jews and Gentiles, women and men.)

6. **Why is it easier for us to serve some people more than others?**
(Some people express gratitude for what is done for them; others
don't. Also, it's often easier to do nice things for people we know and
like than for strangers.) **Why are some people difficult to serve?**
(They don't say thank you; they act like they don't really need your
help; you dislike them and don't want to lower yourself to serve

them; they already act like they're better than you are; etc.) **What example does Jesus set about the kind of people we should serve?** (We should serve everyone who needs our help.)

7. **What was Jesus' ultimate act of service?** (Giving His life for us. [See Philippians 2:8 and Mark 10:45.]) **Do you think He wanted to die?** (He certainly didn't in the Garden of Gethsemane. [See Matthew 26:36-46, a Scripture from last week's study of obedience.] But He was willing to put His own feelings aside to do His Father's will. [See Matthew 26:39, 42-44 and John 6:38.]) **Who did Jesus serve by dying on the cross?** (Everyone—both those who appreciate and receive His provision of salvation, and those who don't.)

APPLYING GOD'S WORD *(10 minutes)*

Have students think about somebody that they would prefer not to serve. Then pass out the 3" x 5" cards and ask them to write that person's name on one side. On the other side, have them write something they can do to serve that person. (This will probably not be a popular assignment.) Emphasize that the proposed acts of service should not be big, showy, phony things. They can be as simple as praying for the person. The receiver does not even have to know how he was served. (Be sure you fill out a card!)

Discuss the attitudes your students have toward serving people they don't particularly like. Use the comments of your group members to lead into a discussion of this week's Life Change sheet about attitudes. Have your group look for inconsistencies between what they wrote and how they actually feel.

Pray about having the attitude of servants toward one another and encourage Discipleship Family members to think of ways they can serve each other this week.

Assignments for Next Week   Give the following assignments:

1. Complete Bible study 7 in *Making Jesus Lord,* **including memorizing Ephesians 5:18 and continuing the daily Bible readings in Mark.**

2. If possible this week, do your act of service for the person whose name you wrote on the card. (Assure students you're going to do yours!)

AFTER THE MEETING

1. Evaluate the meeting: Did students feel hopeful about God's help in becoming a servant, or did they react negatively to the idea?
2. Group members will learn much about being servants by seeing a servant attitude in you. What special things can you do for your students this week?

Turn Him Loose
Bible Study 7

OVERVIEW

Key Concept   Because you have received Christ, the Holy Spirit lives in you and gives you the power to live as a Christian.

Memory Verse   Ephesians 5:18

Goals   *Individual Growth:* To turn the Holy Spirit loose so He can control every action and thought.
Group Life: To become "one" in the Spirit.

BEFORE THE MEETING

1. Pray for your group members individually. Ask God to prompt them to carry out their acts of service this week.
2. Make sure you do your own act of service!
3. Complete Bible study 7 in *Making Jesus Lord.*
4. Memorize Ephesians 5:18.
5. Gather materials for the meeting:
   Bible
   Making Jesus Lord
   Bible memory packet

THE MEETING

BUILDING THE GROUP *(10 minutes)*

Ask: **What's something good that has happened to you this week?** (Group members who remembered to do their acts of service for people they don't particularly like will probably have some good experiences to relate. If no one discusses service, inquire about whether the acts of service were done and what results were apparent. Then tell about your own experience.)

FOCUSING ON LIFE *(15 minutes)*

Emphasize that acts of service for people we don't care for—and for that matter, any good act—can be done only with God in us working through us. That presence of God in us is the Holy Spirit.

Discuss: **When you think of the Holy Spirit, how do you imagine Him?** (Maybe a ghost, an indistinct shapeless fog, an invisible power like magnetism, etc.) **It's easy to imagine Jesus Christ because He was a man and we've seen so many pictures of Him—even though they may not be accurate. And it's possible to imagine God the Father because in our childhood we got impressions of what He must look like—even if they tended toward the "old man with a long beard." But for many of us, our image of the Holy Spirit is kind of vague.**

Jesus compared the Holy Spirit to wind (John 3:8). **What do you think He meant by that?** (Neither can be seen, but their effects are apparent. Also, they go everywhere freely and there is something mysterious and unpredictable about their actions.)

EXPLORING GOD'S WORD *(30 minutes)*

Have group members look over Bible study 7 in *Making Jesus Lord* and ask questions or make comments. Then discuss:

1. **Did it surprise you to learn that Jesus was filled with the Holy Spirit? What does that say about our need to be filled with the Holy Spirit?** (If even Jesus did not depend on Himself but drew on God's power, we certainly need to do the same.)

2. **Were you aware that it was the Holy Spirit who drew you to Christ?** (Some people have dramatic experiences of the Holy Spirit dealing with them to bring them to Christ. Others are gently nudged and may not realize until this Bible study that the Spirit brought them. Others have been Christians since childhood and can't pinpoint an exact time of conversion. But whether or not they are aware of the work of the Holy Spirit, He is responsible for drawing people to Christ.)

3. **Look again at your answers to "Power Fact #6" and "Power Fact #7." They compose quite a list of things the Holy Spirit does in you and for you since you are a Christian! Draw a circle around the ones you're particularly aware of in your experience as a Christian.** (Discuss.) **Draw a square around the ones you don't understand or don't feel you've experienced yet.** (Discuss.) Point out that in all the things the Spirit does, He makes Christians more aware of Jesus.

Ask: **How does that fit with what we saw last week about Jesus' attitude of being a servant?** (The Spirit has that same humility and servant attitude.)

4. **What are some things that keep us from being filled with the Holy Spirit?** (Let volunteers share their answers.)

5. **If the Holy Spirit lives in us, why do you think we don't always feel His presence?** (Perhaps He is more concerned with our obedience and spiritual growth than with our having continual "tingly" feelings. If we felt the Holy Spirit every moment, the way we feel a full stomach or a cold shower, we would have no need for faith.)

APPLYING GOD'S WORD *(15 minutes)*

As a group, pray through the steps of being filled with the Spirit. (See subhead, "The Power Pact.") Give students an opportunity to share their answers in these sections if they wish to. Discuss the Life Change sheet on "Habits," since that's an area where the Spirit's control is particularly needed and where His help will be apparent.

Have a time of prayer, asking the Holy Spirit to make His presence known to yourself and your members individually, and in your group as a whole.

Assignments for Next Week   Give the following assignments:

1. **Complete Bible study 8 in** *Making Jesus Lord.* **Memorize Galatians 5:16 and continue having your daily time alone with God.**

2. **If you did not do your act of service during the past week, remember to do it this week.**

AFTER THE MEETING

1. Evaluate the meeting: Do you find yourself giving answers to discussion questions before students have had much time to consider their answers? Don't be afraid of silence after you ask a question; young people need time to think.

2. Is there still a student who is reluctant to relate to you and the group? Make a special effort to contact him informally this week.

Get In Shape!
Bible Study 8

OVERVIEW

Key Concept With the help of the Holy Spirit, any hindrance(s) to obeying Christ can be overcome.

Memory Verse Galatians 5:16

Goals *Individual Growth:* To recognize specific hindrances to following Christ, confess them, and continue to walk in the Spirit.
Group Life: To encourage each other to honestly identify and deal with any personal hindrances to following Christ.

BEFORE THE MEETING

1. Pray for each student's enlightenment as he works on this week's Bible study. We often don't recognize the things that hinder us from following Christ.
2. Complete Bible study 8 in *Making Jesus Lord*.
3. Memorize Galatians 5:16.
4. Gather materials for the meeting:
   Bible
   Making Jesus Lord
   Bible memory packet
   Toy man such as a soldier or cowboy (not a superhero type). Tie him up with string, small lead weights, and anything else that would hinder him from moving.

THE MEETING

BUILDING THE GROUP *(15 minutes)*
Use this time to evaluate your group members' daily times alone with

God. Discuss any questions, problems, or observations they would like to share. What difficulties are they experiencing? What are they doing to overcome those difficulties? What victories have they had (including small ones)?

FOCUSING ON LIFE *(10 minutes)*

Show the group your "tied-up" toy man. Say something like: **This is Jim. He wants to make the football team and be a Christian witness to the other guys. But as you can see, he has a few problems to overcome before he can accomplish his goal. What would you advise him to do so he can get on with his job?**

Let a student untangle the man. (It could take some doing if you've tied him up tightly! Cut him loose if necessary.) Ask: **How is that toy man like us in our spiritual lives?** (We get tied up with hindrances and must get rid of them.)

(*Option:* You may wish to adapt this exercise using a good-natured student volunteer. He might be wrapped in toilet paper for a comic effect, or tied with fishing line to show that many of our hindrances can be small and barely visible, yet binding. Be creative!)

EXPLORING GOD'S WORD *(35 minutes)*

Have students look over Bible study 8 and ask questions or make comments concerning their responses. Discuss:

1. **Our toy man (or volunteer) would have no trouble figuring out what his hindrances were. Ropes and weights are easy to see and feel. Do we always know what's hindering us spiritually?** (No. We can be deceived by Satan or we can kid ourselves. We can choose to ignore or rationalize hindrances.)

2. **Is it possible to avoid being tempted by the hindrances listed in this week's Bible study?** (We would almost have to become hermits in order to avoid them. Even then, many would pursue us—Satan could find us anywhere we could go. It's not the temptations that cause us the problems. It's how we respond to the temptations. If we let them, our temptations can strengthen our walk with God.)

3. **What do all the hindrances have in common?** (They prevent us from having the closeness with God that He desires.) Have each student examine his list of hindrances to see how he is being motivated by selfishness rather than the fact that Christ lives in him. Be sure to share a hindrance from your own list.

Explain that the presence of hindrances is not the main issue—the big issue is how we respond to them. God wants us to respond by relaxing, letting Him work, and being obedient to what He tells us to do.

4. **When you become aware of a hindrance in your life, what can you do to get back into the habit of walking in the Spirit?** (Acknowledge the hindrance and admit your sin; confess it and consciously decide to put it off; accept Christ's forgiveness; accept the Spirit's filling once again.)

APPLYING GOD'S WORD *(10 minutes)*

Break into pairs, discuss this week's Life Change sheets, and have each person pray for himself and his partner, that each of them will relax in knowing that his life is in God's hands and allow God to make any changes He wants to. (This is a good place for you, as the group's leader, to set an example of honesty about temptations and faith that God forgives and helps you. Assure the group that you are available to talk and pray with them when they struggle with temptation. Encourage group members to reach out to one another as well.)

Assignments for Next Week   Give the following assignments:
1. **Complete Bible study 9 in** *Making Jesus Lord.*
2. **Memorize Colossians 3:1.**
3. **Remain faithful in your daily time alone with God.**

AFTER THE MEETING

1. Evaluate the meeting: Do students freely admit they are tempted, or do some still feel it necessary to put on a show of spirituality?
2. Do you see positive changes in group members' lives as a result of your time together as a Discipleship Family?
3. Does anyone feel put down because he is struggling spiritually? If so, reassure him that he is normal, that God loves him, and that you love him.

Changed and Rearranged
Bible Study 9

OVERVIEW

Key Concept Christ renews our minds and changes our habits—with our cooperation.

Memory Verse Colossians 3:1

Goals *Individual Growth:* To change our thinking by recognizing the newness Christ has already brought about inside us.
Group Life: To see each other as new creatures in Christ and learn to love each other unconditionally.

BEFORE THE MEETING

1. Pray for each of your students' thought lives. Ask God to make them aware of thoughts that are destructive and need to be renewed.
2. Complete Bible study 9 in *Making Jesus Lord.*
3. Memorize Colossians 3:1.
4. Gather materials for the meeting:
   Bible
   Making Jesus Lord
   Two T-shirts: one dirty and sweaty, the other clean (preferably brand-new)
   Bible memory packet

THE MEETING

BUILDING THE GROUP *(10 minutes)*

Since this is the next-to-last meeting of your Discipleship Family, express your appreciation for group members and how they are progressing. Invite group members to comment on the influence of the Discipleship Family on their lives.

FOCUSING ON LIFE *(10 minutes)*

Display a dirty T-shirt. (You could even be wearing it.) Say: **Suppose I want to convince you that I'm a nice, clean-living, self-respecting person. The problem is, every single day you see me wearing this same crummy T-shirt. I never change to a different shirt; I never take a shower. What would you advise me to do?** (Take off the shirt and get cleaned up!)

Now display the clean T-shirt and say: **OK, so I go out and buy this nice new T-shirt. It's mine to wear. But instead of putting it on, I hang it in the closet and continue to wear my old smelly shirt. What would be your advice to me?** (Put on the new shirt.) If you are wearing the dirty shirt, and if decency allows, change into the clean one.

Discuss: **How do these two T-shirts illustrate the way Christ renews our minds?** (He makes us new and clean in our minds. But we have to consciously put off the "smelly" thoughts of our old unchristian lives, and put on the new clean thoughts which He makes possible.)

EXPLORING GOD'S WORD *(35 minutes)*

Ask students to look over Bible study 9. Give them the opportunity to ask questions and make comments. Then discuss:

1. **Can you think of one way you have specifically changed since you became a Christian?** Let group members respond, and then get a little more specific: **Can you think of one way God has helped you change an attitude or a way of behaving in, say, the past year?** (Be sure to share your own experience of how God has changed you, but don't dominate the discussion.)

2. **We should be glad and thank God for every evidence we see that He is making us new people in Christ. But what if it isn't obvious to us that we have been changed inside? What if nothing seems to be happening?** (We must take God at His word that He has made our hearts new and is working in us even when we can't feel it. At the same time we should examine our thoughts and attitudes, and allow Him to bring them into line with our new selves.)

3. **We are commanded to set our** *hearts* **on "things above"** (Colossians 3:1) **and to set our** *minds* **on "things above"** (Colossians 3:2).

What's the difference between the two? ("Heart" indicates your deepest affections, desires, and attitudes. "Mind" indicates your conscious thoughts.) **Since we are told to "set" both heart and mind on God, we are able to willfully decide to act—or not. Think about what you desire to have happen. Is it in line with God's will, or is it self-centered? Pay attention to your thoughts. Are they constructive and wholesome, or are bitterness, lust, and greed present? We can't always control what pops into our heads or hearts, but we can decide whether or not to let it remain there.**

4. Ask volunteers to define renewal. (A simple definition is "to be made new.") Then compare Ephesians 4:22-24 with Romans 12:2. Ask: **Who does the renewing?** (God. Notice that these passages don't tell us to renew ourselves, but to be made new.) **What is our part in being renewed?** (Putting off bad thoughts and attitudes; putting on Christ's thoughts and attitudes.) Explain that renewal requires a conscious decision on our part. It begins with an understanding of what Christ's thoughts are, reached through Bible study and prayer, and results in surrendering to His will daily.

5. Encourage volunteers to share some of the thoughts they need to "put off." It's always helpful for young people to know that others struggle with the same (or similar) problems that they are facing. Honest group interaction can let everyone know he is not alone as he tries to replace unclean thoughts.

6. **In the illustration of how sin "hooks" us, what's the first opportunity sin has to get us?** (Our thoughts.) **Where's the best place to cut sin short?** (Our thoughts.) Summarize: **It often seems Satan knows our weaknesses and knows exactly which "lure" to use. We each have particular "enticements" we must guard against.**

7. **Look at the positive qualities listed in Colossians 3:12-17. How does love bind them all together, as verse 14 says?** (All those good qualities depend on treating one another right and directing our hearts toward God—in other words, loving God and loving our neighbors.)

8. **Last week's Life Change sheet was on temptation. This week's is on your "Thought Life." How are the two topics related?** (If group members put Philippians 4:8 into practice and control their thoughts, they are less likely to yield to temptation.) After discussing the Life Change sheet, move on to related questions under Bible study 9 subhead, "Putting On."

APPLYING GOD'S WORD (15 minutes)

Have group members spend time in silent meditation imagining themselves "in Christ." They may use any mental images that will help them "place" themselves in Him. Ask them to think of themselves as protected and enveloped by Him, so that nothing can touch them without His permission. After silent meditation and prayer, ask students to voice prayers of trust and thanks for their newness of life in Christ.

Assignments for Next Week   Before you give the following assignments, remind students that next week is the final week of this Discipleship Family. Let them know that you will begin the next meeting with a special time of praise to God for His leading throughout this study. Be positive about group members' progress and let them know you look forward to meeting with them next week.

   1. **Complete Bible study 10 in** *Making Jesus Lord.*
   2. **Memorize Romans 12:1-2.**
   3. **Continue having your daily time alone with God.**
   4. **Think of some good things that have happened because of this Discipleship Family.**

AFTER THE MEETING

1. Evaluate the meeting: Did students grasp that they are new people in Christ even though they don't always feel like it?
2. Are there any loose ends to tie up with students? Misunderstandings, lack of communication? Do your best to accomplish that before the next meeting.

Who Owns You?

Bible Study 10

OVERVIEW

Key Concept	Jesus owns your life and has the right to ask you to do whatever He knows is best for you.
Memory Verses	Romans 12:1-2
Goals	*Individual Growth:* To review this Discipleship Family study and recognize Jesus' total ownership of each member's life. *Group Life:* To praise God together for what He has done during this Discipleship Family.

BEFORE THE MEETING

1. Pray for each group member. Thank God for the opportunity to know each one better. Pray for the continued spiritual growth of each person as this study ends.
2. Complete Bible study 10 in *Making Jesus Lord.*
3. Memorize Romans 12:1-2.
4. Write out the good things that have happened in the lives of you and your group members as a result of this Discipleship Family. List constructive criticisms also, and keep them for your next Discipleship Family (or pass them on to another leader).
5. Gather materials for the meeting:
   Bible
   Making Jesus Lord
   A trophy, any type (but not a "joke" type)
   Bible memory packet

THE MEETING

BUILDING THE GROUP *(10 minutes)*

Welcome each group member warmly. Try to say some specific

words of appreciation for each person. (More time should be spent building up one another at the end of this session.)

FOCUSING ON LIFE *(10 minutes)*

Show the group a trophy. Read the name on it and what it was awarded for. Ask: **What does this trophy tell you about** (name of person/team)?

If we're God's trophy, as Bible study 10 says, what does that tell you about God? (He goes to great effort to win us and make us His own, and we're very valuable to Him.)

EXPLORING GOD'S WORD *(30 minutes)*

Have students look over Bible study 10 in *Making Jesus Lord*, make comments, and ask questions. Discuss:

1. **Are there any limitations on that "blank check" Jesus gives you?** (He will only provide things within His will. He won't grant every little whim and desire, but He will provide everything we really need—spiritually, physically, and emotionally.)

2. **Does the thought of giving Jesus a "blank sheet" scare you a little?** (We can't predict what He will bring into our lives—what tests, difficulties, responsibilities, or what joys and accomplishments.) **What makes giving our "blank sheet" to Christ less scary?** (The more we trust Him, the more He proves Himself trustworthy, and the more we discover He has our best interests at heart.)

3. Ask students to share their definitions of a "living sacrifice." Ask: **What's the significance of our being a sacrifice that is still "living"?** (We don't just choose God's will once and then "die." We go on in daily life, thinking and making choices. We are active in God's service. He gives us many things to do even while we're "on the altar.")

4. Review your discussion of the last Bible study concerning the renewing of the mind. (God renews us with our cooperation; we must put off old thoughts and put on new thoughts; renewal is a continual process, etc.) Ask: **Are there areas in which your mind has been renewed during these past 10 weeks?** (Discuss.) **Are there areas in which your mind still needs some renewing?** (Discuss, if students are open.)

5. Ask each student to select one area from the review of the Life Change Sheets that he needs the most help in and discuss it if he

wants to. Encourage group members to continue the life changing process on their own after they leave this session.

APPLYING GOD'S WORD *(20 minutes)*

Encourage students to read their reviews of what they have learned about Jesus' lordship (from end of Bible study 10). Read your own summary also.

At this time you may want to spend a few minutes in songs of praise and prayers of thanksgiving for everything God has done for your Discipleship Family during the past ten weeks. Then close by having each person share the one thing from *Making Jesus Lord* that meant the most to him or perhaps the one person who has done the most to help him make Jesus the Lord of his life. Also take time to encourage students to participate in the next Discipleship Family, using Book 4 in the *Moving Toward Maturity* series, *Giving Away Your Faith.*

Try to talk with each person before he leaves. Thank each one for his faithfulness to the group and to the Lord. Express your confidence that he will continue his life with Jesus as his Lord.

No Assignment

AFTER THE MEETING _____

1. Evaluate: Carefully remove page 145 from this Leader's Guide, and use it to evaluate your 10-week experience with your Discipleship Family. Mail your comments to us right away. Your input is important.
2. Contact each member of the group a week or so before your organizational meeting for the *Giving Away Your Faith* Discipleship Family. Encourage every person to continue his commitment to the group.

Dear Discipleship Family Leader,

After completing your group study of *Making Jesus Lord*, please fill out and mail this evaluation sheet to the editor. Thanks for your input!

1. Did you and your young people enjoy this study? _____ _____

Why? _____

_____

2. How many people were in your Discipleship Family group? _____

3. How many had been in a previous Discipleship Family? _____

4. What benefits and problems did you experience as a Discipleship Family?

Benefits: _____

_____

Problems: _____

_____

5. Do you plan to continue the series as a Discipleship Family? _____

Why? _____

_____

6. What did group members like best and least about the student book?

Best: _____

_____

Least: _____

_____

7. What are the strengths and weaknesses of this Leader's Guide?

Strengths: _____

_____

Weaknesses: _____

_____

8. Were the *Time Alone with God Notebook Inserts* helpful? _____

How might they be improved? _____

_____

Additional comments: _____

_____

_____

_____

_____

_____

_____

_____

**Place
Stamp
Here**

Mail this page to:

**SonPower Youth Sources Editor
1825 College Avenue
Wheaton, Illinois 60187**

GIVING AWAY YOUR FAITH

Leader's Guide
prepared by
Sandy Larsen

Introduction

Moving Toward Maturity is a five-part discipleship training series for young people. It is designed to help them become so independently dependent on Jesus Christ that they can teach others to do the same. This series has three main purposes:

1. To train students in the "how tos" of Christian living.
2. To help students develop strong, Christlike characters.
3. To move students from the point of getting to know Jesus Christ to the point of sharing Him with others.

Giving Away Your Faith, the fourth book in the series, will challenge your students to share their faith with others. Your group members will examine the needs of people, confront their fears, and learn how to relate Jesus Christ to their friends.

The other four study books in the series, and related materials, are described on the outside back cover of this Leader's Guide.

Discipleship Family

Commitment is the key to a successful group study of *Giving Away Your Faith*. So limit the study group to those young people who will commit themselves to study the book and Bible on their own and will faithfully take part in every group meeting. This group of committed young people and their leader are referred to as a *Discipleship Family*. (Turn to page 11 in *Giving Away Your Faith* and read the commitments required of each person.)

By making and keeping these commitments, each Discipleship Family member will:

1. Learn to depend on Jesus Christ.
2. Develop personal discipline in Bible study, prayer, and Scripture memory.
3. Experience the rich fellowship and love of a committed, caring Christian community.

The young people and leaders who commit themselves to this discipleship training will move toward Christ's goal for the church: "His gifts were made that Christians might be properly equipped for their service, that the whole body might be built up until the time comes when, in the unity of common faith and common knowledge of the Son of God, we arrive at real maturity—that measure of development which is meant by 'the fullness of Christ' " (Eph. 4:12-13).*

---

*Quoted from *The New Testament in Modern English, Revised edition,* © J. B. Phillips, 1958, 1960, 1972, permission of MacMillan Publishing Company and Collins Publishers.

You, the Leader

Being a leader of a Discipleship Family will require more time and personal involvement than most Bible studies or Sunday School classes you may have taught in the past. As a member of the group (not just its leader) you should take part in all the commitments, activities, and assignments of the Discipleship Family. To get started, here are some things you will need to do.

1. **Get familiar with the Moving Toward Maturity series** (see back cover) **and your role as a Discipleship Family leader.** Besides the introduction of this Leader's Guide, two other resources by Barry St. Clair can clarify your role: the book *Building Leaders for Strategic Youth Ministry* and the six-part video "The Youth Ministry Puzzle." Both are available in Christian bookstores or from Victor Books or Reach Out Ministries.

2. **Read through** *Giving Away Your Faith* **and this Leader's Guide.** Call each person from your previous Discipleship Family, describe to him the purpose of Book 4, and ask him if he is planning to continue with the Moving Toward Maturity series. Explain the need for him to renew his commitment for the next 10 weeks.

3. **Organize your Discipleship Family.** Pray that the Lord will cause those who need to continue the series to make that commitment. If some students have gone through Books 1, 2, and 3 on their own, or have been members of another Discipleship Family, allow them an opportunity to join your group if there is room. Your group will be most effective with 4 to 8 members, and should not exceed 12. If more people are interested, a second group should be formed.

4. **Purchase the materials you will need well in advance of the first meeting.** Everyone who is leading a Discipleship Family group should have his own copy of the Leader's Guide. Each Discipleship Family member (including yourself) should have his own copy of *Giving Away Your Faith*, a Bible, a 5½" x 8½" looseleaf notebook, a set of *Time Alone with God Notebook Inserts* (you can photocopy them from pages 249-264 of this Leader's Guide), and a supply of paper. Provide these materials for everyone at the first meeting.

You may wish to obtain copies of the *Facts of Life* booklet and the *Getting Started* book. You'll find information on ordering these booklets on page 192 of this guide.

5. **Decide the best time and place to meet.** Have everyone bring their school and work schedules to the first meeting so they can decide as a group when and where to meet for the next 10 sessions. If possible, plan to hold the meetings in your home or the home of one of the group members. Meeting in the informal atmosphere of a living room or around a dining room table will help people open up and join in discussions.

6. **Allow up to two hours for each meeting.** Suggested time allotments for each part of the meeting are given in this Leader's Guide. A total of 60 minutes is suggested for the introductory meeting (ses-

sion 1); 75 minutes are suggested for sessions 2-11. Since these are not instructional classes, but meetings designed to build relationships and share insights, they should be open-ended. If you finish a session in 75 minutes, fine. But you should have the freedom to meet for two hours if necessary (never longer).

7. Be prepared to go with students on their witnessing assignments. Plan to go with each student at least twice during the course of this study. Or pair students up with those already experienced in sharing their faith. If you are not already experienced in sharing your faith, go with a youth minister or pastor at least three times before beginning this study with your young people. Regular witnessing experience is a key to the success of this study.

Building relationships

Your role in the Discipleship Family is that of leader, not teacher. By explaining that you and all members of the group are in the process of becoming more mature disciples of Christ, you will begin to establish yourself as one of the group rather than as the "instructor." But because you are more mature in years and in experience than the young people in your Discipleship Family, they will look to you for organization, guidance, and example.

1. Meet with each group member. Schedule an appointment with each member of your Discipleship Family during the first week or two. Check on his needs, interests, concerns, and any goals he set as a result of previous studies. Share those things about yourself as well. This will help you see one another as unique, important individuals with feelings and ideas. It will also result in more meaningful discussions during your group meetings.

2. Keep your own Time Alone with God Notebook during this 10-week study. In addition to the student notebook assignments, also write your observations about members of your Discipleship Family. Regularly pray for each one by name. Keep track of individual needs and achievements. If someone misses a session, contact him personally. Help him when he has trouble understanding something from Scripture. Talk with him if he seems to be breaking his commitments. Call on him for his opinions during meetings. Build him up so he will be valued and appreciated by the group. You can also use your notebook for writing your evaluation of each session as well as what you plan to do to improve as a leader.

3. Keep your pastor and church informed. While you're building relationships in your Discipleship Family, continue to build relationships within the church as well. Keep your pastor informed as to what is happening in your group. Encourage group members to be involved in the church and to strengthen their relationships with other believers—particularly other young people who are not a part of a Discipleship Family. Group members should continue in the strong relationships they have built with one another, but they should avoid becoming a "clique."

4. Limit group membership. The people who are a part of this group should come from those who have studied Books 1, 2, and 3 with you, and possibly others who have finished those books and want to join the group. Because your Discipleship Family will be building trust based on shared experiences, don't take in any new members once the group has been established. You should also make sure that everyone who plans to join this group has completed all previous group commitments. Anyone who has dropped out of a prior group should not move on until he finishes his work on that book. After completing the study of *Giving Away Your Faith*, challenge each person to renew his commitment and to continue with the group in the study of *Influencing Your World* (Book 5 in the Moving Toward Maturity series).

Effective meetings

The Discipleship Family's meetings are based on biblical principles of discipleship. Each session has at least one *Group Life* and one *Individual Growth* goal. It's important that you work toward accomplishing both.

1. Be prepared. Begin your preparation for each session at least five days in advance. Do the Bible study, answering the questions for yourself, not as you think the students might answer. Then skim through the Leader's Guide suggestions to see if there is anything you need to do right away. Later in the week (one or two days before the meeting) finalize your preparation: Review the material, and study the Leader's Guide suggestions, adapting activities according to the particular needs of your group.

2. Start on time. Since Discipleship Family meetings can last up to two hours, ask everyone to come on time, or even a few minutes early. (Those who arrive early can use the time to share with other group members or review Bible memory verses.)

3. Help students keep their commitments. Students are to complete each week's Bible study **before** each session so the meeting can be devoted to building on what the students are learning on their own. For that reason, the "Exploring God's Word" section of each session does not contain a verbatim review of the Bible study material. Instead students are given an opportunity to quickly look over the Bible study content and their written responses. Then the discussion that follows builds on and reinforces what students have learned during the week prior to the meeting. Group members should also have a regular time each week to share results of their personal times with God.

Be sensitive to group members who may lack self-discipline and need extra encouragement and motivation to keep their commitments. Be positive. Recall how Christ loved, encouraged, and disciplined the early disciples; then follow His example in helping His new disciples along.

4. Continue to develop skill in leading discussions. Here are a few ways to keep your Discipleship Family discussions on track so each member can contribute and learn during each session:

►*State questions clearly and concisely.* You're more likely to get specific answers if you ask specific questions.

After you ask a question, allow time for the group to think. Don't be afraid of short periods of silence. And don't jump in with your own answers or opinions. Don't make a contribution to the discussion that someone else in the group can make.

►*Respect each person's comments.* Encourage each one to say what he thinks, not just what he thinks he should say. Ask additional questions to help him amplify his thoughts and move from ideas to applications.

►*Stay close to Scripture.* The Bible is the authority for this study and for your group discussions. Encourage group members to base their ideas on biblical principles.

►*Challenge trite or superficial answers.* Don't let group members get away with simply rattling off a cliché or a Bible verse. Ask them to explain what they mean or give an illustration.

►*Ask review questions when appropriate to help the group think through things they've studied up to that point.* Use this time for members to raise previously discussed issues with which they're still having problems.

►*If some group members are hesitant to take part in the discussions, ask them direct questions relating to their personal opinions or experiences.* Let them know that you care about them and what they think.

►*If some members answer all the questions, begin addressing your questions to others by name so everyone may be heard.* If a member continues to monopolize the discussions, you may want to talk with him privately after the meeting. Let him know you appreciate him and his contributions, but ask him to give others more opportunity to take part.

5. Evaluate each session. Within 24 hours of each meeting, evaluate how the session went and note the emerging needs of group members. The "After the Meeting" section of each session in this Leader's Guide will help you do this.

As you prepare to lead each meeting, pray that God will help you model the life of a true disciple—especially when it comes to having your own time alone with God and sharing Jesus. Be enthusiastic about growing spiritually, helping others grow, and sharing your faith with non-Christians. Your spirit can be contagious.

If group meetings are enjoyable and helpful to a Discipleship Family member, he will not only grow in his relationships with Christ and the rest of the group, but will probably be eager to commit himself to the Discipleship Family through all five books in the Moving Toward Maturity series. □

Continuing Your Discipleship Family

OVERVIEW

Key Concept
To benefit most from a group study of *Giving Away Your Faith*, we must commit ourselves to the disciplines of a Discipleship Family.

Goals
Individual Growth: To accept the responsibilities and commitments of a Discipleship Family for another 10-week period.
Group Life: To continue the strong fellowship ties within the group established during the first three Discipleship Families.

BEFORE THE MEETING

1. Study pages 148-152 of this Leader's Guide for important background information.
2. In *Giving Away Your Faith*, study pages 5-10, and put together the Bible verse packet in the back of the book.
3. Call each person who said he or she would come to the first meeting. Your group should consist of members who have been through *Following Jesus, Spending Time Alone With God*, and *Making Jesus Lord* Discipleship Families or have completed those three books on their own. Ask everyone to bring their school and work schedules.
4. Be prepared to present the purpose and format of the Moving Toward Maturity series to the group.
5. Pray for each potential Discipleship Family member. Ask God to give you compassion for each person you and the students will encounter in witnessing.
6. Gather materials for the meeting:
   Bible
   Giving Away Your Faith
   3" x 5" cards
   Pencils

Bible memory packet
Student materials (a copy of *Giving Away Your Faith* and a set of *Time Alone with God Notebook Inserts* for each person)

THE MEETING

BUILDING THE GROUP *(20 minutes)*

As each person arrives, greet him or her warmly. Ask everyone to write name, address, and phone number on a 3" x 5" card (unless you already have this information from a previous Discipleship Family).

When everyone has arrived, give each group member another 3" x 5" card and ask each person to write some thoughts about *caring*. They can write a definition or words and phrases that come to mind when they think of the word "caring" or their thoughts about what it means to *care*. (Take part in this activity yourself.) Then let each person share what he or she has written.

FOCUSING ON LIFE *(10 minutes)*

Ask: **Have you ever gotten lost?** (Briefly describe an experience of your own in which you were lost.) **How did you feel? Were you frightened? Did you feel that anyone knew or cared about your situation? Was there anything that gave you hope?** (Discuss group members' stories of being lost.) Ask group members to brainstorm words that sum up the feelings and situation of a person who is lost. Record members' conclusions.

EXPLORING THE CHALLENGE *(20 minutes)*

Have a volunteer read Luke 19:10. The Scriptures describe a person who is without Christ as "lost." Review your group's descriptions of being lost (which you recorded under "Focusing on Life") and discuss which of them also apply to a person who is spiritually "lost." Encourage your group members to begin to have compassion for people who do not have Jesus Christ. Review your group's definitions of "caring" (which they wrote under "Building the Group"). Challenge your teens to have that sense of caring toward those who are lost.

Review the purpose of the Moving Toward Maturity series and the function of the Discipleship Family (page 148 of this Leader's Guide). Let each student share something he or she learned or experienced from being in a previous Discipleship Family. Stress the necessity of commitment to God and to one another in order for the Discipleship Family to be effective.

Distribute copies of the *Time Alone with God Notebook Inserts*. Encourage group members to continue their daily times alone with God as they learn to share their faith. Challenge them to learn and grow independently as they read through the Book of Acts.

Give everyone a copy of *Giving Away Your Faith*. Review the topics to be discussed, and read the group disciplines (page 10). Discuss any questions your students have about the commitments they are expected to make.

Briefly discuss the length and number of meetings (one-and-a-quarter to two hours per week with the group, plus individual study time, for the next 10 weeks). Then have members consult their schedules and decide on a specific time and place to meet.

CONSIDERING THE CHOICE *(10 minutes)*

Ask whether anyone has some fears about learning to share Christ with friends who are not Christians. Above all you do not want these very natural and typical fears to paralyze any student and prevent him or her from joining this Discipleship Family. Assure your students that every Christian struggles with such fears about witnessing. Encourage each student to focus on his desire to share Christ instead of his fear. Let students catch your excitement about witnessing. Explain that you plan to go witnessing with each one several times over the next 10 weeks.

Challenge the group to think and pray about making another 10-week commitment to the Discipleship Family. Anyone who decides not to become a part of this particular Discipleship Family should let you know before the next meeting and return the unmarked copy of *Giving Away Your Faith*.

Encourage everyone to set aside a specific time each week to complete the Bible study to be discussed during the next Discipleship Family meeting. (Note: The *Assignment* section of each Bible study is not to be completed until after the Bible study material has been discussed in the Discipleship Family. For example, your assignment this week will be to complete Bible study 1 [ending with the Making It Personal section] in preparation for next week's Discipleship Family meeting. *After* the next meeting, students should complete the *Assignment* at the end of Bible Study 1 as well as Bible Study 2.)

Close by praying for each person by name, and for yourself. Thank God for your group members, and ask Him to give each of you the compassion and the courage to share Christ with others.

Assignments for Next Week Give the following assignments to those who decide to be a part of this Discipleship Family:

1. In *Giving Away Your Faith*, **read pages 1-10, study and sign the "Personal Commitment" (page 11), complete Bible study 1 (down to the** *Assignment* **section), and put together the Bible verse packet in the back of the book.** (Show your group your packet to demonstrate what it looks like put together.) Remind group members to memorize John 17:3).

2. Bring a Bible, a pen or pencil, and *Giving Away Your Faith* **to every meeting.**

Before students leave this first meeting, try to talk with them individually. See if they have questions or problems. Encourage them to commit themselves to the group, and let them know you care about each of them.

AFTER THE MEETING

1. Evaluate: Did each person become involved in the discussions? Are there people who need to be drawn out to participate more freely? Are there others who dominate? Review "Effective Meetings," page 5 of this Leader's Guide.

2. This week, and every week, begin preparing for the next session at least five days in advance. Complete Bible study 1 in *Giving Away Your Faith*, and read through the Leader's Guide suggestions for your next meeting.

3. Schedule time to accompany students on their witnessing assignments. It is crucial to the success of this study that students go with someone who knows how to witness. Your students will learn to witness by watching you share Christ.

   If you are new at giving away your faith, go with a youth minister or pastor several times before leading young people through this study. Then plan to take two students out witnessing each week, starting with the most experienced. The rest of the group should be paired up as they carry out witnessing assignments. Those with more witnessing experience should team up with students with less experience.

Lost!
Bible Study 1

OVERVIEW

Key Concept In order to witness effectively, you must realize that people are lost without Jesus Christ.

Memory Verse John 17:3

Goals *Individual Growth:* To begin to have more compassion for people who do not have Christ.
Group Life: To agree to support one another in the new adventure of learning to share Christ.

BEFORE THE MEETING

1. Pray for each person who came to the last meeting, asking God to give each one the willingness to commit himself or herself to the group and to sharing Christ.
2. In *Giving Away Your Faith,* do Bible study 1, writing your personal responses to each question. This week and every week, note in the margins other observations or personal experiences that relate to the lesson, and bring them up during your group meeting.
3. Memorize John 17:3.
4. Contact group members who attended the last session and other possible members. Remind them of the meeting time and place, and answer any questions. If someone has decided not to participate in this Discipleship Family, assure the person that you still care for him and that you hope he will be able to participate in a future group.
5. Make a list of the names, addresses, and phone numbers of all the group members (from the 3" x 5" cards filled out last week). Make enough copies for each group member to have one.
6. Begin to think of people you know who do not know Jesus, and ask God to give you

more compassion for them and their need for Christ.

7. Gather materials for the meeting:
      Bible
      Giving Away Your Faith
      Copies of group members' names, addresses, and phone numbers
      Bible memory packet
      A picture of a very well-dressed person (from a magazine ad or clothes catalog)

THE MEETING

BUILDING THE GROUP *(15 minutes)*

Greet each person warmly as he arrives, welcoming him as an important part of the group.

Confirm that by each person's presence, he or she is saying "Yes, I want to be part of this Discipleship Family." Have everyone turn to the *Personal Commitment* sheet (page 11 in *Giving Away Your Faith*). Read it together. Group members should have already signed the commitment sheet, but ask anyone who hasn't to sign now. (Be sure yours is signed!)

Ask volunteers who have been through previous Discipleship Families (*Following Jesus, Spending Time Alone with God,* and *Making Jesus Lord*) to recall how they felt at first about signing *Personal Commitment* sheets. Ask them to tell a little about how God helped them stay faithful to their Discipleship Family commitments, and how He picked them up when they did fall short. Add your own personal experience in keeping your commitment.

Assure your group members that you are always available to help them keep their commitments to this Discipleship Family. Have volunteers pray briefly for the Lord's help in maintaining the discipline and enthusiasm they will need, and for love and concern for each other and for non-Christians.

FOCUSING ON LIFE *(15 minutes)*

Show your students the picture of a very well-dressed person you have cut out of an ad. Give the person a name and summarize the following story:

> This is _____. Just from looking at him [or her] what needs would you say _____ has? Would you say that money is one of his biggest needs? It doesn't look

like it from the way he is dressed. But what if I were to tell you that I know _____ personally, and I happen to know that actually he is flat broke right now and he really does need money pretty badly. You see, _____ had a very good job—that's how he got those nice clothes. But he's just lost that job and has been looking for weeks for another, and can't find anything. Nobody who meets him on the street would know that, because his beautiful clothes are still left over from better days. But pretty soon they'll wear out, and if _____ doesn't find work, he won't be able to hide his true condition any longer.

Explain that this person's situation with money is something like many people's spiritual situation. They don't have Jesus Christ. Spiritually, they are empty. But their lives look pretty good, and we tend to think they don't have any needs. Like fashionable clothes, their good appearances are only temporary and will wear out with time or with stress. The needs are there; it's just that most people don't see them.

EXPLORING GOD'S WORD *(30 minutes)*

(NOTE: Each week this section is based on the work students have done in Giving Away Your Faith. The discussion questions are usually not identical to those in the study book, but they draw from the same Scriptures and assignments. This helps students think through what they have studied rather than simply reading aloud their written answers.)

Allow time for group members to review their written responses for Bible study 1 in *Giving Away Your Faith*. Let them ask questions and make observations. Then discuss:

1. **Do you think Romans 1:28-32 is a fair description of many people in our world today?** (At first glance the passage appears to be talking about the grossest kinds of sinners. Yet it also lists the "little" sins such as envy, senselessness, faithlessness, disobedience to parents, etc.) **How should we look at people who do these kinds of things?**

2. **Recall your description of a time you were lost.** (You did this last week, and this week's Bible Study also calls for it.) **How would it affect our outlook on the people Romans 1 describes, if we knew they felt like that because of their lostness?**

3. **When you think of your non-Christian friends, do you have trouble believing that they are actually in the condition described on page 17?** (characteristics of lost people) **Why is it hard to see some of our non-Christian friends that way?** (They may seem to have everything together—maybe even better than we do!) Remember the diagram is *God's* viewpoint rather than the human viewpoint; He sees where those people really are. Also, they may be like our friend _____ (the cutout from the ad)—looking just

fine on the outside, but with desperate needs that will soon catch up with them.

4. In your Bible study you read about Jesus' attitude toward people who are lost. What would be some examples of showing that kind of attitude toward unsaved friends? Ask group members to share some specific imaginary "scenes" revealing a compassionate attitude.

Invite students to share their responses to "Loving Lost People" (pages 18-21 in *Giving Away Your Faith*). What areas do your students most need to work on? Keep those in mind as you continue working through this Discipleship Family.

APPLYING GOD'S WORD (15 minutes)

Have students look over their answers to "Practical Hints On Loving Lost People" (pages 21-23 in *Giving Away Your Faith*). Ask them to choose one particular "hint" to work on especially this week. Let them know you are available to help them, and encourage them to help each other as they have the opportunity.

Have a time of prayer together. Ask the Lord to give you compassion for one particular lost friend, to see that person as Christ sees him or her and not as that person appears to the world, and to give you love for that person.

Assignments for Next Week As you give the following assignments, express confidence that your students can and will carry them out and will succeed in their commitments to this Discipleship Family.

1. Have a time alone with God every day this week using the Bible readings at the end of Bible study 1 and the helps under "How to Have a Time Alone with God" (page 251 of the *Time Alone with God Notebook Inserts* in this Leader's Guide).

2. Complete Bible study 2 in *Giving Away Your Faith*.

3. Review the memory verses you learned in *Following Jesus*, *Spending Time Alone with God* and *Making Jesus Lord*.

4. Get together with a non-Christian friend and follow the instructions given in the lesson.

AFTER THE MEETING

1. Evaluate the meeting: How was the atmosphere? Relaxed? Too relaxed? Comfortable? If anything about the atmosphere did not seem right, jot it down, try to think of some reason or it, and try to come up with some things you can do to improve it for next week.

2. If any group member expressed special

questions or problems, or was reluctant to sign the commitment sheet, meet with that person this week or call him.

3. Contact other possible group members and offer them a final chance to get involved.
4. Begin talking with students to schedule time to go out witnessing together.

From Fear to Faith
Bible Study 2

OVERVIEW

Key Concept　Natural fears about sharing Jesus Christ can be overcome through supernatural faith.

Memory Verses　Romans 3:23; 6:23

Goals　*Individual Growth:* To acknowledge and begin to overcome fears about witnessing.
Group Life: To accept each other's fearfulness and encourage each other toward faith.

BEFORE THE MEETING

1. Pray for each group member, asking God to give each person honesty and courage.
2. In *Giving Away Your Faith*, do Bible study 2.
3. Think about your own fears about sharing Christ. Your present or past anxieties about witnessing will give you sympathy for your students' fears.
4. Memorize Romans 3:23; 6:23.
5. Gather materials for the meeting:
   Bible
   Giving Away Your Faith
   Bible Memory packet

THE MEETING

BUILDING THE GROUP *(15 minutes)*

Warmly welcome each person. If you know of something specific that happened in someone's life this week (such as a sports event, an award, an illness in the family, a big test) mention it with appropriate congratulations, sympathy, concern, etc.

When everyone has arrived, ask for volunteers to share how the witness of particular people helped bring them to Christ or helped them strengthen their faith through difficult times. Be ready to share your own experience.

FOCUSING ON LIFE *(10 minutes)*

Discuss: **What are some typical childhood fears that you or others have had?** (Let students respond.) **What were some reasons for fearing these things?** (Because they were unknown or unpredictable; because of a bad past experience, etc.) **How did you get over a childhood fear?** (Learned more about it; someone else helped by setting an example; used will power to do it; etc.) Share an old fear of your own as you participate in the discussion. This discussion helps get students talking about their personal fears, but in a nonthreatening way, since they are bringing up past fears which may seem amusing now. For example, a little kid's fear that he might go down the drain when the water was let out of the bathtub!

EXPLORING GOD'S WORD *(30 minutes)*

Have each student review Bible study 2 in *Giving Away Your Faith*. Ask for questions or observations about the study. Then discuss:

1. What might your old fears, those fears you've outgrown that we just talked about, have in common with the fear of sharing Christ with your friends? (The fear may be based on imagination or an inflated idea of how bad the outcome will be.)

2. Why are we ashamed to admit our fears? (Want to appear strong and capable; don't want to admit weakness; scared we'll be laughed at; others depend on us and we don't want to let them down.)

3. What's good about admitting fear? (Gets it out in the open; gives other people the opportunity to help us; shows other people we're as human as they are; makes us more objective and rational about it; assures us we're normal; helps us depend on the Lord.)

4. What are your biggest fears about sharing Christ with your friends? (Lead the way in admitting and talking about your fears of witnessing. As you share your own fears, you will help your students know that you understand and encourage them to voice their fears.)

(NOTE: There *are* individuals who have absolutely no fear of witnessing and do it all the time with no qualms as a natural part of their lives. If you have someone like that in your group, you have several dynamics to deal with. The bold witness may be impatient with those who are more reluctant to share Christ; he can't understand what's so frightening. And the more hesitant group members may feel inferior or less spiritual than the bolder witness. Yet more timid Christians can be spurred on by the bolder witness enthusiasm. It is important for all group members to respect one another's personalities and gifts and to help one another.)

Discuss: **What do you have in common with the disciples in John 20:19-22? Which of the seven reasons for fear** (pages 30-34 in *Giving Away Your Faith*) **have you experienced? Which ones are you experiencing now?** (Encourage students to share openly.)

Ask: **What difference does it make to know that the resurrected Christ is with us?** (We can depend on Him for strength and guidance; we know He won't leave us.) **What practical steps can we take to help remind ourselves of each of the five facts about Jesus on pages 31-34 of** *Giving Away Your Faith?* (Take time to consider concrete ways to be aware of Jesus' presence, peace, plan, penetration, and position.)

APPLYING GOD'S WORD *(10 minutes)*

Have students turn to the prayer concerning fear (page 40 of *Giving Away Your Faith*). If any students have not filled in the blank ("that my fear stems from . . . ") give them opportunity to fill it in now.

Discuss particular fears about witnessing that students would like to pray about. Have a time of prayer about those fears. Then pray (either silently or together out loud) the prayer to overcome fear on page 40 (the individual student fill-in can be read silently by each person).

Have students pray for each other. Have them commit themselves to praying for one other person in the study during the next week.

Assignments for Next Week As you give the following assignments, continue to express confidence in your students. Point out that they are to review verses learned in the previous Discipleship Family (*Making Jesus Lord*) and that those verses will help them in their witnessing.

1. Complete Bible Study 3 in *Giving Away Your Faith.*

2. Continue having your daily time alone with God using the suggested Bible readings.

3. Memorize Hebrews 9:27.

4. Review memory verses from *Following Jesus.*

AFTER THE MEETING

1. Evaluate the meeting: Were students open about voicing their fears about witnessing? Were you honest with them about your own fears?

2. If any student seems to be withdrawing as the issue of witnessing gets more pressing—and threatening—phone or spend some time with that person this week and express your confidence that he or she *will* make it.

3. If anyone is having problems keeping up a daily time alone with God, you could offer to phone the person in the middle of the week to ask how he is doing in his daily quiet times. Or meet with him to have a quiet time together.

Extraordinary Power
Bible Study 3

OVERVIEW

Key Concept	The Holy Spirit makes us powerful witnesses for Christ.
Memory Verse	Hebrews 9:27
Goals	*Individual Growth:* To be continually filled with the Holy Spirit as you witness. *Group Life:* To anticipate seeing the Holy Spirit use your group to bring people to Christ.

BEFORE THE MEETING

1. Pray for a new filling of the Spirit in your own life.
2. Pray for each group member to receive the Holy Spirit's power daily.
3. In *Giving Away Your Faith*, complete Bible study 3.
4. Memorize Hebrews 9:27.
5. Gather materials for the meeting:
   > Bible
   > *Giving Away Your Faith*
   > An electrical appliance such as a hair dryer
   > Bible memory packet

THE MEETING

BUILDING THE GROUP *(10 minutes)*

After you have greeted the arriving group members, ask if anyone has noticed any improvement or other change in the area of fear about witnessing. Ask for volunteers to talk about any particular witnessing experiences they had this week. For some it will be a victory simply to have *thought about the possibility* of approaching someone about Christ! Be positive about your group members' honesty and encourage them to keep on with their witnessing.

FOCUSING ON LIFE *(10 minutes)*

Demonstrate your electrical appliance. Disconnect your appliance and then ask group members why it won't work anymore. (It's cut off from its only source of power. Without the power that it's designed to be run by, it is useless. It does nobody any good. It does not accomplish what it was made to accomplish.)

Point out that the Holy Spirit is our source of power for witnessing (as well as for all other aspects of the Christian life). Cut off from Him, we can do nothing. With His power, we can be strong and effective witnesses.

EXPLORING GOD'S WORD *(35 minutes)*

Have each student review Bible study 3 and ask questions or make comments. Then discuss:

1. What might be some characteristics of a person who tries to witness for Christ without relying on the power of the Holy Spirit? (Argumentativeness, defensiveness, fear to the point of being silenced, attacking the person verbally, lack of love, resentment if the message doesn't get a response.)

2. What difference will it make if we do rely on the Holy Spirit when we witness? (Our attitude and approach will be more Christlike; we'll witness with love, respect for the other person, good will, and faith that God will take care of the results.)

3. In which of the four areas of influence ("Jerusalem," "Judea," "Samaria," and the "ends of the earth," page 46 in *Giving Away Your Faith*) **do you find it easiest to witness? Why?** (Let students respond.) **In which area do you find it most difficult to witness, and why?** (Encourage group members to reveal their feelings as well as their observations.)

Ask students to describe the scene in Acts 2:1-4 when the disciples were filled with the Holy Spirit. Talk about any times that you or your students have been particularly aware of the Holy Spirit's presence and help. Point out also that He is often actively helping us even when we don't "feel" Him. We may not be aware of His help until afterward.

Discuss the five signs of a witness in the Holy Spirit (pages 52-54 of *Giving Away Your Faith*) and ask group members to share recent examples of each that they have seen or experienced.

Ask: **What results of your witness would you like to see? Which results can you expect immediately? Which ones might take longer? Which ones might you never see (although they will happen)?** (Let students respond.) **What's the connection between relying on the**

Holy Spirit and getting results from our witness? (Without the Spirit, we have no hope of lasting results from our witness. Because we can rely on Him, we can count on results even if they don't appear immediately or don't measure up to our scale of what is supposed to happen.)

APPLYING GOD'S WORD *(10 minutes)*

Let students share questions they have about being filled with the Holy Spirit. Have a time of prayer for each student to be filled with the Spirit continually as he or she witnesses for Christ. The Holy Spirit has been offered as a gift; we need only to receive Him (Acts 19:1-7). Explain this to your group.

Assignments for Next Week Notice that under "Making It Happen" your students are instructed to pray for and talk to a friend who doesn't know Christ. Give your students plenty of encouragement in this assignment, because now your witnessing is getting down to hard reality. Invite students to phone you after their conversations and talk about how things went. Better yet, make time each day to take students out witnessing. You go first, then the student. Also give the following assignments:

1. **Complete the Bible study 4 in** *Giving Away Your Faith.*

2. **Continue using the suggested Bible readings for your daily time alone with God.**

3. **Be sure to memorize Romans 5:8.**

AFTER THE MEETING —————————————————

1. Evaluate the meeting: Did students grasp the importance of being filled with the Spirit? Is it still vague to them? How did they react to the assignment to talk with a non-Christian friend?

2. If this first real witnessing assignment seems about to scare somebody off ("I didn't know what I was getting into!") talk with that person privately and do everything possible to help him carry out the assignment—such as going with him to witness.

A Friend in Need
Bible Study 4

OVERVIEW

Key Concept We can make friends.

Memory Verse Romans 5:8

Goals *Individual Growth:* To begin making new friends and renewing old friendships.
Group Life: To look outside the confines of the group to see other people's needs.

BEFORE THE MEETING

1. Pray for yourself and each group member to seek out new friends. Ask God to reveal people He wants each person to befriend.
2. Think of someone to whom you can extend friendship as a witness for Christ.
3. Complete Bible study 4 in *Giving Away Your Faith.*
4. Memorize Romans 5:8.
5. Gather materials for the meeting:
   Bible
   Giving Away Your Faith
   Plastic fencing (from a toy barnyard set) or some similar material to make a miniature enclosure
   Bible memory packet

THE MEETING

BUILDING THE GROUP *(15 minutes)*

After everyone has arrived (greeted warmly by you, of course) ask for volunteers to share their experiences of talking with someone about Christ (part of this past week's assignments). Discuss how the non-Christian friends were approached, how your group members felt as they began conversations, how fears were overcome, and particular responses the friends made (both positive and negative). Rejoice over good responses and offer support to members who found that their friends only tuned them out. You will not have time now to discuss problematic questions brought up by the non-Christian friends in the course of witnessing, but offer to research and talk them over later.

FOCUSING ON LIFE *(10 minutes)*

Build your miniature "pen" and say something like: **Imagine this is a sheepfold, such as Jesus talked about in John chapter 10. Jesus said that He is the Good Shepherd and that we belong in His sheepfold because we belong to Him. But what would life be like for the sheep if they spent their entire lives inside the confines of that little sheepfold?** (Discuss how crowded, dirty, unhealthy, and boring that would be.) Summarize: **Jesus said He would lead us out so we can find pasture. Although it's safe inside the sheepfold, there are many rich blessings outside it, so long as we stay under our shepherd's care and don't run away from Him. Making friends is one of those blessings that can only happen outside the confines of our own group.**

EXPLORING GOD'S WORD *(30 minutes)*

Let each student review Bible study 4 and make comments or ask questions.

Point out that many other things could be considered the main ingredients of friendship (having common interests, sharing similar goals, having similar life experiences); however, a friendship that has no compassion is not a true friendship and will not last when things get tough.

Discuss: **Describe a time when a person showed compassion to you.** (Let volunteers respond.) **How did you react? How did you feel about the person who was compassionate?** (Response.)

Summarize: **As we read the definition of Christian love in 1 Corinthians 13, its easy to see how far we fall short of that kind of love. Read through the chapter again, substituting the word "Jesus" for "love." Reading 1 Corinthians 13 in this way brings home the fact that only Christ can love in such an ideal way. Yet because He is in us by His Spirit (as you studied in last week's meeting) we can show His kind of love, however imperfectly.**

Ask group members to describe how friends have been comforters, counselors, and challengers to them. Discuss how each person can be a comforter, a counselor, and a challenger to a non-Christian friend.

As a group read Philippians 2:3-4. Ask: how can you show the attitude of Christ in your friendships with non-Christians? (Let students respond.)

(NOTE: As the leader, you should be aware that the area of friendships raises several issues—both the area of friendships in general and the area of friendships with non-Christians.

• Some young people make friends very easily and naturally and have already built many bridges with non-Christians based on shared interests and activities. Those teens' naturally winning ways must be supplemented with sincere concern for the spiritual welfare of their non-Christian friends. Otherwise they are merely popular and likable but may not be changing friends' lives. They may even have their Christian and non-Christian relationships segregated so that they live in two different worlds and don't carry over their Christian lives into their non-Christian friendships.

• On the other hand, there are teens for whom friendship is an area of hurt and deprivation. You may have students who make friends very slowly and hesitantly. It may be that their only friends are others in the Discipleship Family. Encourage group members to be loving and supportive of each other, helping each person have the courage to make new friends outside the group.

• Be sensitive to any parental misgivings about non-Christian friends. Many Christian parents do not want their young people to develop close relationships with non-Christians for fear of wrong influences. Certainly a Christian should be wary of developing a close relationship with the opposite sex, outside of Christ, in the hope of winning that person. Talk with any parents who raise objections and explain your witnessing efforts. They may be reassured by the fact that each of your students has the strong support of you and the entire Discipleship Family. But ultimately the wishes of parents must be respected.)

APPLYING GOD'S WORD *(15 minutes)*

Begin to befriend non-Christians by spending time in prayer for particular people your group members know, or have the potential to know better, and would sincerely like to see know Jesus. Be sure members understand that this is not a gossip time, and names of people prayed for are not to get outside this group. While some non-Christians would appreciate being prayed for, others are offended to find out people are praying for them (as though there's something wrong with them). You can use the guidelines under "Making It Personal" (pages 72-73 in *Giving Away Your Faith*).

Assignments for Next Week As you make the following assignments, again express confidence in your students. Give them praise for making it this far in the Discipleship Family, and let them know you know they'll successfully complete it.
1. **Complete Bible study 5 in** *Giving Away Your Faith*.
2. **Continue the daily Bible readings.**
3. **Be sure to memorize 1 Corinthians 15:3-4.**

4. Review all memory verses from *Following Jesus, Spending Time Alone with God,* **and** *Making Jesus Lord.*

AFTER THE MEETING ————————————————

1. Evaluate the meeting: Do students seem eager to reach out to non-Christian friends? Are they reluctant? Dubious? Scared but willing to try?
2. Does your own life reflect your willingness to make friends?

Relate and Communicate
Bible Study 5

OVERVIEW

Key Concept   There are guidelines which can help us turn a conversation toward the subject of Jesus Christ.

Memory Verses   1 Corinthians 15:3-4

Goals   *Individual Growth:* To learn how to make a conversation turn toward Jesus Christ.
Group Life: To practice conversing about Christ.

BEFORE THE MEETING

1. Pray for each of your students, for the friends to whom they want to witness, and for yourself.
2. Recall conversations you have had about Jesus Christ—either someone else's witness to you, or your witness to someone else. Think of crucial points in the conversations and what made them crucial.
3. In *Giving Away Your Faith*, complete Bible study 5.
4. Memorize 1 Corinthians 15:3-4.
5. Gather materials for the meeting:
   Bible
   Giving Away Your Faith
   Pencils and paper
   Bible memory packet

THE MEETING

BUILDING THE GROUP (10 minutes)

If you made a new non-Christian friend this week, share the experience. Ask group members to describe their own experiences. The Holy Spirit may have opened some students' eyes to potential friends for Christ—people they had previously overlooked. Offer encouragement if students are hanging back or unsure how to build friendship bridges. Say: **Tonight we're going to consider and practice some practical, down-to-earth ways of bringing Jesus Christ into a conversation.**

FOCUSING ON LIFE *(10 minutes)*

Ask: **"What was one conversation you had today that wasn't about Jesus Christ? How did you get into the conversation? How did you keep it going? How did the conversation end? Do you think you'll talk with that person about that subject again?** (As students respond to each question, discuss how their answers might apply to a conversation about Christ.)

EXPLORING GOD'S WORD *(20 minutes)*

Have students look over their responses to Bible study 5. Give them the opportunity to ask questions or make comments. Then discuss:

    1. **How did the woman at the well become aware that Jesus cared about her?** (Jesus overcame cultural barriers to speak with her even though she was a Samaritan.)

    2. **What attitudes did He display toward her?** (He was compassionate and loving, as well as concerned about her.)

    3. **What risks did He take in talking with her?** (He might have been condemned for associating with a person considered "beneath" Him.)

    4. **What points in the conversation were crucial (when He could have lost her) and how did He handle them?** (Crucial points came up in John 4:9, 11, 17, 20, and 25 as Jesus fielded her questions and challenges.)

    5. **How did the woman try to distract Jesus from the real issue?** (She asked questions that pointed out their differences and commented on side issues to change the subject.)

    6. How did Jesus get back to the real issue? (He kept returning to her need to know Him.)

    (NOTE: Point out to students that John probably did not give us the entire conversation verbatim; what is written in John 4 may be the high points of a much longer talk.)

    Distribute pencils and paper. Ask each group member to think of a friend that he or she has been particularly praying for and talking with—someone they sincerely want to see know Jesus. Say: **Imagine yourself with your non-Christian friend at a time and place that you usually have an opportunity to talk. Write down all the questions and statements you can think of that could open a conversation for Christ, or turn a conversation that way.** After students have had time to brainstorm their conversation-starters, ask for volunteers to share what they have written.

APPLYING GOD'S WORD (20 minutes)

Divide group members into pairs. (If there is an odd number of students, pair one with yourself.) Have them practice an imaginary conversation about Christ—one person will be the "Christian" and the other the "non-Christian." They should use principles discovered in Bible study 5 and in this session's discussion. (To start this off, you may want to demonstrate a conversation with a voluneer.) It may help if the "non-Christian" plays the role of a particular person to whom the Christian actually desires to witness. Move around the room and tune in to the different conversations as unobtrusively as possible. When time is almost half gone, have the two people switch roles.

After you call time, ask whether anyone has questions or comments about his or her "imaginary" witnessing session. For some, playing the role may have been more nerve-wracking than actually witnessing to a non-Christian! Discuss questions that came up and ask members if they felt they were too "theological" in their answers.

Remind group members that this week begins the weekly assignment to share the Gospel with a non-Christian. Pray briefly for the people to whom group members want to witness, and for wisdom to know what to say and how to say it.

Assignments for Next Week Give the following assignments:
1. **Complete Bible study 6 in** Giving Away Your Faith.
2. **Memorize 1 Peter 3:18.**
3. **Continue to spend time alone with God daily.**
4. **Memorize the four "Bridge Builders" questions and use them to carry on a conversation with a non-Christian friend.**

AFTER THE MEETING ————————————————

1. Evaluate the meeting: Was the role play helpful? Are students coming up with practical and realistic ways to turn a conversation to the subject of Jesus Christ, or is their approach too theoretical, abstract, or phony?
2. Are you meeting your goals of taking students out witnessing?

My Great Discovery
Bible Study 6

OVERVIEW

Key Concept — A thorough preparation helps us present our testimony.

Memory Verse — 1 Peter 3:18.

Goals — *Individual Growth:* To write out a testimony and present it to the group.
Group Life: To hear and give helpful comments about each other's testimonies.

BEFORE THE MEETING

1. Pray for each member of your group. At this halfway point in the Discipleship Family, ask God to encourage each one and give each one renewed enthusiasm.
2. Complete Bible study 6 in *Giving Away Your Faith.*
3. Write out your own testimony according to the guidelines in Bible study 6.
4. Memorize 1 Peter 3:18.
5. Gather materials for the meeting:
   Bible
   Giving Away Your Faith
   Pencils and paper
   Bible memory packet

THE MEETING

BUILDING THE GROUP [10 minutes]

Here is a good opportunity for you to give your Discipleship Family several minutes' worth of appreciation, affirmation, and a pep talk. Remind them that they are now halfway through this Discipleship Family. Let them know you're proud of them for sticking with it—not just enduring it, but actively participating and keeping their commitments to the Lord and to each other. Assure them that you know how tough the challenge of witnessing can be. Once again remind them that you are always available to help answer questions, offer an encouraging word, or go with them. (By this time you should have gone witnessing with each student at least once.) And mention that you pray regularly for each person in the group. Knowing that you care can help faltering group members keep going, and strengthen the resolve of all the group members.

FOCUSING ON LIFE *(10 minutes)*

Have group members pair off and tell each other about something good that happened to them this week. (You can pair up with someone if you have an odd number of students.) After students have shared with each other, get their attention again and say something like: **Wasn't that easy? It isn't hard to talk naturally about something good that we've experienced. Believe it or not, talking about Christ can come just that easily and naturally when we're sure we have experienced Him. However, for reasons we've talked about in our earlier meetings, we sometimes get nervous when the conversation turns to a witness for Christ. That's why it's helpful to have a plan for what we're going to say.** Emphasize that you're not talking about a pre-recorded announcement or a memorized speech, but an intelligent preparation for making a good case for Jesus Christ.

(NOTE: Some Christians think it is unspiritual to have a set plan, either written out or in our heads, for what we are going to say when we witness. They believe—and rightly so—that the Holy Spirit will lead us as we speak. Although Jesus told us not to worry about what we are to say (Matthew 10:19), He did not tell us not to *think* about it. We can best speak for the Lord when we are prepared. When we are unprepared, we might ramble or include irrelevant experiences which could confuse the listener or detract from the main point.

EXPLORING GOD'S WORD *(20 minutes)*

Give students the opportunity to look over their responses to Bible study 6, make comments, and ask questions.

Read Paul's testimony before King Agrippa in Acts 26:1-23. Discuss: **How would you describe Paul's attitude and approach as he gave his testimony?** (Note Paul's respect for his listener; his confidence in his experience with Christ; his brief but honest description of his former non-Christian life; his convincing detailing of his personal encounter with Jesus; and his care in giving God the credit.) You may also want to read verses 24-29 and note the confidence and presence of mind with which Paul rose above Festus' insults and Agrippa's resistance, with calmness and humor.

Hand out pencils and paper and give students the assignment of writing out their testimonies according to the guidelines on pages 90-95 of *Giving Away Your Faith*. Use the three-point outline given, and consider the questions listed. (Be available to answer students' questions and provide help. Your own testimony should be already written out.)

APPLYING GOD'S WORD *(20 minutes)*

Ask for volunteers to present their testimonies to the rest of the group. Present your own testimony after several students have read theirs.

Invite the group to give *helpful* and *positive* criticisms of one another's testimonies following the guidelines in the book. If something in a person's testimony doesn't communicate and doesn't make sense, it's better for him to be told by his supportive Discipleship Family than by the non-Christian he's trying to convince! Yet there are kind and unkind ways to tell a person he's not communicating. Be positive.

The purpose of writing and criticizing the testimonies is to help students continue to polish their testimonies and give them an increasing sense of being well prepared to talk about Christ. Ask them to continue rewriting their testimonies, and assure them you are available to read or listen to their revised efforts.

Assignments for Next Week   Instruct students to continue working on their written testimonies. Give the following assignments:

1. **Complete Bible study 7 in** *Giving Away Your Faith.*
2. **Memorize Mark 1:15 and continue the daily Bible reading in Acts.**
3. **Write, condense, and memorize your testimony.**

AFTER THE MEETING ─────────────────

1. Evaluate the meeting: Did students' testimonies sound natural and convincing?
2. Is there someone who needs special encouragement with his testimony? Make a point of calling or visiting that person this week.

The Message
Bible Study 7

OVERVIEW

Key Concept   We can present the message of Christ clearly.

Memory Verse   Mark 1:15

Goals   *Individual Growth:* To begin to become comfortable with using *The Facts of Life* material in witnessing.
Group Life: To help each other use *The Facts of Life* material to present Jesus Christ.

BEFORE THE MEETING

1. Pray for your group members. Ask God to give them freedom and confidence in their use of a thoughtfully planned written explanation of the Gospel.
2. Pray for yourself, that you will continue to be a good example of a Christian who is enthusiastic about sharing Christ.
3. Complete Bible study 7 in *Giving Away Your Faith,* including becoming familiar with the "Facts of Life."
4. Memorize Mark 1:15.
5. Gather materials for the meeting:
   Bible
   Giving Away Your Faith
   Sets of instructions (such as a recipe, a diagram for assembling a model airplane, rules of a game, etc.)
   Bible memory packet

THE MEETING

BUILDING THE GROUP *(10 minutes)*

As group members arrive, greet each one warmly to let him know that this Discipleship Family is more than a habit or obligation, it's an important time of fellowship.

Pair group members to read their revised written testimonies to each other. Have them share helpful comments.

Say: **We're doing a good job with learning how to present a clear, brief, and convincing testimony about what Christ has done for us. But when our friends ask heavier questions about what it all means, who Christ really is, or how the Christian life works, we need to do more than refer to our personal experiences.** Emphasize the need for solid facts about God and about salvation. Explain that our faith is more than a personal experience inside us; it's the truth.

FOCUSING ON LIFE *(5 minutes)*

Show your students the various instructions you have brought to the meeting. Ask: **Why do we need written instructions for how to do things?** (So we're not left guessing; so we don't waste time making mistakes; so the results will be what they're supposed to be; because the writer of the instructions has better understanding than we do.) Ask for some other examples of things for which students have used written instructions.

Say: **We appreciate and use a good, clear set of instructions for just about anything. Presenting Christ to someone is no different. We can use a clearly written explanation of the facts to help explain the Gospel to our friends. There's a good example of one in** The Facts of Life.

EXPLORING GOD'S WORD *(30 minutes)*

Discuss students' responses to the Bible study questions as you go through *The Facts of Life* material together. Touch on each of the "Facts" even if you do not have time to answer every study question. As you go through the material together, ask students to bring up any questions they think their non-Christian friends might have about any of the points in the booklet. Try to find answers to the questions based on your Bible studies so far. Ask for volunteers to research particularly difficult questions with your help.

APPLYING GOD'S WORD *(20 minutes)*

Have students pair off (as usual, you will be with one student if you have an odd number). One member of each pair will be the Christian using *The Facts of Life* material; the other person will play the role of a non-Christian friend who has expressed interest in knowing about Christ. Have students practice presenting *The Facts of Life* material to one another.

Discuss any snags students ran into during their role playing.

Assignments for Next Week   Give the following assignments:
1. **Complete Bible study 8 in** *Giving Away Your Faith.*
2. **Memorize John 1:12 and continue daily Bible readings in Acts.**
3. **Review your memory verses.**

AFTER THE MEETING

1. Evaluate the meeting: Were students becoming comfortable with using *The Facts of Life* material? Do any students have particular problems using it?
2. As you make increased use of practiced testimonies and witnessing material, is your group's attitude and approach toward witnessing staying fresh and spontaneous, or are you falling in a rut of reciting learned material? As the leader, you can continue to set the example of a person who is enthusiastic and natural about sharing Christ, even as you use preplanned material.
3. Are you going out with students to share their faith each week?

Drawing the Net
Bible Study 8

OVERVIEW

Key Concept
After explaining the Gospel to our non-Christian friends, we should bring them to the point of making a definite decision about Christ.

Memory Verse
John 1:12

Goals
Individual Growth: To develop confidence about bringing someone to a point of decision about Christ.
Group Life: To express confidence in each other's ability to lead someone to Christ.

BEFORE THE MEETING

1. Pray for each person in your Discipleship Family and for their non-Christian friends.
2. Based on your most recent experience of "drawing the net" (leading someone to accept Christ) think about how you reached that point of the conversation, how you led the person to a decision, and how the person responded.
3. Complete Bible study 8 in *Giving Away Your Faith*.
4. Memorize John 1:12.
5. Gather materials for the meeting:
   Bible
   Giving Away Your Faith
   Bible Memory packet

THE MEETING

BUILDING THE GROUP (10 minutes)

After everyone has arrived, ask who they witnessed to this week. Find out what happened, what the response was, and what questions were brought up. If a non-Christian friend has accepted Christ, have a time of prayer of thanksgiving, asking God to strengthen and teach that new Christian.

FOCUSING ON LIFE *(10 minutes)*

Ask: **What's something you have learned to do in the past year? How did you learn about it? Who taught you?** (Discuss answers.) **Could you have learned without someone or something to teach you?** Discuss how good teachers or good instructions help people learn.

Point out that people want to find forgiveness and satisfaction in Christ, but many don't know how. They need someone to help them. Even after they know all the facts about Jesus, they need to make a personal decision to accept Him. Emphasize that if we simply give people the facts and don't give them the opportunity to accept Christ, we've left them hanging without knowing what to do. We need to learn to draw in the net and bring that person to Christ.

EXPLORING GOD'S WORD *(30 minutes)*

Have a volunteer read Acts 8:26-40. This is an excellent biblical example of a faithful witness explaining the Gospel clearly and then effectively drawing the net to bring in a new disciple.

Ask: **Why might Philip have been surprised that the Holy Spirit led him toward Gaza?** (He may not have expected to find any potential converts to Christ there. The road was a desert road.) **What are some unexpected ways that we, or people we know, have come to Christ?** (Discuss answers.) **What does that tell us about what should be included in our witness?** (We should share Christ with everyone.)

How did Philip know the Ethiopian might be interested in Jesus? (He was reading the Scriptures.) **What are some signals our friends send us that indicate they might be interested in Jesus?** (They might ask questions or be reading about spiritual matters.)

The Ethiopian showed unusual willingness to be led and instructed. Discuss what we should do when a person shows some interest in Christ yet also puts up some resistance or apathy. (Listen patiently; pray; keep a loving attitude; etc.)

What sidetracks might Philip have gotten onto in his discussion with the Ethiopian? What did Philip keep as the center of the conversation? (The passage of Scripture and Jesus Christ.)

(NOTE: Verse 37, Philip's "net-drawing" statement, does not appear in all ancient biblical manuscripts and so is relegated to a footnote in modern translations. However, believing in Jesus as the Son of God is crucial in biblical accounts of conversion, such as in

Peter's first sermons in Acts 2—4, Paul's conversion in Acts 9:20, and Romans 10:9. We can be sure that Philip would never have baptized the Ethiopian unless he were sure that the man truly believed in Jesus.)

Ask: **Did anyone act as a "Philip" for you to help lead you to Christ? How did it happen? Would you like to be a "Philip" for someone else who needs Christ?** Point out that any Christian can have that privilege if he or she is willing to draw the net and bring a non-Christian friend to a point of decision.

APPLYING GOD'S WORD (10 minutes)

Spend this time praying for our non-Christian friends and for yourselves. Ask God to give you the wisdom, courage, determination, and sense of timing to bring your friends to a point of deciding about Jesus. Pray for each person to whom your group wants to witness. Pray that their minds and spirits will be open the next time they are approached about Christ. Ask God for sensitivity to friends' moods and feelings and readiness to be serious about Christ.

Assignments for Next Week   Assure your students of your prayers and support before you make the following assignments:
1. **Complete Bible study 9 in** *Giving Away Your Faith.*
2. **Memorize Revelation 3:20 and continue daily readings in Acts.**
3. **Review session 8 and memorize the key questions to ask a non-Christian friend. Be prepared to answer any objections he might present.**

AFTER THE MEETING

1. Evaluate the meeting: Do students have confidence that they can draw the net and help someone actually accept Christ, or are they dubious and nervous?
2. Are you keeping up with your own time alone with God and regular prayer for yourself and your students?
3. Are you going witnessing with students each week?

Hard Questions
Bible Study 9

OVERVIEW

Key Concept Difficult questions about the Christian faith do not have to intimidate us, because there are answers.

Memory Verse Revelation 3:20

Goals *Individual Growth:* To have confidence that tough questions about Christianity can be answered.
Group Life: To assist each other in handling tough questions by sharing answers.

BEFORE THE MEETING

1. Pray for God's insight into difficult questions of the Christian faith and for His insight into the hearts of people who ask them.
2. Complete Bible study 9 in *Giving Away Your Faith*.
3. If one of the questions in the Bible study (or another question) particularly bothered you before you were a Christian, consider how God either answered it or made it become less important to you.
4. Memorize Revelation 3:20.
5. Gather materials for the meeting:
     Bible
     Giving Away Your Faith
     Bible Memory packet

THE MEETING

BUILDING THE GROUP *(10 minutes)*

Since this is your next-to-last meeting as a Discipleship Family, express your appreciation for group members and for their faithfulness and growth. Tell them that next week's meeting will begin with a special time of praise to God for what He has taught you during these weeks. Invite group members to talk about what this Discipleship Family is doing for them, and express your own appreciation for your personal growth.

FOCUSING ON LIFE *(10 minutes)*

Pick out a student who is particularly accomplished at a musical instrument, a sport, or some other acquired skill. Ask the student to describe some of the biggest challenges in becoming skillful at what he or she does. Ask: **When you came up against a "wall"—some technique that seemed too difficult, some level of accomplishment you didn't think you could reach—what did you do?** (The student had to keep working at finding a solution, or else give up. The student's level of accomplishment proves that he or she did not give up, but persevered, seeing the difficulty as a challenge rather than as an obstacle. Of course, there was probably a persistently encouraging coach, teacher, or parent in the background too.)

Summarize: **Sometimes our non-Christian friends will raise very difficult questions about Christianity. We can fold up in the face of those questions, or we can take them on as challenges and find satisfactory answers. We never need to be afraid of investigating the truth of Christianity. Jesus said that He is the truth (John 14:6) and therefore no truth that we find out can ever contradict Him.**

EXPLORING GOD'S WORD *(25 minutes)*

Discuss your students' responses to the Bible study of Acts 17 (page 132 of *Giving Away Your Faith*). Point out how Paul "reasoned with them from the Scriptures" (v. 2) and how he concentrated on the historical person of Jesus Christ (v. 3). Paul kept his purpose clear and founded his arguments firmly on the Word. Notice also that even Paul did not convince everyone, for only "some of the Jews were persuaded" (v. 4).

Ask: **What is the difference between "Epicurean" and "Stoic" philosophers?** (v. 18) (They were from two opposite schools of thought. The Epicureans believed in eating, drinking, and being merry, enjoying life's pleasures to the fullest. The Stoics had a more stark and simplified view of life.) Point out that while we may have friends of both types, both will be attracted to Christ when He is presented convincingly and with love.

Explain that Paul took advantage of the Athenians' natural curiosity about new ideas (vv. 20-21) to introduce the Good News of Jesus. He gave them credit for what they were doing right (worshiping, v. 23, although they did not know the true God).

Ask: **What were the three different responses to Paul's message in verses 32-34?** (Some people sneered; some were interested; some became believers.) Explain that group members will see all three responses as they continue to witness faithfully. It should be a comfort to know that even Paul encountered all three responses to his preaching.

Ask which of the "Tough Questions" dealt with in this Bible study (pages 135-145) have come up in your students' witnessing. How did group members answer them? Which questions do students fear most? For which questions was this Bible study particularly helpful? Ask students to think of other questions which they have, or which non-Christians have brought up.

Try to narrow down the "Tough Questions" to one or two which concern your group members the most.

APPLYING GOD'S WORD *(20 minutes)*

Take the particularly tough question or questions which you and your group have selected, and spend this time talking it over, using Bible study 9, your own study, and your own experience to arrive at useful answers. Urge all group members to participate even if they think their comments are not very profound. Remind them that we can never tell what approach or words will strike the ears and hearts of our non-Christian friends and sound a convincing note.

Have students pair off to discuss the rest of the tough questions in Bible study 9.

Even as you discuss how to answer the objections of non-Christians it is important to remember that some people ask tough questions because they sincerely want answers; others ask tough questions as a distraction. But in either case, when every question has been laid to rest, the person still must make a personal decision about what he or she will do with Jesus Christ.

Pray together for wisdom to understand God's truth and to understand the hearts of your unsaved friends.

Assignments for Next Week As you give students their final assignments in this Discipleship Family, be positive about their progress, and let them know you look forward to a very special meeting next week.

1. **Complete Bible study 10 in** *Giving Away Your Faith.*

2. **Memorize 2 Corinthians 5:17, and continue daily reading in Acts.**

3. **Share your testimony and** *The Facts of Life* **with a friend this week.**

AFTER THE MEETING ————————————————————

1. Evaluate the meeting: Did students grasp

the fact that tough questions don't have to intimidate them, but instead can be challenges they can meet?

2. Are any students discouraged because they haven't led anyone to Christ during these weeks and seem to have "failed" this course on witnessing? Assure them that if they have been faithful witnesses, God considers them a success—and so do you!

3. Have you fulfilled your goal of taking students out to witness?

Getting Started

Bible Study 10

OVERVIEW

Key Concept   New Christians need tender loving care.

Memory Verse   2 Corinthians 5:17

Goals   *Individual Growth:* To commit myself to helping a new Christian grow.
Group Life: To praise God together for what He has done for you in this Discipleship Family.

BEFORE THE MEETING

1. Pray for each group member. Thank God for giving you the opportunity to know each one.
2. Complete Bible study 10 in *Giving Away Your Faith.*
3. Memorize 2 Corinthians 5:17.
4. Write out the good things that have happened in your life and your students' lives as a result of this Discipleship Family. Write out constructive criticisms also. These lists will help you or the next Discipleship Family leader.
5. Familiarize yourself with *Getting Started,* the follow-up booklet.
6. Gather materials for the meeting:
   Bible
   Giving Away Your Faith
   Getting Started or another
      follow-up book
   Set of baby clothes
   Bible Memory packet

THE MEETING

BUILDING THE GROUP *(15 minutes)*

Welcome each group member warmly. Try to say some specific words of appreciation for each person.

As you promised last week, this meeting will begin with a time of praise to the Lord for what He has done for you during this Discipleship Family. Ask students to share particular Scriptures that have been meaningful to them during these weeks. Pray together, thanking God for giving you concern for witnessing to unsaved friends and for equipping you to share Christ with them in confidence as you witness.

Express to the group several special things this study has meant to you. Recall particularly good experiences, and invite members to do the same.

FOCUSING ON LIFE *(5 minutes)*

Although you've been enjoying a time of reflecting and rejoicing over this Discipleship Family, your work is not entirely over!

Show students the set of baby clothes and ask them if they can remember ever wearing clothes of such a tiny size. Of course, none of us can remember that far back, yet we were all babies who needed constant care and attention. Point out that "baby" Christians are like that. Years down the road they will be able to stand on their own, but for now they need an extra amount of care.

EXPLORING GOD'S WORD *(30 minutes)*

Have students look over their written responses to Bible study 10 and ask questions or make comments.

Ask: **What are some practical ways you can show love to a new Christian this week?** (Discuss answers.)

What are some ways you can protect a new Christian this week? (Of course you cannot follow a new Christian around and protect him or her from every ill. Even if you could, it wouldn't necessarily be a good idea. But you *can* look out for a new Christian and notice if he or she is coming under bad influences, is getting discouraged, or is facing temptation. You can step in and offer comfort and help, shielding that person from discouragement or temptation. And you can pray for his protection from Satan.)

Discuss: **How do you feel about taking responsibility for training a new Christian?** (Eager to help; obligated; inconvenienced; glad to be needed, etc.) Explain that Jesus asks us to sometimes inconvenience ourselves for the sake of others, looking "not only to your own interests, but also to the interests of others" (Phil. 2:4). When we lead someone to Christ, or when God brings a baby Christian across our path, we have a responsibilty to help that person as much as possible. It is a commitment we can make to Christ for the sake of that new believer.

Go through *Getting Started* (or another follow-up book) and discuss how to use it most effectively to help a young Christian. Students will be taking on the teaching role which you—the leader of this Discipleship Family—have fulfilled and modeled for them these past weeks. Using the section "Meeting Together" as a guide, students will meet with a new Christian for six weeks of follow-up. Stress that students should have a caring and loving attitude as they offer help to new Christians. They are not simply meeting to "go through a booklet" with someone, but to maintain a warm, personal contact with someone who needs them.

APPLYING GOD'S WORD *(20 minutes)*

Have students decide who they will approach about meeting for one-on-one follow-up. Pray for the new Christians who need follow-up and for your students who will be helping them.

You may close your meeting with another time of singing and prayers of thanksgiving.

You may also use this time to encourage students to participate in the next Discipleship Family, using Book 5 in the Moving Toward Maturity series, *Influencing Your World*.

Try to talk with each person before he or she leaves the meeting. Thank each one for the faithfulness shown to the group and to the Lord. Express your confidence that your students will go on sharing Christ in the strength and love of the Holy Spirit.

Assignments Encourage group members to carry out these continuing assignments.

1. Continue to share your testimony and *The Facts of Life* **every week.**

2. Continue to work through follow-up with a new Christian, helping him grow in his relationship with Jesus Christ.

AFTER THE MEETING

1. Evaluate: Carefully remove page 193 from this Leader's Guide, and use it to evaluate your 10-week experience with this Discipleship Family. Your opinions and experiences are important.

2. Continue taking students witnessing and meeting with them.

3. Contact each group member a week or so before your organizational meeting for the next Discipleship Family, *Influencing Your World*. Encourage each person to continue a commitment to the group.

IMPORTANT

To work through the *Giving Away Your Faith* study, you may wish to obtain copies of the following materials for each group member:

> *The Facts of Life* booklet
> *Getting Started* booklet

If you don't already have these booklets, look for them at your local Christian bookstore. Or write to one of the following for information on how to order:

VICTOR BOOKS
1825 College Avenue
Wheaton, IL 60189

REACH OUT MINISTRIES
3961 Holcomb Bridge Road
Suite 201
Norcross, GA 30092

Dear Discipleship Family Leader,

After completing your group study of *Giving Away Your Faith*, please fill out and mail this evaluation sheet to the editor. Thanks for your input!

1. Did you and your young people enjoy this study? _____

Why? _____

_____

2. How many people were in your Discipleship Family group? _____

3. How many had been in a previous Discipleship Family? _____

4. What benefits and problems did you experience as a Discipleship Family?

Benefits: _____

_____

Problems: _____

_____

5. Do you plan to continue the series as a Discipleship Family? _____

Why? _____

_____

6. What did group members like best and least about the student book?

Best: _____

_____

Least: _____

_____

7. What are the strengths and weaknesses of this Leader's Guide?

Strengths: _____

_____

Weaknesses: _____

_____

8. Were the *Time Alone with God Notebook Inserts* helpful? _____

How might they be improved? _____

_____

Additional comments: _____

_____

_____

_____

_____

_____

_____

_____

- -

Place
Stamp
Here

Mail this page to:

**SonPower Youth Sources Editor
1825 College Avenue
Wheaton, Illinois 60187**

INFLUENCING YOUR WORLD

Leader's Guide
prepared by
Sandy Larsen

Introduction

Moving Toward Maturity is a five-part discipleship training series for young people. It is designed to help them become so independently dependent on Jesus Christ that they can teach others to do the same. This series has three main purposes:

1. To train students in the "how tos" of Christian living.
2. To help students develop strong, Christlike characters.
3. To move students from the point of getting to know Jesus Christ to the point of sharing Him with others.

Influencing Your World, the final book in the series, will challenge students to reach out to others in their own ministries and go on to disciple others. Your group members will explore what their own spiritual gifts might be, learn to help needy people with an attitude of compassion, and plan for a continuing discipleship ministry.

The other four study books in the series, and related materials, are described on the outside back cover of this Leader's Guide.

Discipleship Family

Commitment is the key to a successful group study of *Influencing Your World*. So limit the study group to those young people who will commit themselves to study the book and Bible on their own and will faithfully take part in every group meeting. This group of committed young people and their leader are referred to as a *Discipleship Family*. (Turn to page 11 in *Influencing Your World* and read the commitments required of each person.)

By making and keeping these commitments, each Discipleship Family member will:

1. Learn to depend on Jesus Christ.
2. Develop personal discipline in Bible study, prayer, and Scripture memory.
3. Experience the rich fellowship and love of a committed, caring Christian community.

The young people and leaders who commit themselves to this discipleship training will move toward Christ's goal for the church: "His gifts were made that Christians might be properly equipped for their service, that the whole body might be built up until the time comes when, in the unity of common faith and common knowledge of the Son of God, we arrive at real maturity—that measure of development which is meant by 'the fullness of Christ' " (Eph. 4:12-13).*

---

*Quoted from J.B. Phillips: *The New Testament in Modern English*, Revised Edition, © J.B. Phillips, 1958, 1960, 1972, permission of Macmillan Publishing Co. and Collins Publishers.

You, the Leader

Being a leader of a Discipleship Family will require more time and personal involvement than most Bible studies or Sunday School classes you may have taught in the past. As a member of the group (not just its leader) you should take part in all the commitments, activities, and assignments of the Discipleship Family. To get started, here are some things you will need to do.

1. Get familiar with the Moving Toward Maturity series (see back cover) **and your role as a Discipleship Family leader.** Besides the introduction of this Leader's Guide, two other resources by Barry St. Clair can clarify your role: the book *Building Leaders for Strategic Youth Ministry* and the six-part video "The Youth Ministry Puzzle." Both are available in Christian bookstores or from Victor Books or Reach Out Ministries.

2. Read through *Influencing Your World* and this Leader's Guide. Call each person from your previous Discipleship Family, describe to him the purpose of Book 5, and ask him if he is planning to continue with the Moving Toward Maturity series. Explain the need for him to renew his commitment for the next 10 weeks.

3. Organize your Discipleship Family. Pray that the Lord will cause those who need to continue the series to make that commitment. If some students have gone through Books 1 through 4 on their own, or have been members of another Discipleship Family, allow them an opportunity to join your group if there is room. Your group will be most effective with 4 to 8 members, and should not exceed 12. If more people are interested, a second group should be formed.

4. Purchase the materials you will need well in advance of the first meeting. Everyone who is leading a Discipleship Family group should have his own copy of the Leader's Guide. Each Discipleship Family member (including yourself) should have his own copy of *Influencing Your World*, a Bible, a 5½" x 8½" looseleaf notebook, a set of *Time Alone with God Notebook Inserts* (you can photocopy them from pages 249-264 of this Leader's Guide), and a supply of paper. The leader should provide materials for everyone at the first meeting, and have students reimburse him the next week.

5. Decide the best time and place to meet. Have everyone bring their school and work schedules to the first meeting so they can decide as a group when and where to meet for the next 10 sessions. If possible, plan to hold the meetings in your home or the home of one of the group members. Meeting in the informal atmosphere of a living room or around a dining room table will help people open up and join in discussions.

6. Allow up to two hours for each meeting. Suggested time allotments for each part of the meeting are given in this Leader's Guide. A total of 60 minutes is suggested for the introductory meeting (session 1); 75 minutes are suggested for sessions 2-11. Since these are not instructional classes, but meetings designed to build relationships and share insights, they should be open-ended. If you finish a session in 75 minutes, fine. But you should have the freedom to meet for two hours if necessary (never longer).

7. Get the group together for a fun activity. Before or after session 1, plan a fun get-acquainted activity (softball game, bike hike, retreat, pizza party, picnic) for the participants of the Discipleship Family. This will help them renew the relationships they have developed with one another.

Building relationships

Your role in the Discipleship Family is that of leader, not teacher. By explaining that you and all members of the group are in the process of becoming more mature disciples of Christ, you will begin to establish yourself as one of the group rather than as the "instructor." But because you are more mature in years and in experience than the young people in your Discipleship Family, they will look to you for organization, guidance, and example.

1. Meet with each group member. Schedule an appointment with each member of your Discipleship Family during the first week or two. Strengthen your relationship with each person. Check on his needs, interests, concerns, and any goals he set as a result of previous studies. Share those things about yourself as well. This will help you see one another as unique, important individuals with feelings and ideas. It will also result in more meaningful discussions during your group meetings.

2. Keep your own Time Alone with God Notebook during this 10-week study. In addition to the student notebook assignments, also write your observations about members of your Discipleship Family. Regularly pray for each one by name. Keep track of individual needs and achievements. If someone misses a session, contact him personally. Help him when he has trouble understanding something from Scripture. Talk with him if he seems to be breaking his commitments. Call on him for his opinions during meetings. Build him up so he will be valued and appreciated by the group. You can also use your notebook for writing your evaluation of each session as well as what you plan to do to improve as a leader.

3. Keep your pastor and church informed. While you're building relationships in your Discipleship Family, continue to build relationships within the church as well. Keep your pastor informed as to what is happening in your group. Encourage group members to be involved in the church and to strengthen their relationships with other believers—particularly other young people who are not a part of a Discipleship Family. Group members should continue in the strong relationships they have built with one another, but they should avoid becoming a "clique."

4. Limit group membership. The people who are a part of this group should come from those who have studied Books 1 through 4 with you, and possibly others who have finished those books and want to join the group. Because your Discipleship Family will be building trust based on shared experiences, don't take in any new members once the group has been established. Anyone who has dropped out of a prior group should not move on until he finishes his work on that book. After completing the study of *Influencing Your World,* challenge each person to renew his commitment and to continue by discipling someone else using *Following Jesus* (Book 1 in the Moving Toward Maturity series).

Group ministry project

In addition to weekly Discipleship Family meetings, the group will participate in a group ministry project every week for 1½ to 2 hours. You will need to decide together what your project will be. Consider working with an existing ministry, such as a detention center, a home for unwed mothers, or a halfway house. Or you may want to develop a new ministry among a neglected group in your area.

Effective meetings

The Discipleship Family's meetings are based on biblical principles of discipleship. Each session has at least one *Group Life* and one *Individual Growth* goal. It's important that you work toward accomplishing both.

1. Be prepared. Begin your preparation for each session at least five days in advance. Do the Bible study, answering the questions for yourself, not as you think the students might answer. Then skim through the Leader's Guide suggestions to see if there is anything you need to do right away. Later in the week (one or two days before the meeting) finalize your preparation: Review the material, and study the Leader's Guide suggestions, adapting activities according to the particular needs of your group.

2. Start on time. Since Discipleship Family meetings can last up to two hours, ask everyone to come on time, or even a few minutes early. (Those who arrive early can use the time to share with other group members or review Bible memory verses.)

3. Help students keep their commitments. Students are to complete each week's Bible study **before** each session so the meeting can be devoted to building on what the students are learning on their own. For that reason, the "Exploring God's Word" section of each session does not contain a verbatim review of the Bible study material. Instead students are given an opportunity to quickly look over the Bible study content and their written responses. Then the discussion that follows builds on and reinforces what students have learned during the week prior to the meeting. Group members should also have a regular time each week to share results of their personal times with God.

Be sensitive to group members who may lack self-discipline and need extra encouragement and motivation to keep their commitments. Be positive. Recall how Christ loved, encouraged, and disciplined the early disciples; then follow His example in helping His new disciples along.

4. Continue to develop skill in leading discussions. Here are a few ways to keep your Discipleship Family discussions on track so each member can contribute and learn during each session:

▶ *State questions clearly and concisely.* You're more likely to get specific answers if you ask specific questions.

After you ask a question, allow time for the group to think. Don't be afraid of short periods of silence. And don't jump in with your own answers or opinions. Don't make a contribution to the discussion that someone else in the group can make.

▶ *Respect each person's comments.* Encourage each one to say what he thinks, not just what he thinks he should say. Ask additional questions to help him amplify his thoughts and move from ideas to applications.

▶ *Stay close to Scripture.* The Bible is the authority for this study and for your group discussions. Encourage group members to base their ideas on biblical principles.

▶ *Challenge trite or superficial answers.* Don't let group members get away with simply rattling off a cliché or a Bible verse. Ask them to explain what they mean or give an illustration.

▶ *Ask review questions when appropriate to help the group think through things they've studied up to that point.* Use this time for members to raise previously discussed issues with which they're still having problems.

▶ *If some group members are hesitant to take part in the discussions, ask them direct questions relating to their personal opinions or experiences.* Let them know that you care about them and what they think.

▶ *If some members answer all the questions, begin addressing your questions to others by name so everyone may be heard.* If a member continues to monopolize the discussions, you may want to talk with him privately after the meeting. Let him know you appreciate him and his contributions, but ask him to give others more opportunity to take part.

5. Evaluate each session. Within 24 hours of each meeting, evaluate how the session went and note the emerging needs of group members. The "After the Meeting" section of each session in this Leader's Guide will help you do this.

As you prepare to lead each meeting, pray that God will help you model the life of a true disciple—especially when it comes to having your own time alone with God. Be enthusiastic about growing spiritually, helping others grow, and sharing your faith with non-Christians. Your spirit can be contagious. □

Continuing Your Discipleship Family

OVERVIEW

Key Concept   To benefit most from a group study of *Influencing Your World*, we must commit ourselves to the disciplines of a Discipleship Family.

Goals   *Individual Growth:* To accept the responsibilities and commitments of this final Discipleship Family for another 10-week period.
Group Life: To continue the strong fellowship ties within the group established during preceding Discipleship Families.

BEFORE THE MEETING

1. Study pages 196-200 of this Leader's Guide for important background information.
2. In *Influencing Your World*, study pages 5-11, and put together the Bible memory packet found in the back of the book.
3. Phone each person who said that he or she would come to the first *Influencing Your World* Discipleship Family meeting. Your group should consist of members who have been through *Following Jesus, Spending Time Alone with God, Making Jesus Lord,* and *Giving Away Your Faith* Discipleship Families or have completed those four books on their own. Ask everyone to bring their school and work schedules with them to the first meeting.
4. Be prepared to review the purpose and format of the Moving Toward Maturity series for the group.
5. Pray for each prospective Discipleship Family member. Ask God to give each one the confidence that he or she can help others.
6. Gather materials for the meeting:
   Bible
   Influencing Your World

3" x 5" cards
Pencils
Bible memory packet
Poster board on which you have fastened several objects (such as product labels, money, pens, picture, etc.)
List of questions about the objects on the poster board (see *Focusing on Life* for explanation)
Paper
Student materials (a copy of *Influencing Your World* and a set of *Time Alone with God Notebook Inserts* for each person)

THE MEETING

BUILDING THE GROUP *(10 minutes)*

As each person arrives, greet him or her warmly. Make sure you have everyone's name, address, and phone number on a 3" x 5" card. Inquire about special things that you know are going on in group members' lives (sports, drama, tests, college applications, driver's education, dating).

FOCUSING ON LIFE *(15 minutes)*

Tell the group members you are going to give them an observation test. Hand out paper and pencils to everyone. Say: **I'm going to hold up something for you to look at. I'll give you 10 seconds to observe it. Then I'll give you one minute to write down everything you've seen, and I'm going to ask you a series of questions about what you have observed.**

Hold up the poster board with all the objects and count off 10 seconds.

Turn the poster board around and give students one minute to write down their observations.

Now ask questions to test students' observation skills. (For example: What brand of lemonade was the label from? What color dress was the model wearing? Whose picture was on the bill? Was there a poem on the board?)

Check accuracy of students' answers.

Say: **Some of you may be better observers than others. But one thing about observing is that we can always get better at it. The more you practice observing things, the more you notice. If I gave you the same sort of test next week, you would probably all do even better than you did tonight.**

Ask students to write down the names of one to five people they saw today who had some kind of problem (mental, physical, material). How did they know of the problems? (Person looked depressed; person on crutches; car broken down.) This will focus attention on observing people's needs.

Observing objects on a poster is just a fun exercise. But being able to observe life, to see what is happening with other people, to see their needs—that's something close to God's heart. In this Discipleship Family we will be learning how to see people's needs and how to minister to people in Jesus' name.

EXPLORING THE CHALLENGE *(20 minutes)*

Have group members turn their papers over and make two columns. On the left side ask them to write names of people they know personally who have needs, and on the right side, what those needs are. They will not share these lists out loud.

Say: **If you've been able to write down several names, or even one name, then you have already been observing your friends' lives and have picked up on their needs. But what can we do about those needs? We may not have all the answers, but in Christ we can have compassion and power to help other people. That's what we'll be committing ourselves to doing in this 10-week Discipleship Family.**

Review the purpose of the Moving Toward Maturity series and the function of the Discipleship Family. Invite students to share some things they have learned or experienced through previous Discipleship Families. Stress the need for commitment to Christ and to one another in order for this final Discipleship Family to be effective.

Distribute copies of the *Time Alone with God Notebook Inserts*. Encourage group members to continue their daily times alone with God as they learn to help others. Challenge them to learn and grow independently as they read through 1 and 2 Thessalonians, 1 and 2 Tim-othy, and Titus.

Give everyone a copy of *Influencing Your World*. Review the topics to be studied, and read the group disciplines (page 10). Discuss any questions students may have.

Briefly describe the time required for this study (one-and-a-quarter to two hours per week with the group, individual study time, and practical projects in ministry). This Discipleship Family will probably demand more time than the others. Be up front about that. Encourage them by assuring them they can handle more because of their growth.

Have members consult their schedules and decide on a specific time and place to meet.

CONSIDERING THE CHOICE *(10 minutes)*

Challenge the group to think and pray about making another 10-week commitment to the Discipleship Family. Let them know that you are fully willing to commit the necessary time to *Influencing Your World*, and while school and family responsibilities must come first, you are confident that they can find (or make) time in their schedules to carry out the study and projects. Offer to help them set goals and plan their schedules. You may want to refer to *Building Leaders* by Barry St. Clair (Victor Books) for help in doing this.

Anyone who decides not to become a part of this Discipleship Family should let you know before the next meeting and return his unmarked copy of *Influencing Your World*.

Encourage everyone to set aside a specific time each week to complete the Bible study for the next Discipleship Family meeting. (NOTE: The *Assignment* section of each Bible study is not to be completed until after the Bible study material has been discussed in the Discipleship Family.)

Close by praying for each person there, including yourself. Thank God for each person and ask Him to give each of you the sensitivity to see other people's needs and the willingness to try to meet them in Jesus' strength.

Assignments for Next Week Give the following assignments to those who decide to be a part of the Discipleship Family:

1. In *Influencing Your World*, **read pages 5-11, study and sign the "Personal Commitment" sheet (page 11), complete Bible study 1 (excluding the** *Assignment* **section), and put together the memory verse packet found in the back of the book.** (Show the group your packet to demonstrate what it looks like put together.) Remind your group to memorize Matthew 9:36-38.

2. Bring a Bible, a pen or pencil, and *Influencing Your World* **to every meeting.**

Also remind group members to bring money next week to pay for the student books.

Before students leave this first meeting, try to talk with each one. See if there are questions, problems, or misgivings about participating in the Discipleship Family. Encourage them to commit themselves, and let them know you are committed to each one of them.

AFTER THE MEETING

1. Evaluate: Did each person become involved in the discussions? Are some members too dominant, others too shy? Are group bonds still strong? Was everyone comfortable at the meeting? Review "Effective Meetings," page 199 of this Leader's Guide.
2. This week, and every week, begin preparing for the next session at least five days in advance. Complete Bible study 1 in *Influencing Your World*, and read through the Leader's Guide suggestions for your next meeting.

Broken Hearts
Bible Study 1

OVERVIEW

Key Concept   We should have compassion for people in the same way Jesus did.

Memory Verses   Matthew 9:36-38

Goals   *Individual Growth:* To begin to see the needs of others and become confident that with Christ we can help meet those needs.
Group Life: To be reassured we are not alone as we begin to minister.

BEFORE THE MEETING

1. Pray for each member of your Discipleship Family. Ask God to show you needs of theirs which you can help meet.
2. In *Influencing Your World*, do Bible study 1, writing your personal answers to each question. This week and every week, note in the margins other observations or personal experiences that relate to the lesson, and bring them up during your group meeting.
3. Memorize Matthew 9:36-38.
4. Contact each person who attended last week's session, remind him or her of the meeting time and place, and answer any questions. If someone decides not to participate in this Discipleship Family, assure the person that you still care.
5. Make a list of the names, addresses, and phone numbers of all the group members (from the 3" x 5" cards filled out last week) if your list needs to be updated. Make enough copies for each group member to have one.
6. Gather materials for the meeting:
   Bible
   Influencing Your World

Copies of group members' names,
addresses, and phone numbers
Bible memory packet
Pencils
paper

THE MEETING

BUILDING THE GROUP *(15 minutes)*

Greet each person warmly as he or she arrives, welcoming each one
as an important part of the group. Have everyone turn to the "Personal Commitment" sheet (page 11 in *Influencing Your World*) and
read it together. Group members should have already signed the
commitment sheet; ask anyone who hasn't to sign it now. (Be sure
yours is signed!)

Since this is the final Discipleship Family in the Moving Toward
Maturity series, express again what the previous Discipleship Families have meant to you, and invite group members to do the same.
Ask volunteers to offer brief prayers for the Lord's help in keeping
your commitments to the Discipleship Family.

FOCUSING ON LIFE *(15 minutes)*

Ask students to take paper and pencils and write a list of the five
biggest needs facing American high school students today. You may
have students do this individually or in groups of two or three.

Regain students' attention and ask them to share their lists. Un-
doubtedly many students will have come up with identical needs
while some will have mentioned things others did not think of. Try
to narrow down the lists to five common needs of American high
school students.

Discuss: **Is there any need on this list which Christ could not
help meet?** Some needs, such as purpose in life or forgiveness for
sins, are obviously spiritual, and Christ is obviously involved in
their solution. There are other needs which at first glance don't
appear so spiritual, such as finding a job after graduation. Discuss
how a relationship with Christ can help in those more "down-to-
earth" needs also. For example, a young person looking for a job can
trust the Lord to guide him, to prepare him for interviews, and to
provide for his needs even if he doesn't find the particular job he
wants.

Jesus had compassion on people's needs, whether spiritual or
physical. That's what Bible study 1, "Broken Hearts," is all about.

EXPLORING GOD'S WORD *(30 minutes)*

(NOTE: Each week this section is based on the work students have done in Influencing Your World. *The discussion questions are usually not identical to those in the study book, but they draw from the same Scriptures and assignments. This helps students think through what they have studied rather than simply repeating their written answers aloud.)*

Discuss: **How did Jesus look on the crowd of people in Matthew 9:36? How do each of the three clues ("harassed," "helpless," "like sheep without a shepherd") also describe people today as well as the crowd back then?**

How did you feel when you read the statistics about crime, abortion, abuse, drugs, suicide, etc., in this chapter? What can we do to make those overwhelming statistics more personal? (Think of particular individuals you know who have been victims or perpetrators of crime, have drug or alcohol problems, misuse sex, are in unhappy families, and so forth. Put names on the statistics.)

Jesus saw the hurting crowds as sheep without a shepherd. Then He changed the metaphor (v. 37) and referred to a "harvest." In what sense are those people with such serious problems a potential harvest? (God can bring them in to His kingdom. They are out there waiting to be gathered. It takes work by willing laborers.)

Select one or two specific problems of anonymous friends of your students. Talk about how knowing Jesus can help those friends through their problems and how you can help them. It is important to stress that Christ may not make all the problems go away instantly, but He will be with the person in the problem and help him work through it for good. As the person trusts Christ with the problem, He will solve it. If we don't see Jesus as the ultimate answer, we won't have much motivation to help our hurting friends find Him.

Discuss: **Why do few high school students seem willing to be laborers for Christ in their schools?** (Fear of being laughed at; reluctance to be different from the crowd; too busy with other things; feel no one else is doing it so why should they?)

Does it surprise you that Christ would want to use us as His laborers to help bring people to Him? Why doesn't He do it Himself? (He does do it—through us—though of course He can speak directly to any student's heart. He wants to involve us. For one thing, being involved with others for Him is an expression of Christian love and gets our minds off ourselves and onto Christ and other people.)

How did you feel when you read Making It Personal **(page 23) and saw that you are being asked to become a laborer for Christ during your lunch period at school?** (Scared? Afraid of being used by others? Confused about how to do it? Wishing you'd never gotten into this?) **Don't back out now before you've given it a try.**

Review the five "Rs" in *Making It Personal.* Discuss each one and spend time on any which may not seem clear. On #4, for example, Relate with skill: What particular skills do your students have that will be useful in building bridges with people in the cafeteria?

(NOTE: Don't be discouraged if your students are less than enthusiastic about tackling a lunchtime ministry at school. The idea can be scary, or they may be hazy about how it can be done. Your students may imagine you're telling them to invade their lunchrooms with tracts and Bibles, buttonholing everyone they see. That's not the point. For now, simply help your students begin to be more tuned in to needy people they see every day at noon.)

Some students may have unusual circumstances that make lunchtime not the best time for ministry (regularly going home or running errands at noon, for example). Help those students find different times when they come in contact with the same crowd, with opportunity to talk. What's important is to decide on a definite, regular place and time. Lunchtime would be the best.

Be prepared to answer questions on how to approach a lunchtime ministry. Build on witnessing experience gained in studying *Giving Away Your Faith*. Give them pointers on how to open up a conversation with someone they don't know well. Share with them how to sensitively dig more deeply into another person's life and discover what his needs are.

APPLYING GOD'S WORD *(15 minutes)*

Ask whether students filled in the information on pages 24-25 (person, need, response). Encourage any who didn't to work on it now.

Discuss fears students may have. Be realistic about natural reservations without being negative. Let them know you're available to help and encourage them. Eat lunch with them occasionally if you can.

Spend time praying about your new ministries. Ask God to show you specific people you can begin to help.

Assignments for Next Week As you give the assignments on page 25 of *Influencing Your World*, express confidence that your students can and will carry out the assignments and succeed in their commitment to this final Discipleship Family.

AFTER THE MEETING

1. Evaluate the meeting: Did students participate freely? Are they nervous about their lunchtime ministries? How can you promote

positive rather than negative feelings about it? What can you do to encourage someone who is particularly fainthearted?

2. If any group member expressed special questions or problems, phone or meet with that person this week. If the school and your schedule allow it, go to the lunchroom with students, observing and encouraging them without doing their ministry for them.

Step Out
Bible Study 2

OVERVIEW

Key Concept | God calls each of us to a ministry and enables us to carry out that ministry.

Memory Verse | Jeremiah 1:7

Goals | *Individual Growth:* To identify my particular ministry.
Group Life: To help one another see our particular ministries.

BEFORE THE MEETING

1. Pray for yourself and for each group member. Ask God to continue to give you wisdom and compassion in reaching out to others.
2. In *Influencing Your World*, complete Bible study 2.
3. Identify your own "lunchtime" ministry (at whatever time and place is best for you), and begin looking for your own peers who have needs.
4. Memorize Jeremiah 1:7.
5. Gather materials for the meeting:
   Bible
   Influencing Your World
   Bible memory packet
   Telephone
   Phone book

THE MEETING

BUILDING THE GROUP *(10 minutes)*

Welcome each person warmly. Comment on things you know happened this week in students' lives.

When all students have arrived, ask for their thoughts about the lunchtime ministry you introduced last week. Give positive feedback to any who have begun to make the effort to notice people's needs. Give encouragement to any who would prefer to forget the whole thing! Share your own experience of looking around for people with needs.

FOCUSING ON LIFE *(10 minutes)*

Show your students the telephone and phone book. Ask: **If I wanted to call (someone's name), how would I know the number?** (Look it up in the book. In the case of a student you would probably need to know the parent's name.) **God *calls* each one of us—not on the phone, but in His own unique ways. And you might say He knows your number. He knows just how to get in touch with your spirit and where you are.**

Now suppose this phone were plugged in at your home. How would you know someone was trying to call you? (It would ring.) **And what would you have to do?** (Answer.) We can know that God is calling us through circumstances, our consciences, His Word, prayer, or our desires. He can call us and call us, but we still have to answer His call. That's what Jeremiah did.

EXPLORING GOD'S WORD *(30 minutes)*

Discuss the two misconceptions on page 28 of *Influencing Your World*. The second one may prompt more discussion. It can be argued either way, and endlessly, whether God has a specific will for each person's occupation in life. The point here is that in no matter what occupation a person finds himself, God has a ministry for that person there.

Ask students to summarize what they learned about God's call in the New Testament passages on page 29.

Turn students' attention now to the first chapter of Jeremiah. Ask: **What are some things you have in common with Jeremiah at this point?** (Youth; the call of God; perhaps lack of experience, and doubts.) **How is it helpful to know that the great Prophet Jeremiah felt as you feel and experienced what you experience?**

Discuss some drawbacks that people often associate with being young. (Lack of wisdom; lack of experience; lack of credibility with older people. Life in the teen years is sometimes considered only a "waiting period" until you get enough maturity to begin really living.) Ask: **What are some things you would like adults to know about what young people can really do?** (Encourage your students in the realization that they are important people and have much to give. God treats them as full-fledged human beings and full-fledged Christians even though they are sometimes overlooked by adults.)

Use the students' own statements about what they have to offer to counteract feelings of inadequacy they may be having about their own personal ministries. Discuss the antidotes to inadequacy found in Philippians 4:13, 19.

Say: **Jeremiah was afraid when God called Him. What confidence builders did God give him? Do you need the same confidence builders? What are some specific fears you have or feelings of inadequacy about following God's call in your life?** (Fear of rejection by others and fear that the cost will be too high are two common ones. Another fear may be that of following at all because we may have misunderstood God's call and may be running off in the wrong direction. That fear can paralyze us and prevent us from doing anything useful, and your students need the assurance that God can communicate His call clearly to them. Feelings of inadequacy may be lack of experience, knowledge, and compassion; lack of observation skills and sensitivity.)

If you have had an experience of God confirming His call to you, such as described on page 35 of *Influencing Your World*, share it briefly with your students. Such dramatic things may or may not happen to us in the course of following God, and they will certainly not happen every day, but in some way (or ways) God will let us know we are on the right track.

APPLYING GOD'S WORD *(15 minutes)*

Invite students to share their seven steps of confirming God's call in *Making It Personal*. Let them know that their conclusions don't have to be set in concrete for the rest of their lives, but this exercise can be an important part of the process of finding God's will for their personal ministries. Share the excitement of young people finding out what they can do for God right now in their everyday lives, especially if a student has seen a whole new vision for how God can use him or her.

Pray together about your personal ministries. Pray with confidence and trust that the Lord will carry out what He has begun.

Assignments for Next Week Make the assignments on page 39 of *Influencing Your World*. If anyone is having trouble keeping up a daily time alone with God or memorizing Scripture as assigned, offer help. You or another group member might call that person once or twice this week to check up in a friendly way.

1. Evaluate: Are students beginning to get a vision of what God can do through them? Are some skeptical? Are some scared? Be patient with those who are holding back; not everything will happen in one week.
2. Is there a student struggling with particular feelings of inadequacy? Fear? Make an effort to phone that person or send a nonthreatening note this week. Take him or her out with you to minister.

First Things First
Bible Study 3

OVERVIEW

Key Concept   Prayer is vital to our ministry of outreach.

Memory Verse   Jeremiah 33:3

Goals   *Individual Growth:* To form the habit of praying regularly and confidently for other people.
Group Life: To agree to pray together for people to whom we want to minister.

BEFORE THE MEETING

1. Pray for each person in your Discipleship Family, including yourself.
2. In *Influencing Your World*, complete Bible study 3.
3. Memorize Jeremiah 33:3.
4. Gather materials for the meeting:
   Bible
   Influencing Your World
   Bible memory packet
   Potted plant or tree
   Dead branch or leaf

THE MEETING

BUILDING THE GROUP *(15 minutes)*

After you have welcomed each arriving member of your group, ask students to share some of their experiences in reaching out to others at lunchtime this week. Give all students equal praise for making a start and for trying. Share recent ministry experiences of your own.

FOCUSING ON LIFE *(10 minutes)*

Show your students the potted plant or tree, and point out a particular twig or leaf. Ask: **How does it stay healthy and growing?** (It receives water and nutrients through the stem or larger branch, and ultimately through the main stalk or trunk.) Ask: **What would happen if we cut off this leaf which is out on the end?** (It would shrivel and die because it would be disconnected from its source of life.) Show students the dead leaf or branch and ask what happened to it. (It died because it somehow got disconnected from the main branch, and it can't live on its own.)

Have a volunteer read John 15:1-8. Discuss the main similarity between a living branch and us when we remain connected with Christ, and the similarity between a dead branch and us when we leave Christ out of our lives and ministries.

EXPLORING GOD'S WORD *(45 minutes)*

Discuss: **Why would a person try to carry out a ministry in Jesus' name but forget to ask Jesus for His help in it?** (Pride; ambition to accomplish something so others will think well of us; impulsiveness which doesn't want to wait on the Lord; lack of understanding of how necessary it is to depend on the Lord for success.)

Prayer brings us back to our Source. When we remember to pray, we remember that any ministry we can do is really His ministry. Prayer humbles us by reminding us that without Him we can do nothing for anyone else.

Take a look at the prayer triangle based on Jeremiah 33:3 (page 43) of *Influencing Your World*. Discuss: **What is God's responsibility in the prayer triangle? In other words, what is His part? What is our responsibility? Who can be counted on to faithfully hold up His end of the arrangement? What happens when we fail to do the same? What should we do when we fail?**

Discuss some good results of actively praying for people, even when we know that God already knows our hearts and knows what will happen. (Prayer keeps us in communication with God and changes us. It reminds us of people and their needs and keeps those people on our hearts. And it works! Through it God will change people.)

Discuss the promises students found in John 14-16. You might emphasize the promise of the Counselor, the Holy Spirit, who is in us and who teaches us how to pray and what to pray for. Notice also the emphasis on loving Jesus; if we love Him, our will is going to be in tune with His will, which means our prayers will be answered.

Invite students to talk about answers to prayer they have received, either very recently or in the past. The answer does not have to seem like a big thing to anyone else so long as it was a big thing between that person and God. Share one or two answered prayers of your own.

Note that having a prayer answered by the Lord does not mean dictating to God what He should do and then sitting back while He performs it for us. We cannot tell God what to do, but we can open our hearts to Him and allow Him to reveal His will to us. Then we pray—and act—in obedience.

Discuss: **Prayer is an expression of love, and there is no limit to how far our love can go when we pray. How important is it to feel loving toward the people we pray for?** (It's nice but not necessary. In fact, some of our best praying may be done when we're struggling to pray for God's best for a person who irritates us.) **Suppose you've tried to reach out to somebody in your lunchroom and he shuts you off—even insults you. How can you pray for that person?** (Rather than praying, "Lord, show him he's wrong!" you can pray, "Lord, open his heart to me and to You. Help me be more sensitive to him and even apologize if I came on too strong." You may not feel very loving about that person, but your prayer will be in God's will.)

Share some of your good experiences of praying with others as prayer partners. Ask whether they have had similar experiences. Stress the fellowship and commitment between you as well as the answers to prayer.

Have students begin to divide into twos and threes for prayer for the people God has put on their hearts.

APPLYING GOD'S WORD *(15 minutes)*

Put this chapter of *Influencing Your World* into practice right away by praying in twos or threes for the people to whom you want to minister. Pray also for the items you named on the prayer triangle in *Making It Personal*.

Pray specifically: let your prayers touch particular problems people have (unless they are too personal to share out loud). Pray conversationally: let others offer their prayers for different requests. Pray obediently: leave yourselves open to letting God answer your prayers through you.

Assignments for Next Week   Make the assignments on page 53 of *Influencing Your World*.

AFTER THE MEETING

1. Evaluate: Do students understand and agree that prayer is more than just an "extra" in ministry?
2. Are your students comfortable praying together in small groups? If anyone is hav-

ing trouble, talk with that person and assure him that the intent of the heart, rather than beautiful words, is what God wants. Pray with him this week.

SESSION 5

The Greatest Thing
Bible Study 4

OVERVIEW

Key Concept   We cannot effectively reach out to others unless we love them.

Memory Verses   1 Corinthians 13:4-8a

Goals   *Individual Growth:* To evaluate the quality of our love for others.
Group Life: To help one another resolve unloving attitudes.

BEFORE THE MEETING

1. Pray for your group. Pray particularly for more loving attitudes among you.
2. In *Influencing Your World*, complete Bible study 4.
3. Memorize 1 Corinthians 13:4-8a.
4. Gather materials for the meeting:
   Bible
   Influencing Your World
   Bible memory packet
   Bell, gong, cymbal, or some other noise-maker with a loud, harsh sound

THE MEETING

BUILDING THE GROUP *(15 minutes)*

After group members have arrived and you have greeted each one by name, ask this question: **When was a time somebody really showed love to you? Not romantic love, but think of a time when somebody showed you he really cared.**

Give students time to think. Many experiences will be very personal and students will be weighing whether or not they wish to share them. Don't worry if everybody is silent for a minute. Share your experience first to open them up.

As you and your students share your experiences of being loved, focus on these questions: What did the person do and say? Did you feel you deserved his love? Did he make you feel you had to pay him back? How did it affect your relationship with him?

FOCUSING ON LIFE *(5 minutes)*

Bring out the noisy gong, cymbal, or bell and demonstrate its loud sound. Say: **What would you do if I came up to you and started carrying on a conversation with you, all the time banging this gong so loudly you could hardly hear me?** (You'd probably tell me to get lost!) **With that noise the message is not clear or believable.**

Have a student read 1 Corinthians 13:1. The first verse of this great chapter on Christian love tells us that if we approach people with an unloving attitude, it doesn't matter what we say or how well we say it—people will be turned off by us as surely as though we were beating a gong in their faces.

EXPLORING GOD'S WORD *(45 minutes)*

In Bible study 4 you looked at many negative effects of competition. Some students (athletes in particular) may have questions. Discuss how we can compete in athletic or scholastic realms either with or without love.

Unloving competition is what 1 Corinthians 13 warns us against. It's an attitude of being out to win over others at their expense—socially, athletically, mentally, even spiritually! It does not care anything for the other person, only for itself. Love, in contrast, puts the other person first.

If students feel free to share their answers, discuss the results of the competition scoring you did on pages 58-63 of *Influencing Your World*. Did any of the results surprise you? Did the tests help you discover areas where your attitudes aren't what they should be? (If the tests revealed something to you, the leader, confess it to the class and ask for their prayers as you seek to be more loving in that area.)

Discuss how each of the negative qualities of competition can stifle our efforts at ministry and turn people off.

For example, it is possible to "minister" to others competitively, trying to outdo our fellow Christians: "I witnessed to 27 people this week; I helped Jim solve his problem with his parents." (Competitiveness in ministry may be a temptation for some in your group; watch for it. God calls us to be faithful in the work He has given us, not to be better than somebody else!) If ministering to others is a competition between Christians, it will destroy our fellowship with one another and will make us obnoxious and overbearing with others. We'll minister to non-Christians not because we care about them, but because we're trying to accumulate ministry points!

Focus particularly on your students' particular problems with competition. For example, perhaps arrogance (page 59) isn't a dominant problem with many in your group, but resentment (page 62) may be one they struggle with.

Now turn students' attention to the positive by looking at the section "Love Is."

List the positive qualities of love which students found in 1 Corinthians 13. It's good to hear these things spoken aloud. Discuss: **Why do we sometimes think that being compassionate means being weak and spineless?** (A compassionate person probably comes on softer, less defensive, more open to others, and not fighting for his or her rights. We may have the wrong impression that it's more gutsy to stand up for yourself than to care for others and give way to them.)

Ask: **What kind of real strengths does it take to be compassionate?** (It takes the nerve to put aside our own selfish desires, courage to put up with insults or rejection from those we want to help, and self-control to be quiet and listen when we'd like to jump in with all the "right" answers. It takes patience to wait for the other person to see the truth that we think is so obvious, and to put up with the person's bad behavior.)

Ask: **When have you seen living demonstrations of the positive qualities of love? For example, when has someone been patient with you?** (Giving real-life examples helps students see what love in action looks like.)

Ask students which of the qualities of love they have the most trouble showing. Discuss why these are particular problems.

As you talked about examples of love that have been shown to you, someone may have pointed out that Jesus has shown you all those good qualities of love. Just as He is the only perfect example of love, He is also the only One who can help you show each of these positive qualities of love in your life.

For example, suppose you have trouble being patient. You can manage for a while, on the outside, but eventually your politeness wears off and you blow up in a burst of impatience. How much better to confess your lack of patience to Christ and ask Him—since He is perfectly patient—to be patient in you and through you.

APPLYING GOD'S WORD (10 minutes)

Discuss your students' findings on page 70 of *Influencing Your World:* their high score averages for "Love Is Not" and their leading characteristics for "Love Is." Talk about how you can make improvements, and thank God for the loving strengths He has put into you.

Assignments for Next Week Make the assignments on page 71.

AFTER THE MEETING

1. Evaluate: Are students seeing that love takes real strength and courage? Do any seem put off by the idea?
2. Are there any strains and tensions among members of the group? Here among yourselves is an excellent place to practice Christian love. There may not be any instant cures, but try to talk with each person involved and get them together to begin to work out the problem.

NOTE: For Session 10, five weeks from now, you will need enough copies of *Following Jesus* (Book 1 in the Moving Toward Maturity series) and the *Moving Toward Maturity Series Leader's Guide* for each student to have one of each. Your students will use these books to begin to disciple younger Christians. Contact the publisher to order the books you need.

Gifted Supernaturally
Bible Study 5

OVERVIEW

Key Concept   God gives each of us gifts that further our
ministries.

Memory Verses   1 Corinthians 12:4-6

Goals   *Individual Growth:* To discover our spiritual
gifts and begin to put them into practice.
Group Life: To help each other discover and
practice our spiritual gifts.

BEFORE THE MEETING

1. Pray for everyone in your group (yourself
   included) that the Lord will show each of
   you the particular gifts He has given you for
   ministry.
2. If you have not considered your own spiritual gifts before, or if you are uncertain what
   they are, think, pray, and study about them
   this week. Ask people close to you what
   they believe your spiritual gifts are.
3. Memorize 1 Corinthians 12:4-6.
4. Gather materials for the meeting:
   Bible
   Influencing Your World
   Bible memory packet
   Wrapped gift (make it something inexpensive but desirable, such as a can-
   dy bar, and disguise it by using a
   large or odd-shaped box); or have
   one for each person

THE MEETING

BUILDING THE GROUP *(15 minutes)*

Welcome each person in a special way this week. Let each one know that you value him or her and are glad each person is here.

Give students this time to talk together about their lunchtime ministries. Some may have encouraging things to share with the group. Others may have questions about how to handle a problem or a question which a non-Christian has brought up. Still others may be discouraged at seeing no immediate results. Show your students that they are doing God's will no matter whether others are immediately responding or not, and that they are approved servants.

FOCUSING ON LIFE (10 minutes)

Show your students the wrapped gift or gifts and ask whether anyone would like to receive a present. Some may be willing, and others may be more doubtful. Ask the doubtful ones: **What makes you hesitate to accept this gift? Are you afraid of what might be inside it? Do you think it might not really be for you?** Discuss what makes us willing or unwilling to receive a gift. Note that it makes a difference who the gift is from: if your students know and trust you, they will be willing to accept a gift from you.

If you brought only one gift, select one person (such as the student whose birthday is closest to today) and offer him or her the gift. If that person doesn't take it, select the person with the next nearest birthday and so on until someone takes the gift and opens it.

Say: **God gives us all kinds of gifts such as life, health, and family. But the Scriptures tell us about a special kind of gift that's given particularly for ministry to others. When we know God and know He gives only good gifts, we'll be more willing to take and use the spiritual gifts He gives us.**

EXPLORING GOD'S WORD (30 minutes)

Discuss: **What do we usually think of when we say that a person is "gifted"?** (He or she has special natural abilities that stand out.) **How is that different from having spiritual gifts?** (Anyone, Christian or non-Christian, can have natural, God-given gifts or talents. They can be used to get ahead in the world, to make money, to make others think well of us. They can also be used unselfishly, to serve others. But a spiritual gift is a God-given capacity for service, through which the Holy Spirit ministers to others. It is not a natural ability.)

What are some dangers of envying one another's spiritual gifts? (We tend to think one gift is more valuable than another. For example, we think leadership is better than mercy because a leader is visible while a merciful person is behind the scenes. In truth, each gift is equally valuable and there's no room for competitiveness.)

Discuss the motivations, ministries, and manifestations on pages 78-79 of *Influencing Your World.* Students' lists may vary somewhat. Ask whether students have any particular questions about spiritual gifts. Some may never have considered this topic before. Try to answer the questions through Bible study 5 and the Scriptures referred to. If you have gone through a process of discovering and using your spiritual gift, share that with your students now. Reassure your students that as they pray and learn more, God will reveal their spiritual gifts to them. They do not have to be certain of their gifts tonight, or they may change their minds later as God leads. The point is to seek God, not the gifts.

Discuss how some of the gifts can come into play as you minister to others. For example, how can the gift of encouraging, or exhortation, be a practical help to somebody this week? What about the gift of giving? How might that come into play this week as your group ministers in the lunchroom?

Ask students what they think their gifts might be. Invite other students to give their reactions in a positive way. For example, if Elizabeth believes her gift is prophecy, someone might respond, "I can agree with that. Elizabeth helps us see when we're on the wrong track and puts us back in a loving way." (NOTE: A person can see in himself things he or she would like to be able to do rather than what God actually enables him or her to do! For instance, a bossy person might think he has the gift of leadership. Our true spiritual gifts will be found through seeking God in prayer and experience and will be confirmed by others who know us well. If nobody else thinks you have the spiritual gift you think you have, you should take another look at your gifts and ask God to show you the truth.)

APPLYING GOD'S WORD *(15 minutes)*

Assuming that you at least have a tentative idea of what your spiritual gifts for ministry are, make plans together to put them into practice in your individual and group ministries. This can be an exciting new experience for people who are discovering gifts they didn't know they had.

Assignments for Next Week Make the assignments on page 85.

AFTER THE MEETING _____

1. Evaluate: Are students catching an exciting glimpse of what God can do through their spiritual gifts? Are some students still doubtful or confused?
2. Did students respond in a positive and loving way to each other's thoughts on their own spiritual gifts?

With a Towel
Bible Study 6

OVERVIEW

Key Concept   We must be servants if we want to follow Jesus.

Memory Verses   John 13:14-15

Goals   *Individual Growth:* To look for ways to serve other people.
Group Life: To look for ways to serve one another.

BEFORE THE MEETING

1. Pray for yourself and each of your students. An attitude of serving does not come easily or naturally. It must come from Christ, the great example of a servant.
2. In *Influencing Your World*, complete Bible study 5.
3. Memorize John 13:14-15.
4. Gather materials for the meeting:
   Bible
   Influencing Your World
   Bible memory packet
   Towel
   Container of water

THE MEETING

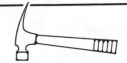

BUILDING THE GROUP *(15 minutes)*

Welcome each person warmly. Remember that you are this group's servant. God has already given you many opportunities to serve your young people, and there will be many more opportunities.

This would be a good time to review some of your conclusions about your spiritual gifts (from last week's session). Ask students whether they have any new thoughts about what their gifts are and whether they have tried to put their gifts into practice this week.

FOCUSING ON LIFE *(30 minutes)*

Display the towel and ask students what it can be used for. Though there are many possible uses for a towel, students should think of "foot-washing" or "service" if they are up on their Bible study.

Ask students whether they would be willing to wash one another's feet tonight. Notice if they balk or seem turned off. Even though your group members are probably friends—and probably fairly clean when they arrive at this meeting—the idea of lowering ourselves to wash one another's feet is not very attractive. Jesus calls us to wash the feet of not just our nice clean friends, but the feet of unattractive and ungrateful people. Like the impossible standard of love in 1 Corinthians 13 (Bible study 4), this standard of service is impossible outside of our example, the master servant, Jesus.

Create a quiet, reverent atmosphere is which members of your Discipleship Family can actually wash each other's feet. You begin by washing someone's feet and letting others do the same. Do it humbly, without talking. This can be a moving experience for your group and a memorable illustration of a servant's humble spirit.

Lead your group in a discussion of what they learned from this experience. Hang up the towel in your meeting room tonight where everyone can see it, as a symbol of service. You may even wish to leave it there as a continuing reminder of the example of Jesus.

EXPLORING GOD'S WORD *(35 minutes)*

Ask: **How does our society teach us to be selfish?** (Advertisements tell us to indulge ourselves by buying more and better things. Many expressions such as "Do yourself a favor," "I'm looking out for #1," "I owe it to myself," "I've got to take care of me" fill our everyday language. It is simply assumed that you will look for the degree and the job that will bring in the most money, the most prestige, the most pleasure. If you give your life to serve others, you will be out of step with our times. People may even question your motives.)

Discuss: **What can we do to counteract all the pressures that tell us to be selfish?** (We can make an effort to tune out the clamor by concentrating on what God wants for us instead. For example, when the slick and persuasive ads come on, we don't have to sit like zombies and absorb them! We can turn our attention elsewhere. Action leads the heart, and to live counter to society we must act. What we do and where we invest our interest and attention will show where our hearts are. If you act as a servant—even when you don't feel like it—you will become a servant. Investing in other people's needs makes you other-centered rather than self-centered.)

Turn to John 13. We know from Luke 22:24 that the disciples had been arguing about who was the biggest and best follower of Jesus. Ask: **What struggles might have been going on inside the Son of God as He got up and took that towel and basin to wash their feet?** (He could easily have wanted to reprimand them harshly. He was about to die and He needed their comfort and friendship, not their bickering. He may not have wanted to serve right then, any more than He wanted to go to the cross when He prayed in Gethsemane a little later. He must have been very lonely as He took up those servant's things and began to do what none of His disciples understood.)

How can that help us as we serve others? (Serving was not always fun for Jesus, and it won't always be fun for us. But God will bless us, as John 13:17 says.)

Discuss: **If you were God and you wanted to show people you were God and what God is like, what do you think you would do?** (Students will have all kinds of answers. From our human perspective we would expect God to create lightning bolts or crush some buildings to show off His power.) **How did Jesus show what God is like?** (He took the lowest role of a servant—and that was *after* becoming a human being with all the limitations that means!) Read Philippians 2:5-8 to see how Jesus humbled Himself to show us what the heart of God is like.

Find out what students have discovered from the Scriptures about being servants (page 91).

What joys await you if you decide to be a servant? (Letting go of the need to protect and defend yourself all the time—looking out for number one can get to be a chore! Knowing you're in God's will and doing things that are close to His heart; seeing others made happy by what you do; feeling worthwhile; feeling needed; having a purpose.)

Discuss what rewards you, the leader, have received from serving. Mention not only the short-term emotional benefits, but stress also the long-term benefits of strengthening your character.

What are some "comfort zones" we are in? (page 93) (Anything that protects us from meeting other people's needs: routine; the same close circle of friends; responsibilities that keep us busy. Even this Discipleship Family *could* become a comfort zone for some if they use it as an escape rather than as a way of learning to obey God.)

What can we "lay aside" (page 93) **to be better servants?** (Answers will be individual for each person, but anything that needlessly takes time may have to be laid aside to give us time to be servants of others.)

Serving is a terrific idea in the abstract and theoretical. **But what reservations do we have about actually getting in there and doing it?** (Discuss reactions such as those mentioned on pages 96-97 and others students may be experiencing about being servants.)

Review the promise of John 13:17. **Think of ways that you might** be blessed if you serve others through Christ. Think of ways you have already been blessed in your ministries and in other ways you have tried to serve. Then count on God to do the unexpected and bless you in ways you never dreamed of. He will bless and reward you in private, personal ways that only you and He understand, and you'll know that He sees and approves of your service.

APPLYING GOD'S WORD *(10 minutes)*

Share together and pray for one another as you look forward to opportunities to serve unattractive people this week. It will be hard, and you will need one another's support. You can serve each other by praying for each other tonight and all week. Ask God to show you specific things you can do to serve others. They may not seem like big acts of service to you, but they will be significant to the people you serve and will show those people the love of God.

Assignments for Next Week Make the assignments on pages 98-99.

AFTER THE MEETING _____

1. Evaluate: Are students looking forward to depending on God in the area of serving others? Are some scared of the idea of getting in the middle of somebody else's problems?
2. If anyone is having a special struggle right now—or if you just suspect he is—pay special attention to that person this week as your way of serving the Lord.

No Limits
Bible Study 7

OVERVIEW

Key Concept Giving is another way of serving God and others.

Memory Verses 2 Corinthians 9:6-7

Goals *Individual Growth:* To plan a budget that includes giving as a vital part.
Group Life: To share problems with managing money wisely and help each other find solutions.

BEFORE THE MEETING

1. Pray for everyone in your group, asking the Lord to give you open minds about the touchy subject of money.
2. In *Influencing Your World*, complete Bible study 7.
3. Think about your own experience with managing money and giving to the Lord. Do you have special problems in this area? Have you found workable solutions to budgeting, tithing, and being in debt? Be prepared to share these with your students where applicable to their situations.
4. Memorize 2 Corinthians 9:6-7.
5. Gather materials for the meeting:
   Bible
   Influencing Your World
   Bible memory packet
   Towel (from last week's session)
   Budget records of your own (if they are organized and clear enough to help your students make their own budgets)

THE MEETING

BUILDING THE GROUP *(15 minutes)*

After everyone has arrived and has been warmly welcomed by you, hang up the "towel of service" from last week's session (or point it out if it is still hanging up in your room) and ask your students how their serving has gone this week. Invite volunteers to tell about any experiences, big or small, they have had in trying to serve others. Tell about anything that has happened to you in the area of service this week. Affirm your students for any efforts at service, no matter how small, and encourage them to continue.

FOCUSING ON LIFE *(10 minutes)*

When Jesus took up that towel on the night of the Last Supper. He was serving His disciples by washing their feet, and He was about to serve all mankind by dying for our sins. He gave His service and His life freely. Read 2 Corinthians 8:9. Jesus' life was a life of giving rather than getting. Giving includes giving time, abilities, attention, and a listening ear—and it includes giving money.

Discuss briefly: **Why is it hard for many people to give away money even to a legitimate need right in front of them?** (Money is precious because it means "power" in our culture; it buys us things we enjoy; it spells security for the future.)

Discuss: **God *could* meet people's needs directly, by dropping food or clothes from the sky, for example. Why do you think He avoids that method and asks *us* to give to people in need?** (Possibly because it builds our character, puts us in contact with real people who have real needs, teaches us to let go of worldly security, and shows us God can provide for us in some other way.)

EXPLORING GOD'S WORD *(45 minutes)*

Brainstorm a list of everything God has given to you. You cannot possibly list everything, but come up with as much as you can. You could continue to list all night and not be finished!

Is God a giver? You bet He is! And since He is our example, He naturally asks us to be givers too. The point is not that God has given us so much that we should feel guilty if we don't give, but that we are more like Christ when we give to others.

Someone might say that it doesn't cost God anything to give what He has given, while it hurts me in the wallet when I give. But the gift of His Son cost Him the ultimate, as John 3:16 reminds us.

Read 2 Corinthians 9:6-11. What is the tone or mood of this passage? Is it saying, "Give, because God will zap you if you don't"? No, it has a positive and cheerful tone. It's saying, "God will bless you when you give."

Discuss the kinds of blessings God gives us when we give to others. (It's not necessarily a guarantee of being paid back materially, although of course God is free to do that; it may be the blessings of feeling useful, knowing we've helped someone, feeling free of the grip of money, peace in obeying God, joy in becoming like Christ.)

How does giving to others help us grow as Christians? (We have to trust God more to provide for us; we obey Him, which always helps us grow; we take Him at His word instead of relying on our feelings; we discover that He is faithful to us; we imitate Christ.)

What are the scriptural uses of money? (It is a legitimate means of exchange, and we don't have to feel guilty about using it to buy what we need or to provide for family members who count on us for support. The wise use and investment of money can provide us with a means of saving and meeting emergencies. But money is also meant to help us learn to be generous. One of the reasons we have it is so that we can give it away!)

What are some advantages of having a planned system of giving rather than doing it hit-and-miss as you hear about needs? (The hit-and-miss method may seem more spiritual to some people because it is spontaneous and seems to rely on God's moment-by-moment leading. But it can easily be based on emotions rather than the Holy Spirit's prompting. When we give to causes that move us the most at the time, we're subject to the most emotional and well-packaged appeal that happens to come in the mail right then. A definite plan of giving, made out objectively ahead of time, takes away that unreliable element of emotionalism.)

Think of a time when someone has been generous to you. How did you feel about the person? How did it affect your relationship? How does giving help your relationships as well as help meet physical needs? (NOTE: *How* a gift is given can affect a relationship for good or bad. Perhaps someone has been "generous" to you but makes it clear that something is expected in return, either materially or in unending gratitude! Giving in the right spirit, expecting nothing back, will help rather than harm our relationships. Of course, there is always the danger that people will misunderstand our motives. But even Jesus took that risk and was misunderstood by many, so we can't expect to be any different.)

How can we begin to put giving into practice, if we aren't in the habit already? (You may want to mention how you began to tithe and/or to give to those in need, how God showed you the importance of giving, and how He has blessed you as a result.)

Ask students about the results of their budget-making. Show them your own budget if you have brought it to the meeting. Of course, your financial situation and that of your students living with their parents are probably quite different, but find as many similar points as possible.

(NOTE: You will have to make many allowances for students' differing financial situations. You will have students who work and must provide for many of their own needs, other students whose parents give them whatever they want, and everything in between. But students need to be aware of the money they spend—no matter where it comes from—and plan their spending. Each person receives X amount of money and needs to spend Y amount of money. Each person needs to learn to give a proportion decided on.)

APPLYING GOD'S WORD *(20 minutes)*

As a demonstration of drawing up a workable budget, ask for a student volunteer to present his or her financial picture, or make up a fictional student as an example. Work together as a group to help that student draw up a budget. Discuss each item and come to conclusions together. (The student does not have to feel bound by the group's decisions, but the exercise should be helpful for the volunteer.)

Assignments for Next Week   Make the assignments on page 115.

AFTER THE MEETING

1. Evaluate: Do students seem to feel freedom about giving away money for the Lord? Does it make them uptight? Are there practical suggestions you can make for how and where they might begin giving?

2. Was any student made uncomfortable because he or she doesn't have as much money as the others? If you have an opportunity this week, try to give that student reassurance that everyone in the group is equal in God's eyes and in your eyes.

NOTE: Have you ordered enough copies of *Following Jesus* and the *Moving Toward Maturity Series Leader's Guide* for each student to have one? They will need these for Session 10, two weeks from now.

In the Dirt
Bible Study 8

OVERVIEW ————————————————————

Key Concept Serving others means inconvenience and cost, but it brings rewards.

Memory Verses Matthew 22:37-39

Goals *Individual Growth:* To become more willing to take risks in ministry.
Group Life: To affirm rather than criticize one another for being involved with unattractive people.

BEFORE THE MEETING ————————————————

1. Pray for each person in your Discipleship Family.
2. Pray for unattractive people you know— people who especially need someone who cares.
3. In *Influencing Your World*, complete Bible study 8.
4. Memorize Matthew 22:37-39.
5. Gather materials for the meeting:
   Bible
   Influencing Your World
   Bible memory packet
   NOTE: Arrange to arrive at this meeting with *dirty hands.* It should be dirt that will rub off on other people but will also wash off easily, such as dirt from a garden.

THE MEETING ————————————

BUILDING THE GROUP *(15 minutes)*

As people arrive, greet them enthusiastically by shaking hands warmly and firmly. Watch people's reactions as they realize they have just gotten dirty by shaking hands with you. Some may refuse to do it if they know how dirty your hands are.

After everyone has arrived, ask: **How did you feel about getting dirty by shaking hands with me?** Discuss people's reactions, including how they looked to those who had already arrived.

Take time for everyone to wash their hands and return to your meeting room before you continue.

FOCUSING ON LIFE *(10 minutes)*

Ask your freshly washed group members: **Suppose I were new here and you knew I was lonely and needed a welcome and I didn't realize how dirty my hands were. Would that change your attitude about shaking hands with me? Would you be more willing to do it, even though it would still be as unpleasant? Why would your attitude change?**

Helping people in trouble may not mean getting dirty physically—though it sometimes means that too—but it always means risk-taking and inconvenience. Yet the rewards are great for us and for the people we help.

EXPLORING GOD'S WORD *(35 minutes)*

Look at Luke 10:25-37. **What answer do you think the lawyer was hoping for when he asked, "And who is my neighbor?"** (v. 29) (Probably someone respectable and easy to care about.)

Why do you suppose Jesus answered by telling this long story? (He often answered that way, in parables, to disarm people. People naturally let their guard down when they listen to a story. Jesus would introduce a situation or principle in a story and tell it so people would agree with Him, whether they wanted to or not. His parables logically led people to see that He was right. In this parable, we see that the command to show mercy to wounded people isn't always easy to accept.)

What kinds of wounds and injuries do you see on the people you come in contact with every day? Why are those injuries harder to notice than the injuries of the man who was robbed on the road to Jericho?

Have you ever felt hurt and wounded, and watched people ignore you? Describe how you felt.

We risk our reputations when we befriend an unattractive person. Christians are supposed to avoid the appearance of evil and care about keeping their reputations pure. How do you bal

ance the two? (You will have to decide if helping a hurting person is worth the risk of giving others a bad impression of you. Will you actually harm your witness, or will you just give negative people a chance to gossip about you? Can you trust God to take care of your reputation as you serve others?)

What other risks do we take when we bother to help people in need? (Losing time; losing popularity; getting distracted from our own ambitions; being thought "different"; getting physically hurt in some cases.)

What risks did the Samaritan take when he stopped to help the robbery victim? (Being robbed himself; losing time; having to spend money even if it wasn't stolen from him; being inconvenienced in several ways, such as having to walk.)

Discuss students' answers to this question: **"What difficulties are you having in letting your compassion flow freely toward others?"** (page 123). Discuss and help each other open up in these areas. (Think of people you know who are particularly good at showing compassion; think of how they express it and the risks they take to do it. Often if we express compassion—whether or not we feel it—the feelings will follow the actions.)

Talk about specific actions you can take to show compassion for people. Notice how seemingly small some of the Samaritan's actions were—going over to the injured man, touching him. Our small gestures can be lifesaving for a person in need. Just stopping where that injured man lay was more than anybody else had done for him all day!

What makes us unwilling to inconvenience ourselves for people? What does that say about our values—what's important to us? (For example, if I don't have time to give an unpopular person a ride home from school when he's loaded down with books because I have to go play tennis, then tennis is more important to me than helping people. It's not that I shouldn't play tennis, or that I have to give everybody I pass a ride home; but it does tell me something about my values.)

Galatians 6:9 says, "Let us not become weary in doing good." Discuss: **Is there someone you've grown weary trying to help in your lunchtime ministry these past weeks? How does this week's Bible study help you see that person in a new light—the light of God's compassion?** Review the promise in the second half of that verse: "for at the proper time we will reap a harvest if we do not give up."

APPLYING GOD'S WORD *(15 minutes)*

Give students the opportunity to consider specific things they will do this week to show compassion for specific people who need help. Let them share ideas with those who are having trouble coming up with something—or getting up the courage to do it! Pray together for the people you want to help, for opportunities to help them, and for willingness and courage to help them.

Assignments for Next Week Make the assignments on pages 130-131.

AFTER THE MEETING _____

1. Evaluate: Are students turned on or turned off by the idea of deliberately "getting their hands dirty" ministering to others?
2. Is one of your own students an "untouchable" who needs a special touch from you or from another student this week?

Multiply Your Life
Bible Study 9

OVERVIEW

Key Concept   We can make disciples and help them grow so they can disciple others.

Memory Verse   2 Timothy 2:2

Goals   *Individual Growth:* To begin selecting people to disciple and understand how to disciple them. *Group Life:* To support each other in the responsibility of discipling others.

BEFORE THE MEETING

1. Pray for each member of your Discipleship Family.
2. Think about how you have gone about discipling your students, what has gone particularly well, and what you could have done better. Your leadership of this Discipleship Family has been your students' chief example of what it means to disciple younger Christians.
3. In *Influencing Your World*, complete Bible study 9.
4. Memorize 2 Timothy 2:2.
5. Gather materials for the meeting:
   Bible
   Influencing Your World
   Bible memory packet
   Paper
   Following Jesus and *Moving Toward Maturity Series Leader's Guide* — one copy of each for each student

THE MEETING

BUILDING THE GROUP *(15 minutes)*

As students arrive, greet each one warmly. You may even want to shake hands with clean hands this week!

Hand out paper and tell students to write their names at the top of a sheet of paper. Then collect the sheets of paper, turn them over, and mix them up. Hand them out again face down and give students these instructions: **Write a message to the person whose name appears on your paper. Tell the person one way in which he or she is a good example to you. For example: "Kevin Peterson, you're an example of cheerfulness even when things aren't going well." Or, "Maria Williams, your sportsmanship in volleyball is a good example to all us poor losers." Now, be serious and be complimentary; no "You're a great example of what God can do with a slow mind!" Don't sign what you write. Hand your papers back to me and I'll distribute them at the end of our meeting.**

Collect the papers and save them for the end of the meeting.

FOCUSING ON LIFE *(15 minutes)*

Ask students: **Who is someone who has shown a good example of the Christian life to you?** Ask what students saw in those people and how those people demonstrated faith in Christ.

(If students mention you, the leader—great! If they don't mention your name, don't be crushed; they may be too shy to say it to your face. You can be confident that if you have faithfully and prayerfully led this Discipleship Family, you have been a good example to your students.)

EXPLORING GOD'S WORD *(35 minutes)*

As students consider taking on the task of discipling younger Christians, ask them what their feelings, hopes, and fears might be. To some it may look like an impossible task. They may be saying, "Who am I to try to teach somebody else? I've had trouble getting through my Bible studies in *Influencing Your World*." Help them voice these feelings out loud in front of each other. This is necessary so they will be able to talk openly and honestly with their disciples. Express confidence that they can do it, no matter how inadequate they feel.

Share with your students any feelings of inadequacy you had as you began this or an earlier Discipleship Family. If you still have feelings of inadequacy, tell students about that too. Rather than lowering yourself in their eyes, you'll be an example of honesty—and how God *can* use a person who doesn't feel adequate, if that person is willing to go ahead anyway.

Discuss: **What can you do well now, but you felt inadequate to do it when you started out?** (Nearly any learned skill or sport works that way.) **How can you apply that experience to beginning to disciple other Christians?** (If you try and keep trying, pick yourself up when you fail, and learn all you can along the way, you'll succeed!)

Discuss: **Do you think you have to be fully mature in Christ in order to teach somebody else?** Notice the definition of "making disciples" on page 135 of *Influencing Your World*. It is "one *maturing* believer"—not a perfect believer—"reproducing other *maturing* believers." If we wait until we are perfect before we try to help anybody else, we will never do anything helpful; we'll never reach Christian perfection in this life. God calls imperfect people to disciple other imperfect people.

Why is it important to stay close to Christ as we begin discipling others? Read John 15:5 together. (Apart from Jesus, we can do nothing. We may be able to recite a lot of Bible facts, but we won't help anybody grow as a Christian because we won't have real spiritual power flowing through us.)

Discuss how to go about approaching someone you think you would like to disciple. **In which cases could you simply say, "I'd like to get together with you regularly and study the Bible and talk about Christ"?** (You could approach a younger Christian friend with whom you already have a close relationship; that way he won't be put off.) **In which cases would you have to spend time building a relationship outside of Bible study?** (Someone you think you can potentially help, but whom you don't know well yet, needs your extension of friendship first; otherwise he'll think you're steamrollering him into Bible indoctrination.) Ask students to think of potential disciples in either category.

Often the best approach is to initially leave out the word disciple. The student can simply ask a younger Christian if he would like to get together to talk about his relationship with Christ, using *Following Jesus* to focus the time.

As you take a younger Christian under your wing and begin to spend time with him or her, what should be your attitude? (Love; caring about the best interests of the person; sensitivity to the person's feelings; a listening ear; firmness in helping the person keep his commitment; belief in the person's full potential. We should not have inflated ideas of our own importance, overprotectiveness of the person, ego involvement in how well the person "succeeds" as a Christian, or a critical attitude.)

Tell your students how you go about trying to be "real" with them (see pages 140-141). What are some advantages of letting students see your faults. Give students the opportunity to tell you what they've learned by seeing you, their leader, make mistakes. (When you're "real" with those you're trying to teach, you show them by example that a Christian is not perfect, but forgiven; that God loves us when we fail; that God will pick us up again no matter how many times we fall down.)

What causes us not to be "real" with people, even other Chris-

tians? (Fear of what people will think, fear they'll reject us, fear we'll damage the Lord's reputation by hurting our witness—but a phony witness is no witness at all!)

What can happen as members of this Discipleship Family take on younger Christians and begin to help them grow? (Let students tell their dreams of what God can do through them. They can change people's lives, change their class, change their school for Christ!)

APPLYING GOD'S WORD *(15 minutes)*

Hand out the copies of *Following Jesus* and the *Moving Toward Maturity Series Leader's Guide*. (Discuss payment as you wish.) Since your students went through this first Discipleship Family (Book 1 of the Moving Toward Maturity series) some time ago, they may enjoy reviewing the course. Talk about how they can use *Following Jesus* and the other books in the Moving Toward Maturity series to help others study the Bible. See pages 146-148 of *Influencing Your World* for suggestions.

Give students the opportunity to talk about people they might wish to disciple. Let them make suggestions to one another. While you don't want to make this into a gossip session, you need to have communication among you to prevent five people from descending on one person whom they have all decided is "their" disciple!

Pray for the people you are considering as potential disciples. Ask God to show each of you who you should disciple and to confirm or revise any choices made.

As students leave, give them their "good example" sheets.

Assignments for Next Week Make the assignments on pages 148-149. The next session is the final meeting of this Discipleship Family! You may want to plan something special for your last time together; make sure someone is in charge of any refreshments or other plans.

AFTER THE MEETING _____

1. Evaluate: Do students believe they can disciple others effectively? Do they understand how to use *Following Jesus*?
2. Does someone need extra encouragement from you this week?

NOTE: In Bible study 10, your students are instructed to consider their priorities in ministry and discuss these with you. This week you should phone or meet with each student and discuss this with him or her. (See pages 155-157 of *Influencing Your World*.)

From Here to There

Bible Study 10

OVERVIEW

Key Concept   We can continue to carry out our ministry through a plan made prayerfully.

Memory Verse   Matthew 10:42

Goals   *Individual Growth:* To decide on ministry priorities and plans.
Group Life: To continue your group ministry projects.

BEFORE THE MEETING

1. Pray for everyone in your Discipleship Family. Thank God for each person's growth and the times of fellowship you have had together. Pray for your continued, growing ministries.
2. In *Influencing Your World,* do Bible study 10.
3. Toward the end of the week, phone each student to inquire about their ministry priorities (see pages 155-157 of *Influencing Your World*).
4. Memorize Matthew 10:42.
5. Gather materials for the meeting:
   Bible
   Influencing Your World
   Bible memory packet

THE MEETING

BUILDING THE GROUP *(20 minutes)*

Make this a time of expressing your special appreciation to this Discipleship Family. Tell them specifically how they've helped you grow, as well as how you've seen them grow. Give your students the opportunity to tell what this Discipleship Family has meant to them; they can refer to their answers on page 152 of *Influencing Your World* if they wish. If you have planned refreshments for tonight, enjoy them together during this time.

FOCUSING ON LIFE *(10 minutes)*

Discuss: **What in your future do you have no control over?** (The economy; international conflicts which might mean being called into military service; parents' job changes; friends becoming fickle; college loans becoming less available.) **What in your future do you have at least some control over?** (Your attitude toward what happens; how hard you study to get the best school record possible; how well you perform your job; how faithful you remain to Christ and the church; how you perform your ministry.)

Our lives go through changes, and we can't foresee where and to whom we will minister in the future. But we can make up our minds that no matter where we are or what we are doing, we will have a ministry to someone.

EXPLORING GOD'S WORD *(45 minutes)*

Discuss: **Sometimes Christians think that the more Christian activities they are involved in, the greater their ministry is. How can good activities, even church activities, possibly harm our real ministries?** (They can run us ragged. They can distract us from people by concentrating on activities and programs. They can keep us surrounded by other Christians so we are insulated from non-Christians who need us. Christian activities are great when they keep their main purposes first, but they can be a distraction from real Christian service if they overload us.)

How can we choose among all the opportunities available to us and decide where we actually belong in Christ's service? (Prayerfully following God's plan, as analyzed in Matthew 10 in this chapter of *Influencing Your World*, and refusing to jump into everything that comes along without carefully considering God's will.)

Why is it vital to know we are called to Jesus rather than to a job, church, cause, or so forth? (Jobs, youth groups, popular causes, and ministry organizations can all break down and disintegrate, leaving their participants disappointed and wondering what happened. Many Christians, deeply committed to a particular ministry, have been left at a loss when that ministry dissolves. They feel abandoned by God. But God calls us to Himself first, and He will then use us in some ministry of His choosing for as long as He chooses.)

What happens when we try to minister to too many people in too many places at once? (We get burned out. We short-change everybody and water down the good that we could accomplish if we concentrated on fewer people. We can't compare ourselves with each other in this; some people have more time and energy than others, and others are better at counseling in depth with one or two people and have no time for more.)

Discuss: **What steps have you gone through to narrow down your ministry priorities?** (You should already have talked with each of your students about this during the week. Let them share their decisions now.)

During these weeks of studying personal ministry, have you changed your mind about what your ministry is or come to any surprising conclusions about how God might want you to minister? (Discuss new insights students have reached.)

How can we have a definite plan for future ministry and yet stay open to God's surprises? (Plan what you can and commit yourself, but don't worry about changing your ministry as God leads you. Make yourself available to His new leadings through prayer and the Word. Keep in mind that no ministry is sacred; only God is perfect and holy.)

Share together the "Practical Ministry Plans" your students have come up with (page 163 of *Influencing Your World*). Help each other make realistic but risk-taking plans for future ministry. Discuss how you can help each other carry out your plans, remembering that each person's plan is also individual and is his or her responsibility.

APPLYING GOD'S WORD *(15 minutes)*

Celebrate your final meeting together as a Discipleship Family by praying and singing together and encouraging each other in your future ministries. If you need to talk about continuing your group ministry project, this would be a good time to plan and pray further about that.

Try to talk with each person before he or she leaves tonight. Affirm each one for his or her faithfulness in ministering for the Lord. The results cannot be tallied on a score sheet or a thermometer; God measures the results in each person's faithfulness.

Assignments Point out the assignments on pages 161-162.

AFTER THE MEETING

Evaluate: Carefully remove page 247 from this Leader's Guide, and use it to evaluate your 10-week experience with this Discipleship Family. Please mail your comments to us right away.

Your opinions and experience are important to those who have put together the Moving Toward Maturity series.

Dear Discipleship Family Leader,

After completing your group study of *Influencing Your World*, please fill out and mail this evaluation sheet to the editor.

1. Did you and your young people enjoy this study? _____

Why? _____

_____

2. How many people were in your Discipleship Family group? _

3. How many had been in a previous Discipleship Family? ____

4. What benefits and problems did you experience as a Discipleship Family?

Benefits: _____

_____

Problems: _____

_____

5. Do you plan to begin the series with another Discipleship Family?

Why? _____

_____

6. What did group members like best and least about the student book?

Best: _____

_____

Least: _____

_____

7. What are the strengths and weaknesses of this Leader's Guide?

Strengths: _____

_____

Weaknesses: _____

8. Were the *Time Alone with God Notebook Inserts* helpful? _____

How might they be improved? _____

_____

_____

Additional comments: _____

_____

_____

_____

_____

_____

_____

_____

. . . .

Place
Stamp
Here

Mail this page to:

**SonPower Youth Sources Editor
1825 College Avenue
Wheaton, Illinois 60187**

SPENDING TIME ALONE WITH GOD NOTEBOOK INSERTS

These sheets provide your Discipleship Family members with suggestions for beginning a time alone with God and daily outlines to keep it going strong.

Photocopy the pages and insert them in a 5½″ by 8½″ notebook. For each Discipleship Family member, make:

1 copy of pages 251–260
5 copies of pages 261–262
10 copies of pages 263–264

Contents of these inserts have been excerpted from *Spending Time Alone with God* (Book 2 of the Moving Toward Maturity series).

HOW TO HAVE A TIME ALONE WITH GOD

By the time you finish this book, your daily time alone with God will include Bible study, praise, thanksgiving, confession, petition, and intercession. Here is a guideline that will allow you to include all aspects of Bible reading and prayer within a 15-minute period of time.

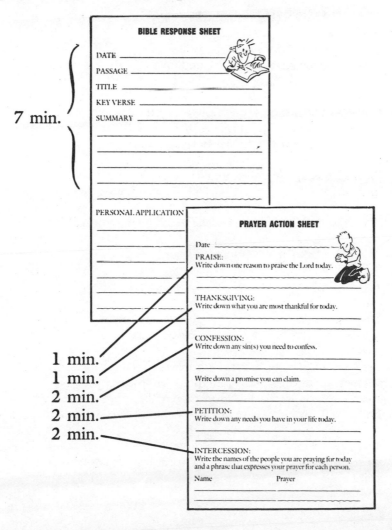

7 min.

BIBLE RESPONSE SHEET

DATE _____

PASSAGE _____

TITLE _____

KEY VERSE _____

SUMMARY _____

_____

_____

_____

_____

PERSONAL APPLICATION

PRAYER ACTION SHEET

Date _____

PRAISE:
Write down one reason to praise the Lord today.

THANKSGIVING:
Write down what you are most thankful for today.

CONFESSION:
Write down any sin(s) you need to confess.

Write down a promise you can claim.

PETITION:
Write down any needs you have in your life today.

INTERCESSION:
Write the names of the people you are praying for today and a phrase that expresses your prayer for each person.

Name   Prayer

1 min.
1 min.
2 min.
2 min.
2 min.

HOW TO STUDY A PASSAGE OF SCRIPTURE

OBSERVATION (Use with *Title* and *Key Verse* sections of your Bible Response Sheet.)

Pray first for the Holy Spirit's guidance, and then read the passage carefully. Read with an open mind, ready to receive and obey what God has to teach you.

INTERPRETATION (Use with the *Summary* section of your Bible Response Sheet.)

Step One — Read the verses preceding and following the passage in order to understand the proper setting and context.

Step Two — Ask yourself these questions about the passage: *Who? What? When? Where? Why?* and *How?* Write down your insights and any unanswered questions you may have.

Step Three — Look up unfamiliar terms in a standard dictionary or a Bible dictionary.

APPLICATION (Use with the *Personal Application* section of your Bible Response Sheet.)

Step One — Look for:
Promises to claim   *Commands* to obey
Attitudes to change   *Actions* to take
Challenges to accept   *Examples* to follow
Sins to confess   *Skills* to learn

Step Two — Describe how the passage applies to your life by asking yourself these questions: "How can I make this passage personal?" "How can I make it practical?" "How can I make it measurable?" Be specific.

MEMORIZATION
Find a verse or passage of Scripture that speaks to you personally, and memorize it.

READ THE PASSAGE SEVERAL TIMES. First read it silently, and then aloud.

UNDERSTAND THE PASSAGE.
 Read it in the context of the passages around it.
Read the comments about the verse in a Bible commentary (for example, *Wycliffe Bible Commentary*).
Write in a few words what the passage is about.

VISUALIZE THE PASSAGE. Use your imagination to picture the passage. For example, Matthew 5:1-12 is part of the "Sermon on the Mount." Picture yourself there on the mountain with Jesus. Then place each of these "Beatitudes" on the side of the mountain. Later, that picture will come to mind and help you recall these verses.

BREAK DOWN THE PASSAGE INTO NATURAL PHRASES. Learn the first phrase of the passage; then add the second. Continue adding phrases until you have memorized the entire passage.

LEARN THE REFERENCE AS PART OF THE PASSAGE. Say the reference, then the verse, and then repeat the reference again at the end. This step helps you fix the location of the verse in your mind, allowing you to turn to it immediately when you need it.

LEARN IT WORD PERFECT. As you are saying the passage over and over to yourself, continue to correct yourself until you've learned it exactly as it is written. You are already taking the time to learn it, so why not do it right! Learning it this way now will give you confidence to quote and use the passage later.

MEDITATE ON THE PASSAGE. As you think and pray about the passage, ask God to speak to you. When the passage becomes meaningful to you, then it will be much easier for you to remember.

REVIEW THE PASSAGE. Each day, review the Scripture passages you have already learned. If you review a passage every day for 30 days, it will be very difficult to forget.

THIRTY DAYS OF PRAISE

Day 1: Psalm 8	Day 16: Psalm 104:1-23
Day 2: Psalm 23	Day 17: Psalm 104:24-35
Day 3: Psalm 34:1-3; 50:1-6	Day 18: Psalm 111
Day 4: Psalm 63:1-4; 66:1-7	Day 19: Psalm 112
Day 5: Psalm 67	Day 20: Psalm 113
Day 6: Psalm 84	Day 21: Psalm 134
Day 7: Psalm 86	Day 22: Psalm 135:1-7
Day 8: Psalm 90	Day 23: Psalm 138
Day 9: Psalm 91	Day 24: Psalm 139
Day 10: Psalm 92	Day 25: Psalm 145
Day 11: Psalm 93	Day 26: Psalm 146
Day 12: Psalm 95:1-7	Day 27: Psalm 147
Day 13: Psalm 96	Day 28: Psalm 148
Day 14: Psalm 100	Day 29: Psalm 149
Day 15: Psalm 103	Day 30: Psalm 150

SEVEN DAYS OF THANKSGIVING

Focus your thanks to the Lord in two areas each day: (1) Bible passages that describe His promises and gifts to you, and (2) your personal thanks for God's working in your daily life.

Day 1
Pray through 2 Peter 1:4 to express your thanks to God.

Lord, thank You for Your great and precious promises that You have given to me that I might be part of Your divine nature.

I also thank You for:
   Your amazing love,
   letting me be in Your family,
   making me really live, and
   life at its most fantastic in Jesus

Day 2
Pray through 1 John 1:7 and Colossians 1:14 to express your
thanks to God.

Father, I thank You for the blood of Your Son Jesus Christ that
cleanses me from all sin and frees me from Satan's power.

I also thank You for:
  Your patience,
  Your comfort,
  Your closeness to me,
  Your disciplining of me, and
  Your love inside me.

Day 3
Pray through 1 Peter 2:24 to express your thanks to God.

Lord Jesus, I thank You that You bore my sins in Your body on the
cross, so that I can die to sin and live righteously, and that by Your
wounds I am healed.

I also thank You for:
  the body of Christ (other Christians),
  the privilege of prayer,
  my home, and
  my parents.

Day 4
Pray through Ephesians 2:8-10 to express your thanks to God.

Lord, I thank You that I am saved by grace through faith, and that
it is Your free gift—I don't have to work for it. But thank You that,
as Your new creation, I can live for You and help others.

I also thank You for:
  my body,
  my health,
  my strength,
  happy times,
  sad times, and
  in-between times.

Day 5
Pray through Psalm 91:11-14 to express your thanks to God.

Lord, I thank You that You give Your angels charge over me to guard me in all my ways. They will steady me with their hands and protect me. You will deliver me because I love You.

I also thank You for:
   opportunities for spiritual growth,
   comfort when I'm depressed,
   joy when I'm sad, and
   courage when I'm scared.

Day 6
Pray through Ephesians 1:3-6 to express your thanks to God.

Lord, thank You for choosing me to be adopted into Your family. Thank You for blessing me with all the good things You have stored up for those who belong to Christ.

I also thank You for:
   food,
   clothes,
   a place to live,
   freedom to say what I feel, and
   freedom not to say what I feel.

Day 7
Pray through 2 Corinthians 8:9 and 9:8 to express your thanks to God.

Thank You, Lord, for paying a debt for me (my debt of sin) that I could never have repaid. Thank You not only for saving me from sin but for giving me the grace I need today to live for You.

I also thank You for:
   saving me from selfishness,
   saving me from pride, and
   saving me from eternal separation from You.

THIRTY DAYS OF CONFESSION

Sins to Confess:

Day 1: 2 Timothy 2:22. Do you have impure thoughts?
Day 2: Philippians 2:14-15. Do you complain or gripe?
Day 3: Ephesians 6:1-3. Do you honor your parents?
Day 4: Ephesians 4:31. Are you bitter toward anyone?
Day 5: 1 Corinthians 6:19-20. Are you careless with your body?
Day 6: Matthew 6:33. Do you seek what God wants first?
Day 7: Matthew 6:14. Do you have a bad attitude toward someone?
Day 8: 2 Timothy 2:22. Do you have impure motives?
Day 9: Colossians 3:9. Do you lie?
Day 10: Ephesians 6:1-3. Do you respect your parents?
Day 11: Ephesians 4:31. Is there anger in your life?
Day 12: 1 Corinthians 6:19-20. Do you have bad habits?
Day 13: Matthew 6:33. Is God the most important person in your life?
Day 14: Matthew 6:14. Are you holding a grudge?
Day 15: 2 Timothy 2:22. Are your thoughts pure toward the opposite sex?
Day 16: Philippians 2:14-15. Do you have a critical attitude?
Day 17: Colossians 3:9. Do you steal?
Day 18: Ephesians 4:31. Do you talk about others behind their backs?
Day 19: 1 Corinthians 6:19-20. Are you lazy?
Day 20: Matthew 6:33. Have you given God everything in your life?
Day 21: Matthew 6:14. Do you have a wrong relationship with someone?
Day 22: Colossians 3:9. Do you cheat in school?
Day 23: Ephesians 6:1-3. Do you have problems with authority?
Day 24: Ephesians 4:31. Are you jealous of anyone?
Day 25: 1 Corinthians 6:19-20. Do you eat too much?
Day 26: Matthew 6:33. Are you trusting God with your life?
Day 27: Matthew 6:14. Is there anyone you resent?
Day 28: Philippians 2:14-15. Does your attitude honor God?
Day 29: Ephesians 6:1-3. Are you rebellious?
Day 30: Ephesians 4:31. Do you argue with other people?

Promises to Claim:

Day 1: Philippians 4:8
Day 2: Psalm 119:9
Day 3: Colossians 3:9-10
Day 4: Galatians 2:20
Day 5: Colossians 3:20
Day 6: 1 John 4:7
Day 7: Hebrews 12:15
Day 8: Ephesians 4:29
Day 9: 1 Corinthians 6:13
Day 10: Colossians 1:27
Day 11: Luke 9:23
Day 12: 2 Corinthians 9:8
Day 13: 1 John 4:4
Day 14: Philippians 1:9
Day 15: 2 Thessalonians 1:12
Day 16: 1 Corinthians 10:13
Day 17: 1 Thessalonians 4:3
Day 18: Ephesians 2:10
Day 19: Colossians 1:13
Day 20: Ephesians 6:2
Day 21: Galatians 5:18
Day 22: Ephesians 4:26
Day 23: 1 Corinthians 3:16
Day 24: Romans 12:1
Day 25: 2 Corinthians 5:17
Day 26: Philippians 2:5-7
Day 27: Matthew 6:12
Day 28: Ephesians 1:3-7
Day 29: Colossians 2:2-3
Day 30: Philippians 3:1

These sins to confess and promises to claim will help you through your first 30 days of confession. During the first month, you will discover several areas God wants to change in your life. From then on, follow the passage that corresponds to that day of the month. Apply it to a sin you need to confess or promise you need to claim.

SEVEN DAYS OF PETITION

Focus your petitions in two areas each day: (1) Bible passages that describe what God wants for you, and (2) your personal requests for God to supply your needs.

DAY 1
(Read Galatians 2:20.)
"Jesus, help me to live as someone who is dead to my own selfish desires. Take charge of my body, my mind, and my emotions. Live Your life in me today."

Other needs: _____

DAY 2
(Read Galatians 5:22-23.)
"Jesus, please help my life to express these qualities to other people."

Other needs: _____

DAY 3
(Read Ephesians 5:18.)
"Jesus, I claim the filling of Your Spirit. Fill me now. I pray for all that comes from Your Spirit: courage, power, wisdom, sexual purity, boldness, compassion, enthusiasm, honesty, and openness."

Other needs: _____

DAY 4
(Read 1 Corinthians 12:4-6.)
"Lord, help me to know my spiritual gift(s) and use it for Your glory."

Other needs: _____

DAY 5
(Read Ephesians 6:10-17.)
"Jesus, it's tough to be a Christian in this world. The pressure gets heavy at times. I ask for Your strength and protection. I put on Your armor: the belt of truth, the breastplate of righteousness, the shoes of the Gospel of peace, the shield of faith, the helmet of salvation, and the sword of the Spirit—the Word of God."

Other needs: _____

DAY 6
(Read Isaiah 41:10.)
"Lord, sometimes I am afraid. But I know I don't have to get scared because You are my help and my strength. Help me today to overcome fear by trusting in You."

Other needs: _____

DAY 7
(Read Acts 1:8.)
"Jesus, I want to be a witness for You to my friends. Give me the power and courage to be Your witness today."

Other needs: _____

PRAYERS YOU CAN PRAY FOR OTHERS

Look at these prayers of the Apostle Paul. They will help you know how to pray for other people. In fact, you can pray these specific prayers for them.

"And this is my prayer: that your love may abound more and more in knowledge and depth of insight, so that you may be able to discern what is best and may be pure and blameless until the day of Christ, filled with the fruit of righteousness that comes through Jesus Christ—to the glory and praise of God" (Philippians 1:9-11).

"I pray that out of His glorious riches He may strengthen you with power through His Spirit in your inner being, so that Christ may dwell in your hearts through faith. And I pray that you, being rooted and established in love, may have power, together with all the saints, to grasp how wide and long and high and deep is the love of Christ, and to know this love that surpasses knowledge—that you may be filled to the measure of all the fullness of God" (Ephesians 3:16-19).

"We always thank God for all of you, mentioning you in our prayers. We continually remember before our God and Father your work produced by faith, your labor prompted by love, and your endurance inspired by hope in our Lord Jesus Christ" (1 Thessalonians 1:2-3).

RECORD OF PETITION

As you begin to pray for yourself, use a form like the one below to: (1) record the things you are praying for, and (2) help you keep up with God's answers to those prayers.

NEEDS FOR MY LIFE

Date Prayed	Request	Answer	Date Answered

RECORD OF INTERCESSION

As you begin to pray for other people, use a form like the one below to: (1) record the things you are praying for each person, and (2) help you keep up with God's answers to your prayers. Fill in the person's name at the top (Mom, Dad, sister, brother, friend, etc.). Don't try to pray for everyone every day—just a few people each day is enough.

Name _____

Date Prayed	Request	Answer	Date Answered

PRAYER ACTION SHEET

Date _____

PRAISE:
Write down one reason to praise the Lord today.

_____

_____

THANKSGIVING:
Write down what you are most thankful for today.

_____

_____

CONFESSION:
Write down any sin(s) you need to confess.

_____

_____

Write down a promise you can claim.

_____

_____

PETITION:
Write down any needs you have in your life today.

_____

_____

INTERCESSION:
Write the names of the people you are praying for today
and a phrase that expresses your prayer for each person.

Name   Prayer

_____   _____

_____   _____

BIBLE RESPONSE SHEET

DATE _____

PASSAGE _____

TITLE _____

KEY VERSE _____

SUMMARY _____

_____

_____

_____

_____

PERSONAL APPLICATION _____

_____

_____

_____

_____

_____